The Effects of Intellectual Property Law in Writing Studies

This book documents the intellectual property experiences of writing studies scholars and challenges naturalized ways of responding to intellectual property concerns.

Analyzing results of a nationwide survey and semi-structured interviews to examine ways decisions about intellectual property (IP) during academic knowledge-making are mediated by histories of enculturation, ethical lenses, and IP sponsors, the book:

- Identifies and illustrates a range of ethical stances that academics might adopt in regard to IP and the range of human, institutional, and technological sponsors that can mediate IP decisions
- Provides evidence that IP affects all of the processes of academic knowledge-making, not just the final product
- Offers heuristic questions that academics can and should ask throughout their teaching, research, and editing to make proactive IP decisions

The book is an essential read for academics working in writing studies and the humanities as well as those interested in IP. This text could also be used in graduate student training in writing studies and related disciplines.

Karen J. Lunsford is Associate Professor of Writing and Director of the PhD Emphasis in Writing Studies at the University of California, Santa Barbara. Most recently, she has co-edited a special issue of the online journal *Kairos* on ownership, authorship, and copyright.

James P. Purdy is Associate Professor of English/Writing Studies and Director of the University Writing Center at Duquesne University, where he received the Presidential Award for Excellence in Teaching. He has co-edited four books and written numerous articles and book chapters on digital writing and research practices and spaces.

The Effects of Intellectual Property Law in Writing Studies

Ethics, Sponsors, and Academic Knowledge-Making

Karen J. Lunsford and James P. Purdy

Routledge
Taylor & Francis Group
NEW YORK AND LONDON

First published 2020
by Routledge
605 Third Avenue, New York, NY 10017

and by Routledge
2 Park Square, Milton Park, Abingdon, Oxon, OX14 4RN

First issued in paperback 2022

Routledge is an imprint of the Taylor & Francis Group, an informa business

Publisher's Note
The publisher has gone to great lengths to ensure the quality of this reprint but points out that some imperfections in the original copies may be apparent.

Library of Congress Cataloging-in-Publication Data
Library of Congress Control Number: 2019952514

ISBN 13: 978-1-03-240092-1 (pbk)
ISBN 13: 978-1-138-49907-2 (hbk)
ISBN 13: 978-1-351-01519-6 (ebk)

DOI: 10.4324/9781351015196

Typeset in NewBaskerville
by Apex CoVantage, LLC

Contents

Tables

Acknowledgments

This project grew out of a conversation at the Conference on College Composition and Communication (CCCC) that followed from our participation in the CCCC Intellectual Property Caucus. We are grateful to the members of the Caucus for their insights, questions, and provocations—and especially their ongoing investment in empowering populations affected by IP decisions. This book endeavors to be part of that mission.

We would also like to thank our study participants who generously answered our survey questions and participated in our interviews to share their reflections. This project would have been impossible without them.

We also benefited from the assistance of several marvelous research assistants who showed care and enthusiasm with everything from data coding to transcribing to preparing the index. Thank you Willard Powell, Indigo Recker, and Kelly Svoboda from Duquesne and Fabian Pacheco from the University of California, Santa Barbara (UCSB). In addition, we thank the students and colleagues from our universities who responded to work in progress and attended our presentations. We are likewise each grateful to have received institutional support for this project. From Duquesne, Jim received a Presidential Scholarship Award and two internal National Endowment for the Humanities grants. From UCSB, Karen received an Academic Senate grant and a faculty fellowship from the Interdisciplinary Humanities Center.

Karen thanks Jim for being an insightful, talented writer and generous collaborator. She also thanks her family, who have always supported her work from both near and far. She honors friends and family who have passed on while this project was underway, including her mother, Beth Lunsford, and IP scholar TyAnna Herrington.

Jim wishes to thank Karen for her intelligence, dedication, and vision. Collaborating was both fun and intellectually rewarding. Jim also wishes to thank his family, including his wife, Mary; mother, Norma; and sister, Amy; who steadfastly supported him in this and in all endeavors. He is grateful to have this bedrock for all of his decisions (IP and otherwise). Finally, he is grateful to Noah and Julia, the next generation of IP decision makers, who bring his life purpose and joy.

1 Introduction

I see IP related issues as inherently fused into the core of our work—what is it to write, [. . .] the role of originality, authorship, etc. Although my experience with the legalistic side of IP is (thankfully) limited, I cannot overstate the importance of such issues to rhet/comp.

—(*Question 20, Response 13*)

The Pervasiveness of Intellectual Property Issues in Academic Life

In *Invention, Copyright, and Digital Writing*, intellectual property scholar Martine Courant Rife reflects on her interviews with seven Web designers, each of whom articulates a different account of how copyright law applies to their work. In response to these differences, Rife argues,

> Misunderstanding and confusion are productive. Misunderstanding is more than just "being wrong." [. . .] Copyright law in all its complexities, and as an interjector in the composing process, likewise begs for misunderstanding and confusion. And to overcome this, participants create stories of the law. Among the interviewees, the proximate law is their story of the law and not really the actual law; it is a story of the law that makes sense to the writer.
>
> (136)

Our book is about such stories of copyright law, including the "[m]isunderstanding and confusion" that emerge surrounding the law, as well as about the influence of intellectual property on academic work in writing studies[1] more generally. By intellectual property (IP), we mean the creations that people can protect with copyrights, patents, trademarks, and trade secrets/proprietary knowledge. In this book, we document reflections of writing studies practitioners[2] about the ways in which IP issues have influenced their work. These reflections illustrate the enculturated practices surrounding IP that have become normalized and show the range of moments in which IP shapes the teaching, research, and editorial work of writing studies professionals—rhetorical moments that recur over and over across colleges and universities. Readers might recognize themselves, their students, their colleagues, or a "friend of a friend" in the following vignettes that represent these moments:

- Vignette #1: An advanced graduate student has just received the publication contract for her first article. She treats it like a click-through license on a piece of software: She skims it, signs and dates the appropriate lines, and sends it back to the publisher.
- Vignette #2: A new faculty member requests copies of documents from a museum archive for a research project and is given a virtually incomprehensible licensing form in return. Noting the irony of having to agree to license materials taken from his own indigenous culture, but needing the materials to do research to achieve tenure, he signs it.
- Vignette #3: The campus librarians sponsor a new event to talk about open-access (OA) clauses in publication contracts, but they cannot recommend a source of funding for humanities scholars to accommodate the high fees publishers now charge to include such OA clauses.
- Vignette #4: A newly hired adjunct is given an employment contract to sign, a contract that includes work-for-hire claims over teaching materials, including materials for online courses.
- Vignette #5: An instructor receives a forwarded email from a student. The email is from an online source that claims a copyright violation because the student has posted a music clip to a website designed for the class. The student's final project—a remixed visual essay analyzing a current political movement—has been removed by an outside entity.
- Vignette #6: A faculty member is considering whether to publish a textbook. On one hand, they[3] need the financial boost (and CV line for promotion) that a successful textbook would provide. On the other hand, their materials were inspired by documents openly shared by colleagues in their program. They debate about their responsibilities to those who have developed materials before them.

As former chairs of the Conference on College Composition and Communication (CCCC) IP Caucus and members of the CCCC IP committee, we have heard such stories about how IP decisions affect the work of teacher-scholars in writing studies. By IP decisions we mean choices such as whether to publish an article with an OA journal, whether to pursue a research project based on whether a desired archive of materials is accessible, whether to ask students to publish their course projects on YouTube, whether to post articles to a course management site, and so forth. Fellow writing studies scholars Heidi A. McKee and James

E. Porter provide the following examples of IP decisions for Internet researchers: "whenever a researcher downloads an online journal article, or quotes excerpts from subjects' writings, or captures screen shots of their web sites, or reproduces their avatar from Second Life or their game character from World of Warcraft" (*Ethics* 56). Stories about these IP decisions are what led to this project. We sought to gather and systemically document these stories through an anonymous nationwide survey and a series of retrospective interviews. When we were initially conceptualizing this research project, we expected horror stories similar to those we had already been told as CCCC representatives: For instance, one researcher shared that a university press refused to publish his print journal article until he removed the one-sentence epigraph. Another researcher explained that a museum archive withheld permissions to reproduce photographs because she planned to submit a copy of her publication to an OA archive. A third researcher reported he had collaborated with an agency to generate survey questions for a study, but he had not anticipated that agency officials would then deem the survey as their proprietary knowledge (i.e., owned by them). Yet another researcher related her saga of receiving permissions from an author to reproduce portions of his rough drafts, only to have the family estate revoke those permissions after he died. Not least, other faculty reported concerns about the Fair Use[4] of instructional materials and the protection of students' rights to engage in critical commentary on texts, multimedia, and cultural artifacts.

While we certainly received some similar stories of specific decisions and events, including, to return to Rife's language, "stor[ies] of the law," our survey and interviews yielded much more, including:

- Discussions of what practitioners might now do differently
- Histories of the evolution of IP (both in terms of changes in IP laws and in terms of changes in personal attitudes towards them)
- Desired past and future developments (i.e., should-have-beens and wished-fors)
- Commentaries on/stances toward IP (both the law and stories of the law)
- Advice about how to approach particular IP issues (e.g., copyright, Fair Use)

When we use the term *reflection* throughout this book, then, we seek to encompass this range. This range of responses speaks not only to the richness of our study participants' experiences, but also to the varied ways in which IP has affected them and influences the broader work of teaching and researching writing.

We next offer one more vignette, with a real name and dates, that hints at this broad impact of and interest in IP issues: In 2015 Creative

Commons creator and perhaps the world's best known copyleft advocate, Lawrence Lessig, ran for president of the United States. Focused primarily on campaign finance and gerrymandering reforms, his platform also articulated an "Innovation Policy" that proposed to create two commissions to write new copyright and patent laws to accommodate new technologies and to reinstate more equitable access to innovations (Lessig "Innovation"). One might argue that it was Lessig's well-known reputation as an IP scholar that scaffolded his presidential bid. We speculate that he might not have reached the fundraising goal that precipitated his run—one million US dollars by Labor Day 2015 from many individual donors (Lessig "Why I Want"; Merica)[5]—were it not for the popularity of his longtime and well-known challenges to prevailing thinking about copyright.[6]

We end this opening section with this vignette because we find Lessig's candidacy in the US presidential election striking. Lessig is an attorney, a scholar, and a university faculty member, not a politician. Even though his campaign lasted only two months (Lessig "Why I Dropped"; Weigel), Lessig's successful bid to have a presence in the election speaks to the currency and urgency of IP issues today. These issues, we argue, are especially pressing for those who both create and teach about IP: members of college and university communities. Moreover, these issues are particularly pertinent to writing studies practitioners, who teach and research major foci of IP: written texts, multimodal compositions, digital webtexts, and multimedia productions. We echo Steve Westbrook's assertion that "copyright law's effects on composition has become a rather exigent matter in our professional lives" ("Introduction" 2). As a field, we have done much work to reflect on pedagogical and research methods, but we have done comparatively little work reflecting on how the IP infrastructure shapes our day-to-day lives as academics in writing studies. Given the larger turn toward metacognition in writing studies (and in higher education more broadly) (McClure and Purdy, Yancey), such reflection is long overdue.

Lessig aside, too few academics are conversant with—much less involved in creating—the IP legislation, policies, and practices that affect their teaching, research, and editing. We invite readers to engage in and influence these conversations about IP. However, we suggest doing so not by memorizing convoluted laws and precedents, but by analyzing reflections like those we share in this book, including stories that writing studies practitioners tell about their IP experiences. In this sense, our book answers Ben McCorkle's call to "create scholarship [. . .] that increases the visibility of intellectual property issues in contexts other than legal discourse" (62). By reporting data from surveys and interviews of writing studies practitioners, as well as offering extended analyses of particular interviews, it also responds to Jessica Reyman's affirmation that "it is only by talking to creators, composers, and authors who rely on digital technologies that we can better understand the need to move beyond considering [the] seemingly universal rule of 'do not steal' to more context-contingent applications of norms" ("Property" 26). Ultimately, writing studies practitioners may (and perhaps should) influence IP law, but first they must understand what ethical lenses writing studies professionals bring to bear on IP situations, who the more proximate sponsors of IP knowledge are, and how IP issues shape our entire knowledge-creating enterprise.

The Need to Document IP's Influence in Writing Studies

Lessig's call for revamping IP, especially copyright, laws in the United States (*Free, Future, Remix*) encapsulates a theme that academics, including those in writing studies, have been hearing for some time: the need to simplify a set of legal concepts that has tremendous influence over the valued products of the information age. The last two decades have witnessed extensive and rapid changes to IP laws and policies in the United States. For those of us in academia, and writing studies in particular, the passage of the Digital Millennium Copyright Act (DMCA), legal cases over peer-to-peer file sharing, the lawsuit at Georgia State over library course reserves, and moves toward open-access (OA) publishing have been notable events. In addition to Lessig, IP scholars such as Heather Joseph, Peter Suber, and John Willinsky have likewise pointed out broad IP trends, such as the erosion of Fair Use and the public domain. They have noted the particular bind for academics, as creators of IP who must participate in a knowledge economy with limited resources, including insufficient knowledge of IP.

Intellectual work has been driving a complex global economy fueled by the online technologies, autonomous vehicles, and handheld devices of the computer industries as well as the texts, music, videos, and movies of the entertainment industries. Intellectual work likewise supports the vaccines, medications, and devices of the medical industries as well as the genetically modified organisms (GMOs), pesticides, and pinpoint machinery of the agricultural industries. Underlying many of these initiatives, of course, is the instruction of new minds, the research, and the intra- and inter-institutional collaborations provided by academia. All of these intellectual areas have to deal with a concept given governmental force some 300 years ago,[7] the idea that products of intellectual labor can, and should, be considered property. Even more, they deal with the idea that intellectual products can, and should, be considered property of individual creators, even though those creators might be employees of large corporations or educational institutions. These assumptions about IP were developed in Anglo-American and Continental contexts, but they also influence, and sometimes dictate, relationships with countries across the world.

Given the range of intellectual work involved, and given 300 years to evolve, it is not surprising that IP laws, processes, and practices appear today to be extraordinarily complex—or, as IP experts in writing studies (e.g., Logie, Reyman, Rife) alongside Lessig have argued, broken. Repeatedly, stakeholders have called for simplified versions of IP to inform (and control) the general public, as when the entertainment industries commissioned public service announcements against peer-to-peer file sharing (see DeVoss and Porter 182–85), or when the US government in collaboration with academic service providers created the Copyright Clearance Center (see Armstrong). Particularly relevant for our project is that teachers and students are two populations especially targeted by messages emphasizing restrictions on sharing materials. For example, the Internet Scout Research Group released a special issue of its Internet Scout Report on March 18, 2016, that compiles, with annotations, instructional resources in two categories: US Copyright, and Intellectual Property and Licensing. The report was published in response to teachers faced with legislation across states echoing a 2006 California Bill (Assembly Bill 307), which mandated that schools receiving funding for technology must also follow and teach "appropriate and ethical use of information technology in the classroom."[8] As we have worked on this research project, we also have been asked—by interviewees, by colleagues, by reviewers—to provide an instructional answer to copyright issues: a handout, a flowchart, a website, something simple to give to academics, especially to undergraduate and graduate students.[9]

However, as the previous vignettes illustrate, writing studies professionals, and academics more generally, are faced with complex decisions about their own and others' IP, and these complex decisions are not reducible to a flowchart or checklist, as much as we might understandably want them to be. Indeed, we would characterize IP decisions as, to borrow a term from design studies, "wicked problems." The notion of wicked problems was advanced by design theorists Horst W.J. Rittel and Melvin M. Webber and subsequently taken up in writing studies. For instance, Richard Marback defines "wicked problems" as problems without a single, knowable solution that are ambiguous, contextual, and iterative and, therefore, must be solved over and over again (W399). Carrie S. Leverenz explains, "By eschewing easy or obvious solutions, wicked problems require us to think creatively about the problem as well as the solution" (7) (see also Purdy "What"). From this perspective, we would argue that the US Constitution, in presenting copyright as both "promot[ing] the Progress of Science and useful Arts" and "securing for limited Times to Authors and Inventors the exclusive Right to their respective Writings and Discoveries" (Article I, § 8, Clause 8), sets up IP as a wicked problem that requires negotiating and balancing competing interests.

The authors of the Constitution might have been more specific and directive, but they recognized the complexities of IP issues. These complexities are sometimes wrapped up in documents, such as contracts and licenses, that attempt to simplify decisions by articulating the responsibilities that different parties have in relation to IP. That effort to simplify, though, often leads to further Byzantine mazes, as stakeholders argue over their relative responsibilities and rights or are unsure what these responsibilities and rights are in the first place. Moreover, the rules and practices that seem to apply in one situation typically do not transfer to others; to deal with IP issues is to deal with a moving target. As many researchers, particularly writing studies IP scholars Jessica Reyman (*Rhetoric*) and Rife (*Invention*) have attested, this approach to IP, one that focuses on how end products are controlled, is neither simple nor has it been attuned to the needs of academics. Fair Use in the United States is one notable example that we discuss in the next chapter.

As academics, and particularly as scholars in writing studies, we must assume a different mindset for handling IP issues—whether these issues are our own, those of our students, or those of the institutions where we work. We argue that instead of a simple flowchart, we need ways of recognizing the different ethical models available to us, the proximate sponsors that so often attempt to define IP on our behalf, the multiple stakeholders involved, and the often tacit or unreported processes by which academics come to resolve IP conflicts. In short, we need critical reflections, including stories of lived experiences. Only through such reflections do we see how someone navigates the complexities of IP laws and practices, the needs of multiple stakeholders, and their own convictions.[10] It is through reflections that we learn what we can and should (and cannot and should not) do. And it is through reflections that we can begin to formulate heuristics for thinking through IP issues that can be useful to other academics as they encounter and contemplate IP issues. With this book, we seek to offer such heuristics (see, in particular, the Conclusion). Instead of flowcharts, then, in this book we offer examples and systematic analysis of writing scholars thinking their way through complex, recurring rhetorical situations in which their intellectual work is mediated by IP law—or rather, by stories about the law.

We affirm that there is a great need to document practitioners' reflections on their experiences with IP in writing studies. First, it is not enough to have "how to" guides. While they can be helpful, such guides often fail to recognize the contextual (i.e., "wicked") nature of IP decisions. Learners must have examples to consider as they also navigate these waters. Some academics are fortunate enough to have colleagues to consult in person. As we have heard repeatedly, though, opportunities for professional development and consultation in IP are often scarce, particularly for the majority of writing specialists who teach as graduate students and adjuncts, and in community colleges.[11] As a result, without documented reflections we lose opportunities to compare and contrast case studies of similar experiences, and we lose exemplars for those who are isolated.

A second reason that there is great need to document writing studies practitioners' IP experiences is that colleges and universities have tended to foreground resources for a narrow (though important) range of IP issues: patent control in computing and the sciences; plagiarism in the classroom and among academics from non-Western cultures; the open-access response to cost increases in academic publication; and guidelines for avoiding legal challenges to online courses or library reserve materials. Conversations in hallways and at conferences, including those represented by our opening vignettes, suggest a need to address a much broader range of IP issues.

A third reason for documenting IP practitioners' reflections is the normalization of IP practices. Certain decisions regarding IP become so commonplace as to become the uncritical norm; consequently, the role of IP in academic work risks erasure. To illustrate, we turn to our survey. An especially provocative version of this tendency to normalize appeared in responses from 19 (of 201) survey respondents who answered "no" when asked whether IP had influenced their research, teaching, or editing work. Three such respondents further elaborated as follows:

> I choose to abide by guidelines to avoid problems.
>
> (Question 20, Response 127)

> I've undoubtedly more or less consciously tried to stay within IP boundaries in all of my work. Insofar as IP laws articulate well-established ethics and conventions I can't say they have constrained the work I've done.
>
> (Question 20, Response 81)

> Not deeply, I don't think. I tend to use copyrighted images in the PPTs [PowerPoints] that I create for in-class use, but seeing as I'm only using the PPTs for educational purposes and in class, and I'm citing the sources of the images (which are often ripped off anyway, I suspect), I don't see it as a problem.
>
> (Question 20, Response 90)

In each of these cases, the IP guidelines—in whatever manner participants defined them—are presented as inconsequential aspects of working as an academic. Yet, these "no, IP has not influenced me" answers are qualified by statements of the labor the respondents report doing to make certain that IP does not affect them deeply: They "choose to abide by guidelines," "stay within IP boundaries," and only use materials "for educational purposes" that are "often ripped off anyway." Such responses signal that respondents are aware that IP work involves labor, yet they do not classify this labor as the result of IP influences. That is, their decisions to "abide by guidelines" become so normalized that they do not see them as decisions at all.[12]

The processes that normalize IP limits, boundaries, laws, and conventions deserve attention. As we discuss in the next chapter, for instance, the "rules" that academics cite for pedagogical, scholarly, and editorial decisions can turn out to be myths that take on a life of their own, as in the case of the CONFU (Conference on Fair Use) Guidelines on Fair Use (Lehman). If nearly all academics within a community see using 10 percent of a text as the absolute maximum allowed under Fair Use, for example, in practice, so it becomes—with the danger that common practice will then be cited in court cases to define more restrictive boundaries on expression than were originally intended by IP law. As Dànielle Nicole DeVoss and Suzanne Webb put it, "If we, as instructors, as researchers, and as composers continue to translate lore into law, we risk chilling the work we can potentially do" (92). Steve Westbrook and James Ryan likewise affirm, "It is not the law itself that is key here but, rather, the cultural perception of legality or, more aptly, the threat of litigation" (101). Normalized practices based on "lore" and "cultural perception" become all the more powerful when they become entrenched within legal, informational, and technological infrastructures.

This book includes critical reflections of higher education faculty on these processes that normalize approaches to IP, concentrating on faculty in writing studies. We chose this focus not merely because writing studies is our disciplinary home but because we see writing studies faculty as especially affected by IP policies and because our discipline's challenges with IP encapsulate challenges experienced by many of our colleagues across the university. Writing specialists engage in research methods shared by other disciplines, often combining close reading and rhetorical analysis of texts and archives (as do humanities scholars more broadly) with the use of surveys, interviews, and observations (as do social science scholars more broadly). All of these methods have IP implications.

In addition to engaging in research methods shared by colleagues across the university, writing studies professionals teach courses (e.g., first-year writing, technical writing, multimedia writing, digital writing) that ask students (and themselves) to think about source use and permissions as well as to engage in research regarding the circulation, delivery, reception, and use of texts and textual artifacts. All of these topics intersect directly with IP issues. Moreover, writing studies professionals, along with librarians, often have the role of explaining IP issues to colleagues across campus—through committee involvement and educational initiatives, such as faculty workshops and professional development. Thus, the reflections of writing studies professionals both highlight IP concerns in ways that might not be visible to others within academia and reflect the larger concerns of higher education faculty more broadly.

IP Research in Writing Studies

Reflections about how IP issues have directly shaped academic work, however, are rarely documented formally in publications. To be sure, scholars in writing studies and English studies have articulated deep histories and thorough analyses of IP regulations as they have affected writing scholars, teachers, and students (DeVoss "Academia," "English"; Herrington; Logie; Lowe "Brief"; Lunsford and West; Ratliff; Reyman *Rhetoric*; Woodmansee and Jaszi *Construction*, "Law"), as well as argued for the necessity of focusing on local, situated cases in considering the ethics of work in digital environments (McKee and Porter "Ethics of Digital," *Ethics of Internet*). A few (Westbrook *Composition*, "Visual"; Galin "Own"; Rife, Slattery, and DeVoss; Bazerman et al.) have offered brief anecdotes of their own or their students' encounters with IP challenges. However, these anecdotes have not been systematically documented and analyzed. These anecdotes, moreover, tend to focus on individual, episodic experiences, such as the unexpected discovery of a lack of open access (OA) to publications or permissions to use images. Such experiences are presented in disconnected, narrative silos. Our more systemic look at the IP experiences of writing studies practitioners, however, offers a fuller picture of the fundamental impact that IP concerns and regulations have on all aspects of constructing and disseminating knowledge in writing studies. Isolated anecdotes overlook how scholars must strategize not only for the short term, but also for the long term of their careers. Most of the published anecdotes, too, come from writing scholars whose research specializes in understanding IP. Several of these scholars are participants in our project, and we share their IP reflections at greater length. With this project, though, we seek not only to extend these scholars' reflections on their experiences but also to situate them within a broader sampling of encounters with IP by writing studies professionals. Our participants, therefore, include mostly scholars who do not identify themselves as specialists in IP, so their reflections represent a wider range of voices talking about ways in which IP issues affect academics going about their daily work of writing, teaching, and editing.

Numerous writing studies scholars, of course, have published important studies on IP, particularly regarding applications of the Fair Use doctrine to teaching writing, especially with digital technologies (Conference on College Composition and Communication Caucus; DeVoss and Porter; Herrington; Logie; McKee; Rife "Fair," "Why"; Shirk and Smith; Spigelman; Westbrook *Composition*, "Visual"); remix compositions, again, especially, though not exclusively, with digital technologies (DeVoss and Webb; Dubisar and Palmeri; Edwards; Ridolfo and DeVoss); and OA considerations of and needs for writing students and faculty (Ballentine "In Defense," "Writing"; Bazerman et al.; Edwards and Reyman; Lowe "Brief," "Considerations," "Copyright"; Lowe and Zemliansky; Ratliff, "Resolution 5"). The field's prominent journals have published special issues on topics surrounding IP, including two special issues of *Computers and Composition,* one in 1998 on *Intellectual Property* (Gurak and Johnson-Eilola) and one in 2010 on *Copyright, Culture, Creativity, and the Commons* (Rife et al.); a 1998 special issue of *Kairos* on *Copywrite, Plagiarism, and Intellectual Property* (Amore et al.), with a follow-up special issue on *Ownership, Authorship, and Copyright* published in Fall 2019 (Lunsford, Logie, and Herrington); a 2010 special issue of *Technical Communication Quarterly* on *Technical Communication and the Law* (Reyman and Schuster); and a 2013 special issue of *College English* on *Western Cultures of Intellectual Property* (Kennedy and Howard). Given the volume of publications on IP in writing studies, a thorough review of this work is beyond the scope of this book. Our study, however, responds to four main gaps in the existing writing studies scholarship.

First, apart from Rife's study, which helped to inspire this work, there are to our knowledge no empirical studies of the influences of IP in writing studies. In publications from her study (*Invention,* "Copyright"), Rife reports survey and interview data regarding how technical writing students and professional writers perceived and understood the influence of US copyright law on their creation of Web content. This important study begins to make the argument that copyright issues affect more than the product of digital writing; they affect process, particularly invention. In reporting results of this study in *Invention, Copyright, and Digital Writing,* Rife calls for follow-up investigation of these effects (150–54).

Our study answers Rife's call. We take up and expand this call in three important ways. First, our study focuses on IP issues beyond just copyright law to approach IP more broadly, including other IP laws, policies, and practices. While copyright was still a main focus of those we surveyed and interviewed, participants in our study also reflected on patents, trademarks, trade secrets/proprietary knowledge, and even plagiarism, as well as copyright. Second, we asked participants to report the effects of IP on their teaching, research, and editorial work—that is, all aspects of their academic lives—not just digital writing or writing for the Internet, the focus of Rife's study. Third, our study includes any scholar who identified with the discipline of writing studies, whereas Rife focused on only one group within writing studies, members of the subfield of technical and professional communication.

A second way our study seeks to complement existing work on IP in writing studies is by focusing on the lived experience of academics.[13] Existing research approaches IP through the lens of the entertainment industry. Such research is helpful, even crucial, of course. As Reyman affirms in *The Rhetoric of Intellectual Property,* IP laws tend to privilege the entertainment industry first; attention to education comes later. But we see value in making higher education activities focal. Indeed, they have too long been disregarded in conversations about IP. In their larger study of the ethics of Internet research, Heidi A. McKee and James E. Porter begin to address IP issues faced by writing studies scholars who do research. They offer one example situation in their chapter of *The Ethics of Internet Research: A Rhetorical, Case-Based Process* on regulatory ethics (56–61). We find great value in their approach of offering example cases, and in this book we share examples representing a wider range of the IP decisions encountered by academics. In other words, we expand our focus beyond just Internet research to address other kinds of research, as well as teaching and editing activities.

A third way our study complements existing scholarship in writing studies is through attention to process. With a few notable exceptions, existing IP research in writing studies focuses mostly on textual products, not processes. Some of this work *talks* about process, but its objects of analysis remain finished products (e.g., laws, student writing, writing curricula). Moreover, existing research in writing studies that does focus on process almost exclusively deals with issues of remix (e.g., DeVoss and Webb; Dubisar and Palmeri). This work contributes significantly to our understanding of ways in which remix practices challenge and complicate conceptions of textual ownership and authorship. As our interview and survey participants make clear, however, there are many more areas of IP's influence to be explored.

Fourth, existing IP research in writing studies focuses on plagiarism more than on legal licensing, contracts, work-for-hire, and other IP issues that affect academics (in writing studies and more broadly). This body of scholarship, like scholarship on remix, crucially informs and enriches our understanding of textual ownership and authorship. Given writing studies' disciplinary foci, the prevalence of this lens for understanding IP makes sense. Indeed, as the special issues of journals highlighted previously illustrate, significant work in writing studies has addressed IP in terms of plagiarism, and several of our study participants shared stories about, experiences with, and commentaries on plagiarism in discussing IP, particularly regarding ways in which they teach students to cite sources and avoid plagiarism. We think it is important, however, to extend the conversation about IP beyond plagiarism. Attention to plagiarism is necessary but not sufficient.

Given these four gaps, there are two areas in particular where writing studies scholars can and should advise colleges and universities about IP. These possibilities for intervention helped motivate our study and, through sharing the reflections we gathered, we hope to begin to offer this advice and intervention with this book. The first area is the particular focus of this study: the day-to-day lived impact of IP on individual academics. Our nationwide survey and interviews affirm that IP concerns play a significant role in determining teaching and research trajectories for faculty at all levels, including contingent faculty and graduate students. For instance, cost burdens (e.g., paying licensing or permissions fees) have shifted to individual academics. Scholars—from PhD students writing dissertations to established faculty seeking promotion—face difficult choices between paying high out-of-pocket costs or simply abandoning a particular image, quotation, video clip, or even a whole project.

Moreover, burdens of proof for Fair Use of IP have shifted to individual academics as well. For example, writers accused of copyright violations (particularly in digital venues) must often demonstrate their innocence to have materials restored. This guilty-until-proven-innocent approach allows for trolling (i.e., deliberately attacking others anonymously online), as opposing agencies use copyright claims to carry out censorship. We found through our survey and interviews that colleges and universities do not always provide legal protection, advice, or support for faculty or students accused of such violations—or, if they do, individual academics are unsure how to access it. Given this shift in the environment of higher education to individual responsibility, we feel it is important to study and document how individual academics are navigating these situations—and to provide example cases for reference.

The second area where writing studies scholars can and should offer advice to institutions of higher education is regarding the shift away from copyright ownership to licensing. Writing studies scholars have addressed the value of, advocated for, and critiqued use of Creative Commons licenses (e.g., Basgier; Galin and Latchaw; Lowe "Considerations"; Zimmerman) and analyzed the (troubling) rhetoric of click-through licenses (e.g., Stedman). In this way, writing studies scholars, along with Lessig and other IP scholars, have done much to inform our understanding of possibilities for and challenges of licensing. Licenses have become so important in discussions of IP because they control access to university library materials and research data and can serve as a move away from Fair Use. For example, in many cases, libraries no longer own physical copies of journals but have licensed the right to allow certain members of the university or college to access digital copies of those journals. Similarly, OA is often controlled through licensing, because authors are asked to pay for the right to place materials into OA repositories. Likewise, control of multimedia—images, music clips, and video clips—has grown increasingly restrictive, sometimes by universities and colleges themselves. As several high-profile cases (e.g., Georgia State,[14] DMCA[15]) have shown, the shift to licensing is involving universities in legal disputes. This shift places an additional responsibility (even burden) on academics; thus, discussions of licensing need to be included as a part of professional development for writing studies faculty and students of all levels. This book offers a start in that direction.

What we found from our study is that many participants indicated that they had not thought about IP issues before—that it is only in retrospect that they considered the influences of IP on their academic work. As one survey respondent put it, "I've not given it [IP] much thought. Until now . . ." (Question 20, Response 154). We see part of the need for this project, then, as helping writing studies practitioners (and academics more broadly) be mindful up front of the shaping force of IP—that is, *before* they make decisions. Thus, rather than be reactive, scholars can be proactive in considering IP.

Personal Stakes

Before we share the reflections of our study participants, we believe it is important to share our own reflections, as several personal experiences have led us to this project. We each have experienced the effects of the changing landscape of IP. For instance, when editing a special issue of a prominent scholarly journal, Karen was surprised when a twenty-second clip of a two-hour movie was challenged as not being under Fair Use; the argument was that there was not sufficient commentary on the clip. Likewise, Jim was told by the editors of another prominent scholarly journal that a short epigraph for his article could not be included without authorial permission; because time did not allow for securing such permission prior to the publication deadline, the epigraph had to be removed. Moreover, as part of a faculty writing group, Karen was asked questions in response to drafts of this project that show popular misunderstanding of Fair Use and a fear of the presence of copyright trolls. Similarly, one of Jim's research assistants for this project requested that he help run a workshop on IP issues for graduate students because they felt largely unsure of how to address copyright issues—or even what IP knowledge they needed (and will need) as students, teachers, and researchers.

We each also have served on committees for which IP concerns have been central. For instance, we both have participated in the Intellectual Property Caucus in Composition Studies (commonly referred to as the CCCC-IP)—with Karen serving as junior chair and senior chair in 2009 and 2010, respectively, and Jim serving as junior chair and senior chair in 2015 and 2016, respectively. From its inception in 1994 through June 2016, the CCCC-IP served as the public counterpart of the Conference on College Composition and Communication's closed Committee on Intellectual Property, and the senior chair of the CCCC-IP served as an ex-officio member of this committee. In June 2016 the Committee on Intellectual Property was not reconstituted; therefore, as of the time of this writing, the CCCC-IP's role has changed and expanded to take on responsibilities of this committee. CCCC-IP has held annual meetings open to any member of the Conference on College Composition and Communication (CCCC). At meetings CCCC-IP participants work to create action plans; develop lobbying strategies; mentor junior scholars and graduate students; produce documents for political, professional, and pedagogical use; and (formerly) advise the Committee on Intellectual Property of desired actions and items to be brought to the larger CCCC and/or NCTE (National Council of Teachers of English) organizations. As members and officers in an organization with this charge, we heard stories like those represented in the vignettes opening Chapter 1, stories of concern, frustration, and uncertainty.

Two other committee affiliations have informed our work on and interest in this research. In March 2015, Karen chaired the CCCC Task Force called upon to update and revise the *CCCC Guidelines for the Ethical Conduct of Research in Composition Studies*, a document that addresses ethical issues in classroom, online, archival, and other empirical research. Jim was also a member of his institution's Institutional Review Board (IRB) from 2012 to 2017. Though not directly charged with considering IP policy or legislation, both committees dealt with ethical research practices and human subjects rights, concerns that intersect with IP issues. Thus, our interest in this project comes directly from our own professional work. It comes from not only an abstract sense of the importance of the topic of IP for academics, but also a tangible felt need of the influence of IP on our own campuses and in our own academic pursuits in writing studies.

In addition to our individual and committee experiences, our research (both individually and collaboratively) led us to this project. For instance, Karen published on the California Open-Access initiative in the *IP Annual*, a publication of the CCCC-IP (Lunsford). Jim published several articles in peer-reviewed journals on plagiarism-detection technologies, with particular attention to their (mis)treatment of students' IP (Purdy "Anxiety," "Calling"). This book is a part of our larger study investigating the influences of IP on academics' research, teaching, and editorial work.

In sum, we have personal and professional stakes in the influences of IP on postsecondary education.

Our Project: Documenting and Analyzing IP Reflections in Writing Studies

Therefore, for this book we sought out reflections and documented the stories writing studies scholars tell. We did so in two ways, a survey and interviews, both approved by our institutions' IRBs. First, we conducted a nationwide, anonymous, online survey, distributed via Survey Monkey, during January to October 2015, with a mix of twenty multiple choice and free response questions (see Appendix A for a copy of this survey). This mix of questions allowed for quantitative and qualitative analysis. Participants could elect to skip any questions they did not wish to answer or those that were not relevant. Questions were aligned with IP issues we had identified through a pilot study[16] as potentially impacting scholars: permission costs (Questions 1–9), challenges to using others' and protecting one's own IP (Questions 10–15), intersections of IP and IRBs (question 16), knowledge of IP (question 17), and intersections of IP and teaching (Questions 17–19). The final question (Question 20) asked participants, "As you reflect on your career, in what ways have intellectual property concerns shaped your teaching, research-writing practices, and/or your editorial decisions?" We recruited scholars who identified themselves as associated with writing studies by advertising through multiple channels: 1) discussion boards/email lists dedicated to writing studies; 2) Facebook posts and tweets; and 3) announcements at the 2015 CCCC and Computers and Writing conferences. In addition, we emailed the editors of journals in writing studies to invite their participation.

This survey was completed (in part or in whole) by 393 teachers-scholars who identified themselves as associated with the discipline of writing studies. Participants were, therefore, self-selected, and the results reflect a population likely interested in IP. Perhaps based on their self-selection to participate, open-ended responses reflect a variety of fields that participants considered as falling under the category of "writing studies," including composition, technical communication, professional communication, multimodal composition, and creative writing. Thus, while this range may not be strictly representative of writing studies as defined at most US colleges and universities, it reflects views across related humanities disciplines and, consequently, is useful for our project. To maintain confidentiality, we did not request demographic information; however, some participants volunteered such information in their open-ended responses. Open-ended responses indicate a range of career experience, from graduate students through professors emeriti, and so offer insight into the effects of IP for the full span of academic careers. The majority of respondents appear to have been located in the United States, although some participants identified themselves as from Argentina, Brazil, Canada, and Iceland. Because different questions had different numbers of respondents, we use response numbers in this book to identify quotes from the survey; thus, response numbers across questions do not necessarily refer to the same person.

Second, we conducted semi-structured interviews with twenty-eight writing studies scholars of varying seniority at various institutions. We asked them questions about the ways in which IP (defined broadly) has affected their research, teaching, and/or editing, including their past experiences and future prognostications (see Appendix B for the interview questions and transcription conventions). These 45–90 minute interviews were recorded via Skype, telephone, or in-person video and audio recording. Participants consented to the use of their real names.

While our request to use real names was grounded in practical concerns (we wanted to use video and sound clips in publications and presentations), it was also crucial in allowing us to give participants ownership over their stories and to emphasize the ways in which particular people have been influenced by and grapple with IP in their professional work.

Equally as important, in this project we sought to document the experiences of members of writing studies who have been touched by IP concerns. Academics' encounters with IP have brought productive initiatives for disseminating research and teaching materials through open source and OA venues as well as alternatives to strict copyright ownership (e.g., Creative Commons). Too often, however, our needs as academics have been disregarded by entertainment and other industries because we have lacked a strong voice in national IP discussions. Too often, our needs as individual scholars have been subsumed under the claims of an academic institution because we lacked data to support our arguments. To redress these problems, we offer here data on the range of media/texts and the range of academic processes affected by IP.

In addition to documenting these reflections, we analyzed them. Along with reviewing the quantitative responses in the survey data, we coded answers to free response questions to identify trends. Likewise, we transcribed the interview recordings and, once participants had the opportunity to approve those transcriptions, coded these individual transcriptions as a group to determine themes. More specifically, we coded the explanatory comments respondents provided for the first nine questions of the survey regarding the financial costs of securing IP permissions. Doing so allowed us to discover that many participants reported low or no costs paid for IP permissions because they decided not to include desired materials, and thus did not pay for them. We also coded Questions 10 and 11 for the reasons why respondents chose not to include desired materials in publications or course materials. Doing so allowed us to discover that cost, time, hassle/effort, permission denial, and orphan works were the main reasons. In analyzing our participants' interview transcripts, we were struck by the variety of ethical lenses participants used in making IP decisions and the sponsors, particularly gatekeepers, that participants identified, implicitly and explicitly, as mediating their application of these lenses. In turn, for Questions 12–20 in the survey, we coded open-ended responses for the ethical lenses and sponsors that emerged from the interviews.

Another theme that emerged from the survey responses is that IP issues impacted not just end products, but the entire knowledge-making process. Thus, we also coded responses to the final, open-ended question of the survey (Question 20) regarding ways in which participants described the impact of IP on work over their career. To arrive at this emergent coding scheme, we first separately coded the 201 responses to this question and then compared our individual coding, negotiating to agree on all codes. Doing so allowed us to determine that respondents indicated IP influenced five parts of the knowledge-making cycle: 1) choosing topics to study and teach; 2) collecting data and materials; 3) negotiating procedures and products for publication; 4) disseminating and storing texts; and 5) employing materials and technologies in face-to-face and digital classes. Chapters 3, 4, and 5 identify and discuss these ethical lenses, sponsors, and knowledge-making processes, respectively.

To provide context for our participants' reflections in their survey and interview responses, Chapter 2, "Histories of Intellectual Property in Academia," centers on the question, What histories and legislation set the parameters for an IP decision? This chapter offers a brief history of IP, particularly copyright, and the academy. This chapter reinforces that there are, in fact, multiple histories of IP. In particular, Anglo-American and Continental approaches to IP have evolved to privilege different figures in the rhetorical triangle. The Anglo-American system favors the audience, while the Continental system favors the author (though, as we affirm, the Anglo-American system has come increasingly to favor the author). By discussing two significant facets of US IP law, Fair Use and the Bayh-Dole Act, Chapter 2, "Histories of Intellectual Property in Academia," chronicles how time has allowed certain choices about IP to become routinized among postsecondary institutions.[17] The chapter situates our analysis of these aspects of law, as well as the 2001 boycott of scientific journals, within larger conversations of IP in critical university studies in order to acknowledge broader cultural and economic trends that have changed and challenged the role of IP in institutions of higher education. As a result of these trends, and as our study participants attest, IP legislation and its varied interpretations may exert unacknowledged influence over choices that writing studies professionals make in regard to their teaching, research, and editing. This chapter helps to illustrate that the complex, sometimes invisible histories of IP legislation likewise suggest why IP procedures often come across as intimidating, a comment we repeatedly heard from participants in our nationwide survey, in our interviews, and in our work with members of CCCC. Faced with this complexity, academics can learn ways in which to respond to IP situations through critical reflection.

Chapter 3, "Ethical Lenses Academics Bring to Intellectual Property Decisions," provides such reflections from our study participants that show them to approach IP issues through a range of ethical lenses (not limited to legal or Western views). It seeks to answer the question, What values guide writing studies practitioners' IP decisions? We found participants apply a range of ethical lenses and sustain multiple, even contradictory, ethical lenses simultaneously. These approaches emerge from participants' understandings of themselves as academics in writing studies. Drawing on McKee and Porter's work on ethical approaches to research in writing studies, which emphasizes the value of looking beyond laws to case-based reflections in making (and understanding) complex decisions, this chapter shares ways in which participants recounted experiences that show them using different sophisticated lenses to provide models for how to understand and/or negotiate IP issues, to offer alternative views that writing studies practitioners need to consider in challenging existing entrenched perspectives, and to highlight policy debates occurring in the discipline of writing studies and in academia more broadly. For instance, one of the participants offers a Native American perspective on IP that approaches IP as collectively rather than individually owned, another offers an industry perspective that establishes academic work as entrepreneurial, and another provides a classical rhetoric perspective that situates IP decisions as based in considerations of ethos. In this chapter we provide data from our study showing writing studies practitioners view IP as part of business practice, IP as part of economic systems, IP as fundamental to democracy, IP as protecting individual expertise, IP as part of ethical systems, IP as collective development of a culture, and IP as about disciplinary relationships. Ultimately, this chapter argues that it is crucial for writing studies scholars to recognize this range of ethical lens options, in order to consider alternatives for the complex teaching, research, and editorial situations they encounter, as well as to recognize the lenses that prevail in current US legislation, in order to understand the perspectives privileged in the law.

Our survey and interviews reveal that these ethical lenses are instantiated and enacted through sponsors. These sponsors are the subject of Chapter 4, "Sponsors that Mediate Academic Intellectual Property Decisions," which addresses the question, Who and what offer guidance about IP decisions, and what advice do they offer? We use the term *sponsor*, following Deborah Brandt's term *literacy sponsor*, because we argue IP knowledge is a type of literacy. As our survey and interviews show, academics' IP decisions routinely are shaped by sponsors, including gatekeepers, who provide both accurate and misapplied information. Such sponsors have significant, but often invisible, influence, and this chapter seeks to make such sponsors more visible. By analyzing survey responses, this chapter illustrates that these sponsors can be human (e.g., editors, department chairs, interview participants themselves), institutional (Fair Use guidelines, publishers, cost), and technological (e.g., YouTube, content management systems, Google). The chapter then provides two extended examples taken from our interviews that demonstrate the influences of IP sponsors. We first analyze a trend that characterized the majority of our interviews, attention to the changing conditions of—and roles of sponsors in mediating—archival research. We close by offering an extended example of the interview of one participant, Cruz Medina,[18] whose reflections illustrate a subtle, cumulative change in IP practices based on the interventions of various IP sponsors.

Taken together, participants' reflections in Chapter 4 offer data about the multiple forces that shape what writing studies practitioners learn about IP and that direct what decisions they make (or think they can make) regarding IP. In this chapter we argue that knowing these sponsors can make practitioners more mindful of decision points as well as ways in which they can and should be sponsors. Moreover, these reflections document misinformation, where gatekeepers misguide through inaccurate advice or directives, and show instances of missed opportunities for faculty to pursue teaching and scholarship as well as for universities to intervene on behalf of their faculty and students.

Our study shows that survey and interview participants bring ethical lenses to bear on and sponsors influence work at different parts throughout the academic knowledge-making cycle, not just at the end with textual products. These different parts are the focus of Chapter 5, "Effects of Intellectual Property on the Academic Knowledge-Making Cycle," which explores the question, When are IP decisions made in academic knowledge-making? Our study participants revealed that elements of the knowledge-making cycle affected by IP include choosing topics and texts to research and teach, collecting data and evidence, negotiating procedures and products for publications, disseminating texts, and using materials in face-to-face and online classes. Through first analyzing survey responses, this chapter both recounts ways in which study participants changed what they did for their research and teaching because of IP encounters as well as identifies ways in which study participants changed what and where they published based on IP encounters. The chapter then offers more extended analyses of interviews from two study participants, Damián Baca and Cheryl E. Ball, to reinforce that IP concerns influence the full knowledge-making cycle in systemic, pervasive, and sometimes in more insidious ways. Taken together, participants' reflections in Chapter 5 offer data about the multiple instances and places where writing studies practitioners at all levels are blocked from or enabled in doing their work because of IP.

The final chapter of the book offers a concluding reflection and call to action. In this chapter, we address the challenges of increased focus on IP in writing studies and identify ways in which this book helps writing studies practitioners meet those challenges. We then, based on analysis of findings from our survey responses and interviews, offer heuristic questions to guide writing studies professionals in making IP decisions that influence their teaching, research, and editorial work. We organize these questions by the foci of our chapters: ethical lenses, sponsors, and steps of academic knowledge-making. Each set of heuristics is followed by a hypothetical scenario, drawn from vignettes we offer in Chapter 1, that walks readers through applying these questions to IP decisions they may face. Next, we consider three future trajectories of IP—nonhuman agents, artificial intelligence and bots, and licensing—that will inevitably affect writing studies practitioners in their future teaching, research, and editing. Finally, we close the book with two reflections: We tell our own IP story connected with writing this book, reviewing our own IP choices. Then, to echo the story of Lessig's run for president that we offer in this introductory chapter, we return to a story that connects IP, particularly copyright, and the presidential office of the United States, the proposed Register of Copyrights Selection and Accountability Act, which assigns the president, rather than the librarian of Congress, the authority to appoint the register of copyrights.

But first, to better understand these and our study participants' reflections, we look back at the history—or, rather, the histories—of the academy's complex relationship with IP.

Notes

1. Charles Bazerman defines writing studies as "the study of writing—its production, its circulation, its uses, its role in the development of individuals and societies, and its learning by individuals, social collectives, and historically emergent cultures. [. . .] Inquiry into the skills, practices, objects and consequences of reading and writing" (32).
2. When we reference professionals from writing studies, we assume—and wish to highlight—that they are "teacher-scholars" by default. That is, because of the discipline's historical grounding in and emphasis on pedagogy, practitioners both teach and research. Both roles are integral. Thus, both roles should be understood for writing studies professionals even when we use the terms *scholar* or *practitioner.*
3. We use *they* as a singular pronoun to avoid binary gendering (with a recognition that some non-binary individuals are using other pronouns). We intend this pronoun to be inclusive.
4. In Chapter 2, we define and discuss the Fair Use exemption to copyright law (Section 107 of the US Copyright Act of 1976).
5. Lessig's fundraising efforts reflected his platform to reform campaign financing laws so that corporate entities or a few big donors would not wield so much influence over the federal government.
6. Lessig's ideas about reforming copyright are perhaps most famously developed in *Free Culture: How Big Media Uses Technology and the Law to Lock Down Culture and Control Creativity.*
7. Most visibly, in England, by the Statute of Anne, 1710.
8. The enacted language of the Bill called on schools "to educate pupils and teachers on the appropriate and ethical use of information technology in the classroom, Internet safety, the manner in which to avoid committing plagiarism, the concept, purpose, and significance of a copyright so that pupils are equipped with the skills necessary to distinguish lawful from unlawful online downloading, and the implications of illegal peer-to-peer network file sharing" (California, AB 307 ¶3). The regulation was incorporated into California's Education Code in 2006, amended again in 2007, and repealed in 2017.
9. In this way, our experience reflects that of McKee and Porter, who note that in their work on Institutional Review Boards they encountered "reviewers and researchers who when reviewing Internet research projects desperately [sought] some clear-cut, absolute answers to thorny questions" (*Ethics* 151).

10. At the end of his *Law and Literature* article "Fair Use and Education: The Way Forward," legal scholar Peter Jaszi makes a similar claim and call for teachers to tell their stories, in his case stories about how teachers' work with copyrighted material is necessarily transformative (45).
11. Jody Millward et al. found that "[t]wo-year colleges teach an estimated 50% of all college-level composition and an estimated 70% of all developmental composition courses" (8). These instructors typically are expected to invest in professional development through research and/or the development of instructional materials.
12. Notably, we also found language pointing to similar labor among survey respondents who answered, "yes, IP has influenced me." Among the interviewees, we received extended reflections by participants who both challenged and abided by IP guidelines, and we analyze some of these responses in later chapters of this book.
13. Certainly, we are not the first to survey or interview academics about their research-writing practices. For instance, Ithaka S+R has conducted surveys of US and UK faculty regarding their work (Housewright et al. *Ithaka S+R | Jisc*; Housewright et al. *Ithaka S+R U.S.*; Wolff et al.). Jennifer Rowley et al. also used surveys to gauge UK academics' attitudes toward and participation in OA publishing. Yet these surveys only indirectly touch on IP issues—in particular, faculty members' use of OA materials. Such surveys do not yet address how IP issues directly affect research and teaching activities. That is one reason why we conducted our own survey.
14. In *Cambridge University Press et al. v. Patton*, also known as the "Georgia State" case, several academic publishers, including Cambridge, claimed that the Georgia State University Libraries illegally posted digital copies of texts on reserve. Georgia State claimed doing so constituted Fair Use. The case rulings and appeals have highlighted the murkiness of applications of the Fair Use exemption. We discuss this case further in Chapter 2.
15. The DMCA, or Digital Millennium Copyright Act, is the 1998 US copyright law that criminalizes use of technologies to intentionally circumvent copyright protections and increases penalties for infringing copyright on the Internet.
16. We developed the survey through a pilot study during November–December 2014 in which we invited ten experienced scholars to test 20 questions; seven respondents were able to provide comments. We used their feedback to refine the survey for general release, but we do not include their responses in the survey results and totals we discuss in this book.
17. One such choice is the precedent that faculty at research universities typically are granted copyright ownership of their intellectual works by the institution's hiring contract, even though such agreements may become tenuous (Rooksby "Copyright" 199–204, 220). Time has also allowed conceptions and misconceptions of IP to become entangled, as when teachers, students, and other composers must consider the extent to which digital copying intersects with plagiarism (Rife "Why"). Even when IP procedures are rendered more visible, as when peer-to-peer file sharing visibly challenged the procedures of traditional publishers and music distributors (DeVoss and Porter; Logie; Reyman), IP protocols have many facets that must be learned, and academics do not always have the resources at hand for learning them.
18. See Appendix B for the interview questions and transcription conventions; see Appendix C for the position titles and affiliations of interview participants from at the time of their interviews.

2 Histories of Intellectual Property in Academia

IP rules help motivate me to publish because I know I will get credit for my work. Research is hard work—I want to be recognized for it.

—(*Question 20, Response 69*)

Historical Shifts in IP Legislation: Toward More Author-Centered Practices

Before we turn to the reflections from our interview and survey participants, we present a larger picture of the historical and cultural exigencies that have brought us in higher education to our current relationships with IP. This historical trajectory emphasizes the need to approach IP as continuously in process, rather than as a set of rigid rules or procedures that academics can and should memorize, as IP legislation itself has developed over time through frequently rancorous debates. Time has buried the initial historical exigencies for IP legislation, as well as the fact that US legislation has been influenced repeatedly by global (especially European) legal mores. We need to make visible the major IP developments that establish why IP matters to academia in order to better understand our study participants' reflections on IP.

In this chapter, then, we provide the historical background and context to help readers understand the data we share in the following chapters. We sketch a tale of the complex development of IP legislation in the US, especially copyright, and offer a closer look at Fair Use, particularly the story of Fair Use that has been promulgated throughout academic institutions through both official channels and lore. This story about Fair Use serves as an example of the power of stories in shaping our understanding of and reactions to IP and the need to look beyond just legislation in considering the influence of IP. We then examine current economic exigencies through the lens of critical university studies, particularly to consider the impact of the Bayh-Dole Act and 2001 journal boycott in fundamentally changing the role of IP in academia.

To sketch our historical tale, we turn to historian Peter Baldwin's book *The Copyright Wars: Three Centuries of Trans-Atlantic Battle* as a framework for understanding historical events surrounding IP. We know there are other histories, particularly English studies and legal scholars Martha Woodmansee and Peter Jaszi's *The Construction of Authorship: Textual Appropriation in Law and Literature.* We reference Baldwin here, however, because, as important as lawyers and legislators are for defining IP legalities, Baldwin's cultural history emphasizes that people are not actuated by the letter of the law, but rather are motivated by cultural assumptions and by contradictory goals. We see Baldwin as aligning the stakeholders in the debates over IP legislation with a rhetorical triangle; they include the author, the distributor, and the audience. Such an alignment reinforces writing studies and IP scholar Martine Courant Rife's point, with which we begin Chapter 1, that non-lawyers tend to make sense of the law by telling stories about the law, including stakeholders and sponsors as characters in these stories (*Invention* 136). And this alignment reinforces the value of considering IP from the perspective of writing studies. IP legislation attempts to define relationships between individuals, states, and innovations—or, in other words, authors, audiences, and distributors—and attempts to answer questions such as What is at stake in this property-sharing, power-sharing agreement? as well as Who has a voice, and, more pointedly, who has the dominant voice in this agreement? Baldwin's triangle of author, distributor, and audience provides a rhetorical means of tracking the different answers that cultures have devised.

Our book's ultimate intervention in IP issues, then, is not legal but rhetorical. As writing studies scholars rather than attorneys/legal scholars, our focus is the ways in which our colleagues make meaning of and about IP through reflecting on their experiences, including the stories they tell, the advice they offer, and the prognostications and commentaries they make. That is, we are interested in their rhetorical constructions of IP, including the lenses they use as authors of their own experiences to frame and make sense of IP (which we address in Chapter 3), the mediators they encounter who shape how they come to understand and respond to IP (which we address in Chapter 4), and the moments throughout their professional work of knowledge-making when such considerations occur (which we address in Chapter 5).

Our historical narrative begins 300 years ago, when legislators in England and on continental Europe debated how to define a new type of property, the property of intellectual labor. In part, these debates marked an addition to a palimpsest of previous practices that governed intellectual innovation, including systems of patronage, monopolies granted by royalty, and the residual practices of trade guilds. Crucially, in their debates, the Anglo legislators and those on continental Europe constructed different balances among authors, distributors, and audiences.

Simply put, the Anglo system tended to favor the public domain (the audience), while the Continental system tended, and still tends, to favor an author's rights (Baldwin; see also Woodmansee and Jaszi *Construction*). When the US founders wrote the Constitution, they aligned their IP code with the Anglo one. The Constitution sought to support new innovation by granting only a limited monopoly to creators: "Congress shall have power [. . .] to promote the Progress of Science and useful Arts, by securing for limited Times to Authors and Inventors the exclusive Right to their respective Writings and Discoveries" (Article I, § 8, Clause 8). The limited time for copyright protection was set as fourteen years, with the possibility of one renewal (via the Copyright Act of 1790). After that, the work would be considered in the public domain and open for improvement or further development by others.

Even this initial sketch begins to provide context for some of the moral, legal, and power conundrums we as academics find ourselves in today. As academics (and as writing studies practitioners, in particular), we are living in an IP milieu in which we have inherited at least two different legal responses that articulate different ways of thinking about IP and that privilege different players in what we see as Baldwin's rhetorical triangle.[1] These differences are in direct conflict with each other. The Anglo-American system answers the question about how a culture might best foster innovation by limiting an author's monopoly over intellectual work in favor of allowing others to adopt, adapt, build upon, or otherwise exploit it. The Continental system, on the other hand, operates from the assumption that authors should be rewarded long term for their efforts, and they should retain some say over the future of their intellectual products. Since academics are both creators and consumers of others' creations, each system may be attractive under different circumstances.[2]

Frankly, though, neither of these approaches has been primarily concerned with academic needs, as we explore later in discussing adaptations and accommodations that institutions of higher education have made in regard to Fair Use. In addition, neither the Anglo-American nor the Continental system acknowledges non-Western ways of thinking about intellectual labor, a fact reinforced by several of the academics we interviewed (see Chapter 3). As universities increasingly participate in a global economy, we argue that academics must also consider these non-Western systems as part of our IP palimpsest.[3]

To fully understand our options, we must further sketch the history of this palimpsest and tease out its multiple layers. As a starting point, we need to recognize that IP itself is not monolithic as a concept. Several different categories have been defined according to different types of intellectual processes and products. As defined in US law, these categories include copyright, patents, trademarks, and proprietary knowledge (or trade secrets). Often these categories have been challenged or stretched, as new technologies and concepts have been created: For instance, critical university studies and legal scholar Jacob H. Rooksby (*Branding*) explores the question of whether patent law applies to living things, including the human genome (122–30), as well as whether Internet domain names are covered by trademarks or should be considered an additional IP category (218–34). The magnitude of this challenge is further illustrated by Lessig's 2015 presidential run platform, which we discuss in Chapter 1, which called for new copyright and patent laws to account for new technologies (Lessig "Innovation"). In this book, we are primarily interested in copyright, although the other categories of IP, along with concerns about plagiarism, arose in the survey responses and interviews, showing how layered and interrelated these components of IP are.

Even when we focus on just copyright, however, we are again faced with a multilayered concept. *Copyright* can be expressed as a singular noun, but it actually encompasses a bundle of different rights that have been legally defined as belonging, initially, to an author. As Rooksby (*Branding*) as well as English studies and legal scholars Martha Woodmansee and Peter Jaszi (*Construction*) explain, these rights include, for example, who has exclusive control over making (and selling) copies, whether that control is time-limited or perpetual, whether derivative works can be made, and so on. According to Baldwin, both the Anglo-American and the Continental systems identify bundles of rights; however, these bundles do not entirely overlap, and the two systems have different interpretations of the relative rights of the author, distributor, and audience. The Anglo-American system predominantly has defined the bundle of rights as *alienable*, which means that when the author sells or signs away rights—that is, signs a publication contract—the author is divested of the specified rights. The distributor owns them. Likewise, if an employee performs work-for-hire, the employer owns the IP rights (and, in legal terms, is called the author) (Baldwin 25, 72, 95–97, 269–71).

These assumptions contrast sharply with those embedded in the Continental system, which takes for granted that authors have natural rights to their IP products. As Baldwin recounts, some of the rights the Continental system defines are *inalienable*. They cannot be sold or given away or otherwise divested from the author. These inalienable rights are referred to as *moral rights*. They include the right of disclosure (control over whether, when, and how a work is initially released), attribution (acknowledgement of authorship and protection against having works attributed by others to the author), and repenting (a right to withdraw a work from circulation, even if it has been sold or licensed to others). The most important moral right, and the greatest contrast with the Anglo-American system, is called *integrity*. An author retains control over how a piece is presented, staged, or employed, even if other aspects of the copyright have been turned over to another entity (Baldwin 9–18, 29–34,

72–73, 126–27; Reyman *Rhetoric* 52–54; McKee and Porter *Ethics* 64–65; see also Woodmansee and Jaszi *Construction*). In other words, an author can continue to look over the shoulder of a distributor to control how a piece appears in the world. In some parts of the world, the author's right of aesthetic integrity can trump a contract that has clauses that conflict with it, as integrity is an inalienable right. Even a work-for-hire author can have a say in the integrity of a work otherwise owned by an employer (Baldwin 2, 25–26). Perhaps the ultimate surprise for those of us used to the Anglo-American system is that these moral rights are inheritable. An author's heirs or estate can withdraw a piece or exert aesthetic control over a piece long after the author's death—perhaps in perpetuity, although that is currently being debated. For these reasons, argues Baldwin, the Continental system is said to privilege an author's rights in contrast to the Anglo-American system's privileging of the public domain (94–98, 145–53, 200–13).

To make matters even more elaborate, these systems have been changing over the past 300 years. Several scholars (e.g., Baldwin, Logie, Rooksby *Branding*, Woodmansee and Jaszi *Construction*) have claimed that the US system has edged closer to the Continental perspective that grants authors (including corporations) more extensive and longer control over their intellectual work. This shift has happened despite some stakeholders' opposition and reluctance. The initial copyright term limit, fourteen years, was extended over the following decades. However, according to Baldwin, throughout the nineteenth and twentieth centuries, the US continued to privilege the public domain in two major ways. First, it required "formalities" to assert and maintain a copyright, such as registering the copyright and using the copyright symbol on all copies. In other words, works were not automatically protected upon their creation but were assumed to be in the public domain and/or subject to state laws. A registered copyright meant that the author or distributor asserted the protections offered by federal law (Baldwin 213, 219, 257–59). Second, the US did not fully recognize foreign copyrights. In taking these two stances, the US resisted the Berne Convention, which had been established among European countries, including the United Kingdom, in 1886. The Berne Convention was an agreement among nations to mutually recognize each other's copyrights, rights that were granted automatically upon the work's creation in a fixed form. In contrast, the US reluctantly extended copyright to foreign authors only as of 1891, and the Copyright Act of 1909 continued to require that foreign authors/entities physically manufacture books and other texts within the US to be granted copyright protections for them (Baldwin 11–13, 20–22, 119–22, 154–56, 160–61).

It was not until 1989 that the US became a member of the Berne Convention and began to more nearly, albeit not completely, align with the Berne Convention's regulations. As a prelude, the Copyright Act of

1976 began to align US practice with the Berne Convention practice of granting copyright protection beyond the death of the author (at the time, 50 years beyond the death), instead of from the time of publication (Baldwin 200, 219). Moreover, copyright became automatic once an original concept was rendered in a fixed medium, although an author might gain legal benefits by formally registering the copyright (Baldwin 135–36, 213–17, 219). In 1998, the Sonny Bono Copyright Extension Act was passed to extend copyright to equal the term established by European legislation: life of the author plus 70 years. Likewise, work-for-hire copyrights were extended to 95 years from publication, or 120 years from creation (Baldwin 248–50, 302–4; Logie 101, 141).

This shift from privileging the audience to privileging the author had several consequences. One impact of these Acts is that the US removed from the public domain a large swath of texts that had been available to be used. Another impact was to exacerbate the problem of orphan works, in which texts are considered to be under copyright because of their creation or publication dates, but the copyright owners are unknown or cannot be found. Moreover, copyright applies to films and to software, and those commercial industries, alongside for-profit authors, were major stakeholders in arguing for these extensions of copyright terms (Logie 5–6, 105–6; Rife "Why"). Thus, in 1998 (with implementation in 2000), the Digital Millennium Copyright Act (DMCA) was passed. It specifically addressed challenges brought by digital technologies by forbidding the circumvention of embedded technologies designed to prevent piracy (Logie 113; Rife *Invention* 65, 133–34; Reyman *Rhetoric* 2, 56–57). Baldwin argues that this move towards privileging the author over the audience appears to have accompanied a shift over the centuries in the US economy towards being a larger global exporter of intellectual products (283–88)—that is, in wanting to establish its presence as "author" in the global economy.

For the nonprofit world of academia, all of these extensions of copyright protections and incursions into the public domain have been troubling, not least because the categories of author, distributor, and audience have been blurred. And this blurring is where the story grows even more complex for professionals in writing studies (and higher education more broadly). In the last two decades, the most visible flashpoints have been debates and legal cases over peer-to-peer file sharing and over remix composing. Peer-to-peer networks allow users to bypass traditional models for distributing films, music, software programs, images, and texts, and they were initially promoted by developers as a means to distribute digital files more efficiently by harnessing the power not of a single mainframe computer, but of thousands of personal computers. Opposition to peer-to-peer networks typically has been led by the entertainment industries, which, in their advertisements and lawsuits, often portray a peer-to-peer user as an anonymous student using educational computing resources to pirate materials (Reyman *Rhetoric* 3, 7, 44; Logie 129). That is, college and university students were cast as IP pirates (Logie 14–16).

Similarly, an emergent remix culture has challenged traditional definitions of authors and audience, as composers clip or sample published materials and use them to stitch together new songs, videos, images, and other texts. In some cases, this use of others' copyrighted materials is justified as parody, and thus as Fair Use. Increasingly, however, the reuse and recontextualization of these materials, that is, the remix, is considered to be a derivative work and thus a violation of copyright protections, especially when the remix may be commercially distributed. For instance, YouTube's official explanatory video on copyright explicitly declares that remix is not protected by Fair Use (@YouTube). Full accounts of lawsuits associated with these positions, as well as analyses of the rhetoric used in conversations about them, have been thoroughly covered elsewhere, including in the scholarship of Reyman (see especially *Rhetoric* 34–36, 84–89, 144–46), Logie, Rife ("Why"), and the *IP Annual* of the Conference on College Composition and Communication (CCCC) IP Caucus.

Our historical narrative arc extends into the future, as scholars have speculated on challenges to established IP legislation that new technologies and global economics will bring, especially for academics. For example, Rooksby warns of an upcoming debate over whether scholars or their institutions own the copyright over smartphone apps that faculty and students create ("Copyright" 217). The Electronic Frontier Foundation (EFF), a nonprofit advocacy group, is already tracking the impact on scholars inflicted by copyright "bots" (automated software that comb the Internet for matching metadata, text, and code), copyright trolls, and patent trolls (people or automated software who claim ownership over innovations for the sake of threatening expensive lawsuits). So far, the bots and trolls have issued thousands of demands that have been proven spurious, but the EFF expects them to continue until IP legislation changes to forestall them.[4] Likewise, the Scholarly Publishing and Academic Resources Coalition (SPARC), with over 200 institutions of higher education as members, advocates for OA materials in academia, including publications, data, and instructional resources (SPARC). As OA advocates such as Heather Joseph ("Future," "Open"), Lawrence Lessig (*Free, Remix*), Peter Suber, and John Willinsky argue, however, SPARC's goals will be met only after a thorough overhaul of current IP policies. Our study participants, too, meditated on the future of IP, and their reflections on and predictions about issues such as these appear in the following chapters. In our Conclusion, we likewise gesture to future trajectories of IP that we believe will be significant.

For now, though, we turn our narrative arc back to our central point: Across the history of IP legislation, regardless of the actual legal language, people have attempted to deal with the laws' complexities and high stakes by telling stories. As Baldwin argues, across time and across nations' legal systems, authors, distributors, and audiences have been granted different privileges in both the legislation and its concomitant stories. Whenever established IP protocols are challenged—whether by new innovations, new economies, or new theories of who the stakeholders may be—the stakes are high. Fights over existing and evolving standards carry risks to scholars' reputations and jobs, risks to future educational projects and practices, and risks to budgets. Lawsuits over IP issues are notoriously expensive: Legal scholars Deidré Keller and Anjali Vats cite American Intellectual Property Lawyers Association data indicating that, in 2013, "litigating a copyright infringement case in which less than $1 million was at stake through the discovery phase cost approximately $150,000." As a result, they claim, administrators of institutions of higher education fear to become entangled in such cases, and, they remark, "risk aversion seems rational" (186). Such conditions of high risk lend themselves to the creation of policies, memes, and lore that purport to prevent faculty, students, and staff from becoming liabilities.

Of the recurrent legal battles, those over Fair Use have been particularly visible in academia, especially as the US has drifted towards granting authors rather than audiences the priority of control over texts, images, and other materials that might serve educational purposes. Much lore about Fair Use circulates among academic hallways, but that lore is neither incidental nor innocent. There is a larger, more systemic story to be told about Fair Use, a story that illustrates the cultural processes we summarize. In the next section, we analyze a problematic interpretation of US law, Section 107 of the Copyright Act of 1976, that has been routinized and widely promulgated in place of the law's own words. It is, in fact, based in myths.

Fair Use and Its Myths

Our cultural historical overview brings us to the story of Fair Use, Section 107 of the Copyright Act of 1976, which offers limitations to copyright. Of all the stories of copyright law that academics tell, Fair Use is perhaps most mythologized—and the story that is most under pressure—as the survey results and interviews we discuss in later chapters help illustrate. For instance, in his interview, Carl Whithaus,[5] shared an instance of this myth at work:

> You sometimes get contortions from instructors around Fair Use of source material I'm not sure are needed. But it's like it develops as an urban myth within a writing program or at an institution, and it would be nice if [. . .], in terms of composition studies, CCCC, or NCTE, there was a way to go to very clean clear examples that were updated about Fair Use. So that when someone was told, "You can't put up that

> PDF file in a Moodle-protected site for your class because the University doesn't support Moodle; the University only supports Blackboard. So you have to, even though you're running your class through Moodle, you still have to reference for all of your source articles back to a file in Blackboard." That sort of contortion wasn't necessary.

Here Whithaus emphasizes that myths of what Fair Use allows result in "contortions" that ultimately are not "necessary." Kathleen Blake Yancey, in discussing the postcard archive at Florida State University, offered a reflection that similarly highlights the power of myths about Fair Use:

> So the rules of the road, there's a lot of ambiguity here. [. . .] I say, "the rules of the road"—I don't think we really want rules, exactly. But I think even Fair Use in terms of 250 words is a guideline. What are they going to do? Come put you in prison if you have 251? I mean, you know it doesn't actually work that way; it's a guideline. [. . .] What can you use [from] this material? Can you use all of it? Do you use part of it? Do you have to represent it in full? Can you crop an image for example and just use that? [. . .] That is, it's more about the spirit of these conventions then it is about the letter of the law.

Here Yancey recognizes the arbitrary nature of a limit of using 250 words from a copyrighted source, joking "What are they going to do? Come put you in prison if you have 251?" As she explains, "it doesn't actually work that way; it's a guideline. [. . .] it's more about the spirit of these conventions then it is about the letter of the law." She casts this "ambiguity" as necessary to some extent: "I don't think we really want rules exactly." Her point about image use illustrates the necessity of flexibility: What would be the 250-word equivalent of an image? Would it be a cropped portion?

Yet the myths persist. Among other interviewees, Naomi Silver, when she discussed giving advice to students on course projects, illustrated how lore replaces legality: "I don't think I have necessarily a legal basis for this. But my understanding is that if you're using short clips from a video, that's not violating Fair Use." Silver acknowledges her uncertainty surrounding a Fair Use rule on source length. She is correct that this is a myth: While Fair Use decisions are more likely when shorter rather than longer portions of an original text are used, the law itself does not provide a strict guideline regarding the length of video clips. And this uncertainty raises anxiety for members of the field.

Ben McCorkle provided an additional example of this anxiety. In response to a question regarding why he felt his remix work had not been targeted for takedown notices, he explained,

> I don't know because . . . I want to say because a lot of my content lately has probably legitimately used open content and/or original

> content. And so maybe I haven't raised the hackles. But I would like to think that it might also be because they're not as vigilant about policing as before. I don't know that to be true. Plus, I'm not studying it too closely, but it seems like this is part of the cultural anxiety about utilizing content and producing derivatives: that no one really knows the rules. And so we make them up as we go along. And sometimes we overreach and then the crowd yells back at you—then you pull back. I think this is part of a figuring-it-out kind of process.

McCorkle's profession "I don't know that to be true" supports that he, like Silver, recognizes there is a myth at work, in this case that the work of teachers and scholars in writing studies is not high profile enough to warrant attention by copyright enforcers (so "they're not as vigilant about policing as before"). But the myth is so deeply entrenched that it continues to hold sway—even if (and perhaps partly because) it is part of a larger "cultural anxiety . . . that no one really knows the rules." Thus, many practitioners simply hope to fly under the radar but are also aware that the current balances among IP stakeholders are tenuous.

Because US academia is so imbricated in the myths of Fair Use, we want to pause here to consider its foundation in the 1976 legislation. Why should the law contain a Fair Use exemption for classrooms and other nonprofit educational spaces such as museums? To return to our reading of Baldwin's formulation, IP legislation strikes a balance among authors, distributors, and audiences. The Copyright Act of 1976 shifted a historical preference for audiences to a balance more favorable to authors; however, legislators recognized the need to protect First Amendment rights to free speech, especially critique, as well as the public good of an educated populace (Baldwin 126, 135–36). As legal scholar Kenneth D. Crews puts it, "Without a fair-use right, all copying of materials for the simple pursuit of classroom handouts would be prohibited" ("Law" 617). Moreover, the material conditions for distributing copies created limits: Photocopying stores such as Kinko's were available, but were not yet considered a sizable threat to authors' profits, and a widely available Internet was still over a decade away.[6] With Section 107 on Fair Use, the Copyright Act of 1976 thus reaffirmed the principles of the audience's rights, while at the same time it specified precise protections for authors to align the law with the Berne Convention.

The legal formulation for Fair Use lends itself to storytelling because the four factors employed to determine Fair Use are not hard-and-fast criteria, but are open for interpretation. These four factors include:

1. The purpose and character of the use, including whether such use is of a commercial nature or is for nonprofit educational purposes;
2. The nature of the copyrighted work;

3. The amount and substantiality of the portion used in relation to the copyrighted work as a whole; and
4. The effect of the use upon the potential market for or value of the copyrighted work. The fact that a work is unpublished shall not itself bar a finding of fair use if such finding is made upon consideration of all the previous factors (17 USC § 107; see Conference on College Composition and Communication Caucus on Intellectual Property 486; Crews "Law" 608).

The idea codified by Fair Use is that each author or educator, at each instance of employing some textual material, should consider the four factors to determine whether the use constitutes Fair Use. Potentially, that is a lot of pressure on individual academics, especially if IP training is not a regular part of professional development, an issue raised by several of the academics we surveyed and interviewed. Because of the vagueness of the criteria, because of the costs of gaining permissions,[7] and because of the extreme cost of IP litigation, it is no wonder that stakeholders have attempted to simplify them.

This attempt at simplification led to stories. We use the term *story* purposefully here to emphasize that what many (if not most) academics understand about Fair Use is the narrative about it, not the law itself. In other words, the story became the law. Indeed, Crews even explicitly points to the "illusion" of Fair Use in the title of his *Ohio State Law Journal* article "The Law of Fair Use and the Illusion of Fair-Use Guidelines," which traces the legislative documents and court decisions that contributed to this illusion. Similarly, Rife calls such guidelines "imagined," designating them as "widely circulating myths about 'educational' Fair Use" ("Why"). As Siva Vaidhyanathan reinforces in his *Intellectual Property: A Very Short Introduction,* "Contrary to many popular assumptions, there is no formula that determines when a use is fair and when it is not. There is no maximum number of words, percentage of a work, length of a song clip, or similar measurement that will certainly be considered fair" (24).

These stories about Fair Use have led writing studies professionals (and academics in general) to believe certain practices are (and are not) allowed under the Fair Use exemption. Rife describes these as "myths such as using a certain percentage is acceptable, using for non-profit is alright, using a predetermined number of minutes for sound recordings is fine, etc." ("Why" Conference). These myths have held such power, in fact, that in their *College Composition and Communication* article "Use Your Fair Use," the CCCC Caucus on Intellectual Property urges readers that under the provisions of Fair Use "legally, we are allowed much more than many of us have been led to believe" (485). That is, the stories that circulated about Fair Use became myths, scary tales that offered a more restrictive set of guidelines than the law actually stipulates. The CCCC Caucus on Intellectual Property's efforts to correct these myths have been shared by others. Crews (*Copyright*) and media literacy scholar Renee Hobbs also offer detailed explanations to educators on how to apply the four factors of Fair Use, including checklists that have been taken up by educational institutions.

The other related story that is often overlooked in higher education today is how "Fair Use" itself came to be defined. Indeed, this myth about Fair Use is so common and naturalized in academic culture that it has become a major IP sponsor and a changeling for the actual wording of the law: the incomplete and not fully accepted Fair Use Guidelines for Educational Multimedia. This "Guidelines" document was an appendix to a report developed by the Conference on Fair Use (CONFU) through various meetings between 1994–1998 and was a response to new technologies that allowed for more widespread copying and dissemination of texts.[8] However, the guidelines were never endorsed by academics.[9] In fact, the guidelines document was not even formally endorsed by CONFU, whose subcommittees ultimately reached a stalemate in their discussions in 1998.[10] In the conclusion of CONFU's 1998 "Final Report to the Commissioner on the Conclusion of the Conference of Fair Use," Bruce A. Lehman, then assistant secretary of commerce and commissioner of patents and trademarks and chair of the Working Group on Intellectual Property Rights of the Information Infrastructure Task Force, writes,

> Not all participants supported the goal of developing and adopting educational fair use guidelines, preferring to seek legislative action on the issue. Some participants opposed the process, as well as the results, while others strongly supported both. Others strongly supported the process, but determined that they could not, or would not, support the results. Most participants concluded, however, that it had been an instructive, if not always productive, endeavor.
>
> As CONFU concluded, it was clear that fair use was alive and well in the digital age, and that attempts to draft widely supported guidelines will be complicated by the often competing interests of the copyright owner and user communities.
>
> (18; see also Woodmansee and Jaszi *Construction*, "Law"; Rife "Why")

So while the CONFU Report contains the proposals and recommendations discussed at its meetings, it does not offer conclusively endorsed or legal guidelines.[11]

Despite this lack of formal endorsement, the Fair Use Guidelines for Educational Multimedia were promulgated as though they were accepted. As Reyman points out, guidelines that were intended to be minimum starting points for negotiation transformed into maximum allowances for Fair Use (*Rhetoric* 49–50). In other words, guidelines intended to be a safe harbor became "rules" for maximum usage. Hence, writing studies teacher-scholars have been taught "rules," such as a certain number of words or a certain number of seconds of an audio or video recording, are permissible to use without granted permissions. Another popular myth is that it is Fair Use to copy for students' classroom use up to 10 percent of a published textual work. Crews notes such precise guidelines were advanced in the Agreement on Guidelines for Classroom Copying in Not-for-Profit Educational Institutions (also known as the "Classroom Copying Guidelines" or "Classroom Guidelines"[12]), a document produced by educators, authors, and publishers in anticipation of the 1976 Copyright Act ("Law" 617). Keller and Vats describe the Classroom Guidelines as

> the result of long and arduous negotiations among representatives of publishers, educational institutions, and other stakeholders. The intention was for the negotiating parties to propose statutory language embodying a fair use provision specific to education. However, the ultimate result was a non-binding document that has been influential in shaping educational fair use jurisprudence.
>
> (180)

All of these "rules" reinforce the move toward expanding authors' rights at the cost of the public domain, resulting in a focus on products rather than processes, which Reyman (*Rhetoric*) and Rife (*Invention*), as well as computers and writing scholars Jeffrey R. Galin and Joan Latchaw, identify as problematic.

What makes this myth even more powerful is that these "rules" are cited as precedent in the legal system. An example is the Georgia State case (*Cambridge Univ. Press v. Becker* and the appeal *Cambridge Univ. Press v. Patton*), which centered on whether Georgia State University committed copyright infringement by putting portions of texts on its library's electronic reserves.[13] Galin explains the role of supposed Fair Use guidelines in the Georgia State decision and its appeal:

> For years, the 1976 Classroom Copying Guidelines have been mentioned, particularly in case dicta, footnotes, or as references to minimal standards against which fair use violations might be measured. Until this case, however, no Federal court had ever directly ruled on what role these decidedly narrow legislative guidelines for brevity, spontaneity, and cumulative effect should play for a fair use case for non-profit institutions. The plaintiffs asserted vehemently that these guidelines should be used as the standard for fair use practices. Judge Tjoflat put this issue to rest noting that although they are "part of the legislative history of the Copyright Act," they "do not carry force of law." [. . .] This statement is a direct rejection of the Classroom Guidelines as legally binding and as a set of bright line rules for determining fair use.
>
> ("Keep" 24)

From Galin's perspective, then, the Georgia State case appeal ruling helps make explicit the problem of relying on the non-legislative guidelines—that is, myths—about Fair Use, in this case, the 1976 Classroom Copying Guidelines: They "do not carry force of law."

Other scholars likewise point to the shaping power of the story of Fair Use in the Georgia State case. In his response to the initial ruling, "Fair Use and Education: The Way Forward," which was published while the ruling was under appeal, Jaszi writes about the problematic influence of the supposed Fair Use guidelines. He notes that the judge, while drawing heavily on Georgia State's status as a "nonprofit educational institution," also focused on how much material was copied, "measured as a percentage of the source work," and the lack of transformative use. He concludes,

> [T]he courts have given us little, if any, specific guidance on how to think about fair use and education, and it seems unlikely that one district judge's opinion will be the last word. In fact, this essay concludes that, whatever the result of the Georgia State case, the education community has some urgent work to do if we really care about explaining why we sometimes should be allowed to "use" copyrighted material without getting permission or paying license fees. (34)

In their response to Jaszi's article, Keller and Vats explain, "Jaszi argues that the idea of 'educational exceptionalism' is a *myth.* [. . .] Rather, as the Georgia State decisions exemplify, educators and educational institutions are treated like every other unlicensed user of copyrighted materials" (176, our emphasis). In other words, the Georgia State case suggests that educators are not granted Fair Use as outlined under the law but rather held to the guidelines circulated in the story of Fair Use (which do not, in fact, grant educators an exemption). The process Rife (*Invention*) identifies, then, whereby we make sense of the law through narrativizing the law, comes full circle: The law and the story of the law become conflated, even indistinguishable.

Given the significant effects of such Fair Use myths, we see a gap in existing scholarship: There is little work on the power that these stories of IP have had in shaping practice in everyday academic life. Academics in writing studies and several other disciplines interested in scholarly communications have addressed Fair Use, of course, but influential resources outside of legal scholarship have appeared in the domain of library and information science (e.g., Association of Research Libraries), as librarians are often in the role of IP literacy sponsors.[14] Crews's work (*Copyright*), for instance, is directed explicitly towards librarians, and the Georgia State case was over library reserves. Meanwhile, thousands of first-year college students who have library orientations are introduced to standards of source use based on CONFU Guidelines. In this way, this story of Fair Use has become enormously powerful, and it should not be forgotten.

The Bayh-Dole Act, the 2001 Journal Boycott, and the New University Economy

As the example of Fair Use indicates, institutions of higher education are implicated in and deeply affected by changes in IP legislation. The historical narratives we trace in this chapter indicate the different balances among authors, distributors, and audiences that Western cultures have defined for copyright. In this section, we aim to situate such choices within a larger picture of the impact of IP regulations on university economies, for changes in IP regulations have led to changes in funding streams and in definitions of academic labor. To sketch this larger picture, we build on the work of scholars in critical university studies (e.g., Cantwell and Kauppinen; Donoghue; Ginsberg; Newfield *Unmaking*, *Mistake*; Rooksby *Branding*, "Intellectual"; Welch and Scott) who focus on the broad cultural and economic trends that have energized and challenged institutions of higher education, especially in the wake of the Great Recession of 2008. In addition to tracking these larger trends, we argue IP research needs to document the impact of legislative changes on individual scholars, especially in writing studies, and especially those whose voices have been muted.

From the perspective of scholarship in critical university studies, institutions of higher education have seen substantive shifts in power in the last few decades. Several scholars explore the decline of tenured faculty in general and the diminishment of humanities departments (both in number and in influence) in particular. For example, Christopher Newfield (*Unmaking*, *Mistake*) and Frank Donoghue each (separately) warn academics about the decline of institutional support for the humanities, and, together with Benjamin Ginsberg, note the rise in administrative, as opposed to faculty, control over defining the purposes for higher education. In essence, they explain that science- and technology-oriented departments have been highly privileged voices in US universities for some time; however, because these departments now attract the bulk of available federal and state grant funding, as well as attention from the public at large, they now have become overwhelmingly dominant voices. Responding to deep cuts in public funds for education, administrations have likewise tended to skew budgets and attention to these disciplines. (For instance, Newfield [*Unmaking*, *Mistake*] tracks how public funds for students are largely diverted to these departments.) In this new university economy, events that affect faculty in the sciences and technology—including debates over IP issues—tend to impact the university at large.

To illustrate this dynamic of a rather large tail wagging the dog, we examine two crucial events whose stories continue to define the terms for IP debates for scholars across campus. The first event is the passage of the Bayh-Dole Act in 1980. The second is the worldwide boycott of academic journals in the sciences in 2001, a boycott that was the prelude to the founding of the Public Library of Science (PLOS) and the OA movement. Together, these events illustrate the tension between institutional and/or individual ownership of IP and the public good embedded within higher education's approaches to IP.

The Bayh-Dole Act

Critical university scholars (e.g., Morris, Newfield *Unmaking*, Rooksby *Branding*) have singled out the Bayh-Dole Act as the key piece of US legislation that signaled a change in how the public views and how the government funds universities. This legislation was a game changer for academia. It affected the mission of universities, making the goal of academic work more economic.[15] Bayh-Dole allowed universities to own and make money from IP (through patents). As Galin put it, "the Bayh-Dole Act [. . .] legislation created a new gold rush mentality for potential revenue that could distract universities from their central mission of creating and disseminating new knowledge and training future generations of American citizens" (205). The story about the Bayh-Dole Act's effects on patents parallels the story about copyright we have already seen: The legislation signaled a shift in US policy to privilege creators over public ownership. Before this Act, universities and their faculty members were not allowed to hold patents on intellectual products developed with federal funding. Instead, the legal code had been guided by assumptions about the public good: Universities were engaged in basic research already paid for by the public, so members of the public had the right to build on that work by conducting applied research and developing products. The concern that led to the Act, though, was that patentable innovations were languishing within universities because potential developers did not see a way to gain exclusive profits from them. In other words, because a university could not sell or license exclusive rights to a patented creation, no commercial entity would be able to prevent other commercial entities from also using that innovation. As a result, no commercial entity could be certain of earning profits, and so the commercial sector declined to invest in further developing creations first developed on a college or university campus. The Bayh-Dole Act was intended to remedy this situation by allowing colleges, universities, and their faculty to claim patents, with provisions for a funding agency to claim a patent if they did not exercise that right. Universities could then recoup funds either by selling or leasing their patent holdings.

The Bayh-Dole Act has had significant impact on higher education as a whole, although perhaps not quite in the ways that its authors intended. It has raised questions about potential conflicts of interest, as when a faculty member founds a startup company to exploit a research finding funded by government resources (Morris, Rooksby *Branding*).[16] Likewise, as Rooksby affirms, it has unintentionally raised questions about whether institutions that provide "substantial university resources" to students should have an acknowledged stake in students' profitable innovations (*Branding* 178–82). To respond to questions such as these, some universities increased their levels of administration and established Technology Transfer Offices. Despite these efforts, scholars such as Emily Morris, Newfield (*Unmaking*), and Rooksby (*Branding*) who have studied the Bayh-Dole Act conclude that it has not fulfilled its overall purpose. It has not radically increased the applied development of concepts or innovations discovered on university and college campuses. Rather, most patents still languish because universities do not have the infrastructure needed to market them or to develop them into profitable products. Except for a handful of universities—Newfield (*Unmaking*) points to fifteen (202), primarily those with medical schools—patents have not become a significant, fruitful revenue stream for colleges or universities (201–7).

Even so, the Bayh-Dole Act and its history of implementation both reflect and define a cultural milieu in which US institutions of higher education are expected to become more business-like, even though corporate practices may be contrary to academic purposes. As Rooksby puts it, "As the United States moves further toward an information- and knowledge-based economy, the impetus to lay claim to intangible intellectual outputs is increasing" (*Branding* 254–55). This impetus, Rooksby argues, applies not only to science and technology departments, but to academic fields, like the humanities and social sciences, governed less by patent legislation and more by copyright. Academic activities across campus are being increasingly viewed with an eye towards raising revenue.

For instance, to turn to a critical example raised by our study participants, throughout the 2000s many university and college administrators began claiming exclusive university/college ownership over instructional materials that faculty, adjuncts, and graduate students developed for online courses (see Porter; Samuels "Future," *Why*). Frequently, instructors found that they lost control over the copyright; in fact, some of our participants reported that when they moved to another institution, they lost access to their materials entirely. Faculty protested, as they had operated under the assumption that they maintain copyrights over their own research publications and instructional materials. That faculty keep the copyright on their work until they sign it over to journals or universities is a "gentleman's agreement" holdover from the pre-Bayh-Dole Act approach to IP. As new technologies, such as course management systems and video conferencing technologies that facilitate online teaching, came along, the post-Bayh-Dole Act approach increasingly took hold. Thus, administrators countered that digital materials are work-for-hire, particularly because the technologies employed to create them are considered to be substantial university resources.

As of the time of this writing, the outcomes of these negotiations have been mixed. Some administrations have elected to preserve traditional faculty contracts (but not necessarily those of adjuncts and graduate students) that maintain the pre-Bayh-Dole "gentleman's agreement." Others have decided to assert the institution's control over the copyright in part or in whole, even explicitly stipulating work-for-hire arrangements in contracts where universities own course materials used for online teaching (see Ahmadi). Either way, these decisions are likely to be only temporary for two reasons. First, instructors continue to develop not only texts using digital technologies and environments but also entire digital technologies and environments themselves. Second, administrations continue to renegotiate IP ownership. These developments and negotiations raise questions such as Who or what owns a collaborative MOOC (massive open online course) (Porter; Aaron and Roche)? and Who owns what when resources developed for tutoring services are outsourced to a for-profit instructional company? In perhaps an ironic touch given the recent emphasis on makerspaces and technology development in the digital humanities, these questions extend to whether patent legislation is likely to become more relevant (Rooksby, *Branding* 178–82).

The 2001 Journals Boycott

The second critical event we explore is the 2001 boycott of closed scientific journals. We focus on this event not only because it gave fire to the OA movement, but also because many details of this story are primarily recorded in transitory online venues and are at risk of being lost. Although the 2001 and subsequent boycotts[17] have not received the same attention from critical university studies that the Bayh-Dole Act has, they likewise inspired new IP legislation, and they have been significant in defining new economies of university publication not only for the sciences but also for writing studies and academia at large. According to one of the leaders, Michael Eisen (see his blogged interview with Richard Poynder), as well as researchers on scholarly communications (e.g., Kimbrough and Gasaway; Rizor and Holley), the 2001 boycott arose as academic scientists became frustrated by rapid hikes in journal subscription prices that were far outpacing university library budgets. These price hikes, in part, were prompted and enabled by the changing material conditions of publishing. Traditional publishers were faced with challenges of shifting from print-based to new, digital forms of producing and distributing materials, including challenges to the economic models guiding their business decisions. Some publishers (e.g., Elsevier, Springer) began to assert control by consolidating rivals into near monopolies.[18] As biologist Carl T. Bergstrom and his economist co-author Theodore C. Bergstrom explain, such monopolies took advantage of journals' entrenched position in academic reward structures, as publication in and access to high-impact scientific journals are key to academic tenure and advancement (see also Kimbrough and Gasaway). The stakes on both sides were high. Unlike publications in many humanities disciplines, journal publication profits for STEM disciplines can be substantial. Julie L. Kimbrough and Laura N. Gasaway summarize reports of $9.4 billion in overall revenue in 2011 and an "estimated profit margin of 20 to 30 percent" (279).

These profit-seeking tactics were particularly irksome to academics since authors provided content (i.e., their articles) and peer-review services at no cost to the publishers. Moreover, as psychologists Lisa A. Curb and Charles I. Abramson relate (building on Bergstrom and Bergstrom), since the 1930s, several journals have required authors to pay to be published, including page fees (costs per page) and/or other "publication fees (submission fees; fees for use of color, figures, exceeding a page limit; or a combination of these)" (1). These fees used to be primarily charged by nonprofit journals to supplement their lower subscription costs (Bergstrom and Bergstrom), but they expanded to the for-profit sector (Curb and Abramson). As subscription prices skyrocketed, academic scientists, especially those in medical research and the life sciences, began asking why they were paying to be published, and were signing away their copyrights to entities that would then deny them access to their own research unless their institutions paid high subscription prices to regain that access. They also questioned how these restrictive conditions would affect the integrity of their research. For example, they worried how research studies could progress when co-authors—especially those from developing economies—were denied access to publications because their institutions could not afford to pay to access them.

In answer, an advocacy group of scientists co-founded by Harold Varmus, Patrick O. Brown, and Michael Eisen asked colleagues to sign an open letter to journal publishers in 2001 (Public Library of Science "*PLOS* Open," *PLOS* Story"; Poynder "The OA Interviews: Michael"). The open letter, available in Appendix D, was signed by nearly 34,000 scientists from 180 countries and laid a foundation for the next two decades' conversations and battles over scholarly communication practices.

Signatories of the letter characterized themselves as nonprofit authors and audiences of scientific texts, as opposed to for-profit distributors. Their narrative extolled the public good of OA to texts: an increase in interdisciplinary research, greater international collaboration, and a better mechanism for creating permanent archives. To achieve these goals, signatories agreed to boycott certain publishers by withholding all forms of intellectual labor from which the publishers profited. The publishers, for the most part, "blithely ignored" them (Poynder "The OA Interviews: Michael").

As the 2001 boycott collapsed, the co-founders and signatories turned to several initiatives that became stepping stones within the OA movement. In 2002, the Budapest Open Access Initiative (BOAI) was founded to declare forcefully, again, the public good of OA for research, to define different levels of OA, to develop economic models to support OA, and generally to produce scholarship on OA (Joseph; Rizor and Holley). By 2003, Varmus, Brown, and Eisen had reimagined the PLOS advocacy group: Their organization became an OA publisher by launching the digitally native journal *PLOS Biology*. In 2005, another of their journals, *PLOS ONE*, became a multidisciplinary OA competitor to *Science* and to *Nature* (Public Library of Science "*PLOS* Story"; Poynder "The OA Interviews: Michael").

Subsequently, academic societies, universities, and governmental agencies developed and expanded OA repositories. The PLOS/BOAI grassroots OA campaigns gained considerable momentum after 2005 when federal and state officials began passing IP legislation to mandate OA repositories (Joseph; Kimbrough and Gasaway; Lunsford). As of 2005, the US National Institutes of Health (NIH) began requiring that recipients of NIH research grants deposit versions of any resulting publications in the government-sponsored OA repository, PubMed.[19] Publishers resisted this requirement, arguing that the deposited copies of publications violated their copyrights. However, the federal government doubled down on the requirement, with proponents arguing that since taxpayers had already provided funds to support the research projects, they should not have to pay again to learn about the results. Moreover, proponents argued, OA not only to final publications but also to datasets would reduce redundant studies, and thus save taxpayer costs. In 2008, the NIH Public Access Policy was codified into law as part of the federal Consolidated Appropriations Act. In 2013, an Executive Directive on Increasing Access to the Results of Federally Funded Scientific Research expanded the scope of the NIH policy to include over 20 federal granting agencies in the US (e.g., Department of Defense, Department of Education, National Science Foundation, Smithsonian Institution). To a lesser extent, US state legislation has paralleled federal efforts, with Illinois passing legislation in 2013 requiring its universities to develop OA repository policies, California passing a law in 2014 requiring OA to research funded by the California Department of Public Health, and New York currently considering OA legislation (Kimbaugh and Gasaway; Lunsford). Meanwhile, several university systems have undertaken on their own to establish OA infrastructures, such as the eScholarship repository, which in 2012 allied with the California Digital Library, California State University, and University of California systems (Lunsford).

The OA movement, however, has become somewhat co-opted. One OA economic model has been to charge OA fees in place of subscriptions, with average rates ranging $1,000–$5,000 per STEM article (Kimbrough and Gasaway; see also Poynder "The OA Interviews: Michael"), and $300–$800 for other OA venues (Rizor and Holley). Existing OA venues such as *PLOS* have come under criticism for not lowering their rates (Poynder "The OA Interviews: Michael"), and, as university press publisher Michele Myatt Quinn points out, there is a concern that OA costs to authors might ultimately exceed the costs of subscription models (see also Rizor and Holley). Moreover, commercial journals across the disciplines have built OA clauses into their publication contracts, so that relatively high OA fees may be charged in addition to other fees and subscriptions. As our survey and interview participants shared, individual scholars have had to pay publishers, at times out of their own pockets, to make their work OA (and, indeed, we encountered the same situation for this book as well; see Chapter 6). Such OA payments can be more feasible for those in the sciences who have grant funding and greater institutional support, leaving humanities scholars to make difficult decisions about OA to their work (Quinn; Rizor and Holley). Equally troubling, relatively few OA repositories exist that are dedicated to humanities scholarship and to the types of archival, qualitative, and quantitative evidence that humanities scholars, including writing studies scholars, collect. Moreover, the interest in OA publishing has led to the rise of predatory journals and publishers that scam authors by falsely presenting themselves as peer-reviewed, OA academic venues (Poynder "The OA Interviews: Jeffrey"; Quinn).

The full ramifications of the 2001 boycott and the ensuing OA legislation, for writing studies and for academia at large, are still to be determined. These conflicts are ongoing, as illustrated by the University of California (UC) system's and Louisiana State University's 2019 cancellations of their contracts with Elsevier, which occurred as we were writing this book and followed similar cancellations by Florida State University and institutions in Germany and Sweden in 2018 (McKenzie "UC," "Another," "Florida"). The UC system, which had paid Elsevier over $10 million annually, wanted a "read-and-publish" deal[20] without increased subscription costs (McKenzie "UC") that conformed to its *Declaration of Rights and Principles to Transform Scholarly Communication.* This *Declaration,* among 15 other rights and principles, includes "No waivers of OA Policy," "No deals without OA offsets," and "No new paywalls for our work" (Schneider et al.). Though Norway has since reached a read-and-publish deal with Elsevier (at increased cost) (McKenzie "Elsevier"), as of the time of this writing, the UC system has yet to do so. Undoubtedly, despite its lack of a firm resolution, the scientific OA campaign has significantly altered the landscape of academic publishing both for scholars in the sciences, as publishers of scientific research have worked to accommodate OA mandates by allowing deposits into institutional repositories, and scholars across the disciplines, as journals in multiple fields have responded to the OA movement and new OA publication venues have been created.

In sum, both the OA repository mandates and the Bayh-Dole Act have had direct consequences for the knowledge-making and instructional functions of educational institutions. They define mechanisms for how IP is (and should be) exchanged with other scholars and the general public, and thus they intervene in how academic knowledge is circulated, co-constructed, and archived. Yet, despite these substantive impacts on academic missions, the primary approach by educational institutions to IP remains legal rather than academic. As Rooksby notes, "On most campuses today, deans, provosts, presidents, and boards of trustees are given legal and business guidance about intellectual property, but rarely do they receive academic advice on this topic" (*Branding* 284). The same is true of faculty in writing studies. Fortunately, as we cover in the following chapters, there is a lot of academic advice for them to consult.

Conclusion

Given the complexity of the histories of IP and the economic forces that have shaped the university, as well as the gaps in the current research in terms of the effects on individual scholars and ways in which they respond to them, in the following chapters we provide reflections from scholars in writing studies. These reflections both document and reinforce the complexities of IP that make simple checklists or flowcharts inadequate as well as provide examples—even models—of scholars seeking to understand and respond to these complexities in their daily work in writing studies. We argue that these reflections support and demonstrate that we must attend to three aspects of the IP landscape in particular: 1) the ethical lenses academics bring to bear on their negotiation of IP issues, 2) the sponsors, particularly those that act as gatekeepers, of IP knowledge and decisions, and 3) the effects of IP on the entire knowledge-making cycle. In the next chapter, we turn to the ethical lenses.

Notes

1. Heidi A. McKee and James E. Porter indicate in their 2009 *The Ethics of Internet Research: A Rhetorical, Case-Based Process* that they see "a very broad" "global human rights perspective" on IP emerging, largely from Article 27 of the Universal Declaration of Human Rights, which they present as "something like an international principle regarding intellectual property," together with the Berne Convention and the Trade-Related Aspects of Intellectual Property Rights Agreement (52, 66). Yet it is what they identify as the shared feature of

these documents—a "view of intellectual property that affords moral rights to the author stronger than those recognized in US copyright law" (69)—that suggests we have yet to see such a consensus position emerge. In other words, the Universal Declaration of Human Rights, the Berne Convention, and the Trade-Related Aspects of Intellectual Property Rights Agreement counterpose US copyright law on the idea of moral rights.

2. In our nationwide survey, we received responses taking a range of perspectives: a desire to protect one's own work alongside a desire to employ others' work alongside a desire for more flexibility in acknowledging collaborative work.
3. Our history in this chapter does not include non-Western views because US universities are modeled on European universities, especially German ones, and the Anglo IP tradition became embedded in US law. In later chapters, we discuss the non-Western views brought up by the writing studies scholars we interviewed.
4. Adi Kamdar et al., for example, note that in a single case, "a secretive troll called MPHJ sent over 13,000 letters to small businesses demanding payment" for a spurious patent claim to "'scan to email' technology" (23). Mitch Stoltz, referring to Matthew Sag's research, likewise argues,

   > Copyright trolling is a widespread problem. Although one notorious outfit known as Prenda Law ceased its lawsuit campaign in January 2013 and was later sanctioned for fraud, copyright troll suits (identified in one study as copyright suits against multiple John Doe defendants) were nearly one-third of *all* the copyright suits filed in the US in 2013. In Illinois, Indiana, and Wisconsin, these suits were over *half* the copyright suits filed in that year (8, emphasis in the original).

5. See Appendix B for the interview questions and transcription conventions; see Appendix C for the position titles and affiliations of interview participants from at the time of their interviews.
6. Kinko's was founded by Paul Orfalea at the University of California, Santa Barbara in 1970; the lawsuit against Kinko's on the basis of copyright infringement would come in 1991 (Crews "Law" 641). Tim Berners Lee's proposal for the World Wide Web overlay on the Internet is dated to March 1989 (Greenemeier).
7. Two respondents to our nationwide survey reported having paid between $20,001–$25,000 via a publisher or deducted royalties to secure permissions to include materials in a scholarly publication. For textbooks, two respondents indicated that grants had paid career totals of over $50,001 for such permissions expenses, and two more respondents indicated that the publisher and/or royalties had covered totals over $50,001.
8. CONFU's "Final Report to the Commissioner on the Conclusion of the Conference of Fair Use" explains the charge of CONFU as "to bring together copyright owner and user interests to discuss fair use issues and, if appropriate and feasible, to develop guidelines for fair uses of copyrighted works by librarians and educators" (Lehman 2). The report suggests that the failure to decide on such guidelines may have been more the result of lack of consensus about the guidelines' content and less the belief that such guidelines were not "appropriate and feasible."
9. Indeed, several library and higher education organizations publicly opposed most or all of the CONFU "guidelines." These organizations include the American Association of State Colleges and Universities (AASCU), American Council on Education (ACE), American Historical Society (AHS),

American Library Association (ALA), Association of American Universities (AAU), and Association of Research Libraries (ARL), among others (Crews "Law" 610).

10. Some organizations, however, publicly supported parts of the CONFU guidelines. These groups include the Association of American Publishers (AAP), Association of American University Presses, Inc. (AAUP), Broadcast Music, Inc. (BM1), and Motion Picture Association of America (MPAA), among others (Crews "Law" 610).
11. Moreover, many of the IP scholars we cite in this book, as well as the writing studies faculty we surveyed and interviewed, might challenge the conclusion that "fair use [is] alive and well in the digital age" (18).
12. Computers and writing scholar Jeffrey R. Galin references the Agreement on Guidelines for Classroom Copying in Not-for-Profit Educational Institutions as the 1976 "Classroom Copying Guidelines" ("Keep").
13. The initial ruling in the Georgia State case found only four or five cases of infringement in the more than 74 charges brought (there seems to be some disagreement about the number: Jaszi indicates four [33–34]; Keller and Vats indicate five [175]). Therefore, this ruling was seen by some as a victory for educational Fair Use; however, the appeal was viewed less so. In his discussion of the appeal for the CCCC *IP Annual*, Galin explains the judgment of the appeal this way: "In essence, the higher court agreed with the overall logic of the decision (with some important qualifications) but not the method for determining fair use. For the time being, the injunctive relief that the lower court established and the award of litigation costs to the Defendants have been vacated" ("Keep" 21). Keller and Vats similarly characterize the appeal as less positive for educational institutions: "Judge Vinson's derisiveness toward the notion of educational exceptionalism leaps off the page" (177–79). Jaszi defines "educational exceptionalism" as "the notion that teaching and learning are so special, and so highly favored in copyright policy and fair use law, that it ought to be possible to get courts to cut education some special slack, beyond that which they extend to uses of third-party copyright material by filmmakers or musicians or publishers" (36). For Galin ("Keep"), as well as Keller and Vats, then, the appeal ruling threatens the notion that educational institutions should receive special consideration in making Fair Use judgments.
14. We discuss in Chapter 4 the role of literacy sponsors in mediating academic IP decisions.
15. That faculty keep the copyright on their work until they sign it over to journals or universities is a "gentleman's agreement" holdover from the pre-Bayh-Dole Act approach to IP. As new technologies, for instance, course management systems and video conferencing technologies that facilitate online teaching, have come along, the post-Bayh-Dole Act approach has increasingly taken hold (e.g., in university IP agreements that stipulate their ownership of patents and in faculty contracts that stipulate work-for-hire arrangements where universities own course materials used for online teaching).
16. CITI training for Institutional Review Board (IRB) members, in its module on conflicts of interest, quotes David C. Mowery and Arvids A. Ziedonis to note explicitly that "In the past few decades, advances in technology coupled with a change in federal law that allows universities to retain title to intellectual property developed using federal funds, have resulted in significant improvements in commercialization of technologies developed in academia." That is, since the Bayh-Dole Act, universities have been able to monetize new technologies developed and used by their faculty, which, for

CITI training purposes, can result in conflicts of interest that must be considered when IRBs decide whether to approve research protocols.

17. For instance, publishing giant Elsevier was boycotted in 2011 in response to its support of SOPA (the Stop Online Piracy Act). Similarly, the University of California threatened to boycott the Nature Publishing Group in 2012.
18. This history of consolidation is eloquently summarized in the copyright notice of The Nature Publishing Group. As of this writing, the footer of the *Nature* journal pages, such as its current homepage, www.nature.com/nature/index.html, reads, "© 2017 Macmillan Publishers Limited, part of Springer Nature. All rights reserved. Partner of AGORA, HINARI, OARE, INASP, ORCID, CrossRef, COUNTER and COPE."
19. It should be remembered that Harold Varmus was the director of one of the NIH agencies at the time, the National Cancer Institute.
20. Roger C. Schonfeld, director of Libraries, Scholarly Communication, and Museums for Ithaka S+R, defines a read-and-publish deal as one that "bundles together access to a publisher's subscription content with the ability to publish openly through its journals without paying individual APCs [article processing charges]," or publication fees. In other words, a read-and-publish agreement combines access to subscription content behind paywalls with immediate OA to journal articles.

3 Ethical Lenses Academics Bring to Intellectual Property Decisions

[IP] is a concern, but much like speeding, I comply only enough to, hopefully, not get into trouble.

—(*Question 20, Response 119*)

Introduction

In the last chapter, we discuss histories of the evolution of IP to note the different (and competing) trajectories offered under the Anglo-American and Continental models for IP. We pay particular attention to the case of Fair Use both to illustrate that the US system now privileges more of the Continental model, which grants most rights to authors (or, more precisely, copyright holders, which may not be authors), and to illustrate the power of stories (or myths) in shaping IP's role in the decisions writing studies practitioners make with respect to IP. The preceding chapter also discusses the Bayh-Dole Act and its significant influence in fundamentally changing academia's relationship with IP, making it possible for individual institutions to own IP. Finally, the prior chapter discusses the academic journal boycotts of the early 2000s, as well as more recent extensions of this activism, namely, the 2018 University of California's (UC) *Declaration of Rights and Principles to Transform Scholarly Communication* and resultant 2019 boycott of Elsevier, to illustrate higher education's more proactive stance vis-à-vis open access (OA) and the IP created by its faculty. The UC *Declaration* articulates a strong ethical position regarding IP—especially that faculty should have "more control over the fruits of their labor" (Schneider et al.), in other words, their IP, and that research publications, particularly from faculty at public institutions like UC, should be published OA.

We found participants in our study likewise to apply ethical lenses in making decisions about IP. These ethical lenses are the focus of this chapter. In his "Defense of Obfuscation," technical and professional communication scholar Brian D. Ballentine calls for greater attention to ethics in studying IP: "[T]he instruction and the understanding of intellectual property and ownership in digital environments must include and go beyond the rule of the law to incorporate the 'effects on culture' and our system of values. [. . .] Ethics takes us beyond the letter of the law" (81). Our project, in attending to ways in which writing studies scholars make IP decisions, as well as the myths that circulate regarding IP, heeds this call to look beyond the letter of the law. This chapter, in particular, takes up Ballentine's admonition to consider ethical perspectives by turning explicitly to the range of ethical lenses writing studies teacher-scholars use to approach IP decisions.

By ethical lenses we mean the fundamental premises and frameworks from which teacher-scholars operate, the foundational beliefs and rationales that shape their practices and the ways in which they reflect on their lived experiences. We contend that ethical lenses necessarily shape the perspectives from which we, as writing studies practitioners, make decisions and, indeed, which decisions we choose to make. Our interviews and survey reveal that, because IP involves a bundle of negotiable and inalienable rights, writing studies scholars' IP decisions are equally multifaceted and complex—especially because individuals approach IP issues through a wide range of ethical lenses that are not limited to legal or Western views. In this way, IP is like other ethical dilemmas: One must simultaneously consider multiple perspectives and balance competing goals. We see writing studies practitioners' applications of their ethical lenses as particularly helpful in showing this process of consideration. As Heidi A. McKee and James E. Porter put it, laws alone provide insufficient guidance for ethical questions: "[R]esearchers should not see laws and regulations as providing definitive answers to ethical questions" (*Ethics* 73). Thus, we in writing studies need reflections borne out of lived experience.

Our study reveals that writing studies practitioners negotiate among and prioritize different lenses in different contexts of their professional work. In other words, they simultaneously occupy multiple different subject positions (e.g., author, editor, user, teacher) that might privilege different (or even conflicting) ethical stances. For instance, while as a teacher someone might privilege an activist lens, advocating OA or copyleft by instructing students to assign Creative Commons (CC) licenses to their course projects, as a scholar that person might privilege a professional lens, concentrating on tenure and promotion concerns by publishing in a closed, peer-reviewed journal. In his interview, Michael A. Pemberton[1] highlighted such distinctions in describing his approaches to IP as a researcher, a teacher, and an editor. We quote him here at length:

> What I think about in terms of being a researcher, I guess the most prominent and obvious one is, making sure I'm aware of important citation practices, and that I give credit and recognition to people

> upon whose work I'm building which have informed my own scholarship. As a teacher, I think intellectual property has shaped what I do, in part as a way of [determining] the topics I introduce, in [that] each of the courses that I teach have some IP concerns, and also in the sense that I make some distinctions between how I look at my own personal intellectual property as a researcher as opposed to being a teacher because as a researcher I have, perhaps, much more of a vested interest in what I write and publish, and retaining my own intellectual property rights is fairly important. But in terms of teaching materials, it's not because I usually don't have much concern about intellectual property with those; when people ask me for teaching materials, I openly share them and say "just use them however you want." It doesn't really matter to me. I think that's part of what it means to me to be a good teacher—is to share that knowledge. And then as a publisher, it has shaped my editorial vision in some important ways; since I am the editor of an open access journal, the whole point of that is to distribute information as freely and as openly as possible. So when people submit and have articles published in *Across the Disciplines*, it's generally . . . we don't ask them to sign contracts of any sort. We don't require any kind of rights other than relatively minimal ones. All rights remain with the authors of the pieces.

Here Pemberton discusses—and applies—multiple different ethical lenses. As a researcher, he seeks both to acknowledge his use of the IP of others in sanctioned disciplinary ways and to protect his own IP. That is, he sees IP as about disciplinary relationships and as protecting his own expertise. As a teacher and editor, he takes another approach, promoting and engaging in the free circulation of IP by openly sharing his teaching materials and by editing an OA journal that allows authors to maintain full copyright. That is, he sees IP as part of economic systems and (again) as about disciplinary relationships. At least three lenses (as we label them) are at play here: IP as about disciplinary relationships, IP as protecting individual expertise, and IP as part of economic systems. And one lens, IP as about disciplinary relationships, results in different kinds of decisions depending on which relationships are the focus: citing carefully as a way to respect relationships among texts and among authors, circulating teaching materials freely as a way to share knowledge and promote best practices among teachers, and publishing OA as a way to grant authors agency in publishing relationships. Given such multifaceted reflections, which characterize responses across our interviews and survey, we contend academics should consider the multiple ethical perspectives that might guide their decision-making rather than simply accept someone else's dictates about IP law. The complex nature of IP decisions makes universal application of decontextualized rules and flowcharts difficult—and is a main reason why other practitioners' reflections on how they have made IP decisions are so important.

Ethical Lenses and IP Decision-Making

Our approach to ethical lenses draws on McKee and Porter's rhetorical, case-based approach to ethical decision-making. Like them, we believe that "ethical decision-making requires attentiveness to 'people's lives'—and to the complexities, differences, and nuances of human experience" ("Ethics of Digital" 724). McKee and Porter assert, "there is a need in the realm of Internet research for greater sharing and dissemination of such [individual] cases," though not just individual cases "alone." They call for striking a balance between a "formulaic" approach that offers decontextualized yes/no answers and a "personal" approach that offers "*ad hoc* particularism" (*Ethics* 149). In outlining these poles, they draw on the work of media studies professor Charles Ess, who they note identifies two major approaches to research ethics: the US utilitarian approach, which privileges the benefit to society over the individual, and the European Union approach, which protects individual research subjects' innate rights (*Ethics* 150). This categorization seems to parallel closely the Anglo-American and Continental approaches to IP that we outline in Chapter 2. To illustrate the need for a case-based approach that mediates these two poles, McKee and Porter offer an example from Institutional Review Boards (IRBs). They contend that the Office for Human Research Protections flowchart[2] that researchers are to use to determine if their research requires IRB review is too reductive to use effectively for complex issues such as human subjects Internet research. Yet they profess researchers still require some guidance to make decisions. For them, this guidance can come through a collection of individual cases, examples from the lived experiences of practitioners (*Ethics* 37–41). We agree and affirm the same applies to IP decisions. We take up their call in this chapter.

By providing a variety of examples of writing studies practitioners thinking through IP decisions, we seek to strike the balance between formula and relativism that McKee and Porter advocate. Thus, our goal in this chapter is not to tell readers the one "right" lens to choose in making IP-related decisions or to offer a diagram to walk readers through which lenses to adopt in particular situations. As a result, while we, as authors of this book who are heavily invested in IP issues, have personal preferences for the lenses we privilege in particular teaching, research, and editing situations, we seek not to create a hierarchy among the lenses we found.[3] Rather, through sharing the reflections of other writing studies professionals (what McKee and Porter might call "cases"), we endeavor to make professionals aware of the multiple options available. Such awareness can allow them to consider lenses they might not otherwise have known about, which can both guide their own IP decisions and help them understand what may motivate the IP decisions of others. This awareness is so important because we found study participants' reflections on IP to be embedded within overarching ethical approaches as academics—that is, their identities as writing studies teacher-scholars. Moreover, we do not see the range of ethical lenses that we found study participants to apply being taken up in the law or in stories of the law. That is, while it may seem obvious that academics approach IP from different perspectives, the law (and stories about it) seems based on a narrow set of ethical positions, for instance, IP as part of economic systems and IP as protecting individual expertise. Other lenses our study participants used, for example, the notion of IP as the collective development of a culture or IP as part of an honor code/ethical system, are absent or less represented.

The lenses we discuss in this chapter emerged from our participants' reflections on, including stories about, IP, particularly in interviews. For each lens we discuss, we identify a few responses from the survey that illustrate that lens and then bring in extended examples from the interviews. Because part of our goal with this project is to document writing studies scholars' experience with IP, we sometimes quote at length. Participants' ethical lenses emerged particularly in response to the interview question "Tell us the salient part of your IP story. As you reflect on your career, in what notable ways have intellectual property concerns shaped your teaching, research-writing practices, and/or your editorial decisions?" These lenses also emerged from questions 10–15 and 17–20 in our questionnaire (see Appendix A for the full list of our survey questions). These lenses, though, were present throughout the interviews and survey responses. That is, throughout their responses, study participants offered reflections premised on particular definitions of and stances toward IP.

Despite the range of ethical lenses we found, our participants' reflections about IP decisions were characterized by similar rhetorical moves. Participants' stories in interviews, in particular, followed a recognizable arc (though not necessarily in this order):

1. Acknowledge the complexity of IP.
   Twenty-three of twenty-eight interview participants explicitly indicated that IP is complicated or complex. Michele Eodice, for instance, noted of IP that "there are layers . . . layers of things." Timothy R. Amidon similarly asserted that "there's paradoxes and contradictions built into the systems in which we operate. [. . .] [T]his gets really complicated." Ellen Cushman's acknowledgement of the complexity of IP was quite personal: "I'm pretty much stuck in a system of imperialism that I don't necessarily feel comfortable with, but I've also benefited from pretty greatly. So, it's a thorny one." Mike Palmquist, in fact,

noted "that it's complicated" is the most important thing that writing studies teacher-scholars need to know about IP. Christa J. Olson offered a similar response to this same question: "It is complicated. It's okay to feel frustrated by it, like you aren't sure what to do and you're running into walls. In some ways, that acknowledgment—that not everybody knows how it works and that people who do know how it works still run into trouble—might be, in some ways, the best thing we can do."

2. Offer a provisional associational definition of IP.
   Participants associated IP with something, for example, an economic system, individual expertise, honor, a collective cultural development, disciplinary relationships, and so forth. These associations form the basis of the categories of ethical lenses we discuss in this chapter.
3. Apply an ethical lens given this definition.
   Participants then used these associations as lenses when recounting IP decisions and experiences (e.g., if IP is X, then the ethical way to approach IP is Y). Examples of these applications are the stories we share in this chapter.

As we listened to interviews and read interview transcripts and questionnaire responses, we found our interview and survey participants to use ethical lenses that fall into three broad categories: professional, social-cultural, and activist.[4] We selected these categories because we found them to be three areas of high contrast. That is, while reflections from interviews or survey responses often fell into more than one of these categories, we found we could easily designate particular responses as fitting into one of these classifications. Thus, we began the process of coding interview and survey data by identifying reflections that fell into these categories. We then performed content analysis to look for examples within these broader categories around which multiple participants converged. For example, within the "professional" category we found participants to discuss IP as essential for a functioning democracy as well as IP as a standard part of business practice. We then used these areas of convergence as the basis for the seven ethical lenses we share in this chapter.

This coding scheme was emergent; we added to it as we encountered new lenses in participants' interviews and survey responses. We do not have space in this chapter to report on all of the lenses we found. For this chapter, we report examples of those lenses that were especially prevalent (i.e., that we encountered over and over across participants) or provocative (i.e., that stood out in our data). For instance, one of the participants offers a Native American perspective on IP, another offers a religious perspective, and another provides a classical rhetoric perspective. No participant espoused only one lens, and we selected particular examples from interviews and survey responses to show applications of and conversations surrounding the different lenses, not to characterize particular individuals as representatives of those particular viewpoints. Indeed, we reference some participants in multiple categories. These ethical lenses are not mutually exclusive. They overlap. For the most part, participants did not explicitly indicate that they were invoking a particular lens in reporting their stories and decision-making. Thus, we named the ethical lens categories we offer here. Others, we realize, might name these categories differently or disagree with our classifications.

This chapter adds to the existing literature on IP in writing studies. Previous literature has addressed differing viewpoints that opposing stakeholders might have in an IP dispute (Reyman *Rhetoric*) as well as has analyzed technical writers' reflections on how IP issues affect their decision-making processes for Web writing (Rife "Copyright," *Invention*). However, to our knowledge no previous study has identified the wide range of often tacit ethical lenses that writing studies teacher-scholars bring to IP decisions and the ways in which these lenses play out in academia. We seek to do that here.

Awareness of these ethical lenses is especially important for writing studies scholars for two reasons. First, we attest writing is fundamentally an ethical activity. Thus, the work of writing studies professionals cannot help but entail and instantiate perspectives regarding suitable ways of being writers; thinking about writing; and engaging in practices associated with creating, teaching, and studying writing. Not surprisingly, the field of writing studies has a long history of considering ethical issues, particularly regarding the ethics of research methods (e.g., Anderson; Kirsch and Sullivan; McKee; McKee and Porter "Ethics of Digital," "Ethics of Archival," *Ethics, Professional*; Mortensen and Kirsch), including, through the Conference on College Composition and Communication, issuing the *CCCC Guidelines for the Ethical Conduct of Research in Composition Studies* and "Guidelines for the Ethical Treatment of Students and Student Writing in Composition Studies." To our knowledge, however, the field has not yet applied this ethical perspective to the IP decisions that underlie the work of writing studies.[5] A second reason awareness of these multiple ethical lenses is important is that writing is a (if not the) major site of IP decisions. That is, the products of writing comprise the IP covered by IP legislation. Thus, the work of writing studies professionals is always already imbricated in IP decisions, and they benefit from making more visible the ethical stances toward making these decisions.

In this chapter, we share reflections study participants offered that show them using different sophisticated lenses. These reflections provide examples of ways in which writing studies professionals understand and/or negotiate IP issues, offer alternative views that writing studies teacher-scholars might need to consider in challenging (or reinforcing) existing entrenched perspectives, and highlight IP-related policy debates occurring in the discipline of writing studies (and in academia more broadly). In these ways, these examples can help writing studies practitioners make more informed, mindful IP decisions for their own academic work as well as better understand, participate in, and shape IP discussions at both local and national levels.

IP as Part of Business Practice

Several study participants shared reflections that show them viewing IP through the lens of business practice. That is, in making and responding to IP decisions, they considered whether the context was academic or business, approaching IP differently for academic work and for business/entrepreneurial work or explicitly approaching academic work as business/entrepreneurial work. One survey participant, for example, indicated, "When I worked in industry, IP was a part of daily life" and noted, therefore, that preparing students to work in the business world entails teaching students about IP (Question 20, Response 110). For this respondent, in other words, instruction in IP is a necessary part of training students for a career in industry. Other survey respondents contrasted their experiences with IP in academia and industry. For instance, one noted, "I have been in education most of the time since [1968] but have also had sojourns in business practice. The sensitivities in business practice were far more critical and litigious" (Question 20, Response 177). Such responses signal participants made IP decisions based on whether they were operating in educational or business contexts.

In interviews, participants provided more extended examples of this lens. For instance, throughout his interview Patrick W. Berry highlighted contrasts between business and academic approaches to IP. He noted, for example,

> I think that in academic publishing there's much more of a generosity. [. . .] Like right now I work with CCDP [Computers and Composition Digital Press]. It's open source books, but the press is not making any money on those publications. I don't know if that has any play, but I think it does. To me, it's like a different world. I think sometimes our issues of intellectual property and copyright [are] unlike my experiences working in commercial publishing where there was incredible anxiety because of the legal consequences.

Here Berry draws attention to what he sees as stricter approaches to IP, particularly copyright, in the business world, where there is "incredible anxiety because of the legal consequences." He elaborated, "I would say that if you published something [in academia] that you thought met Fair Use guidelines in a non-commercial open source publication, the worst thing that would happen would be that maybe someone would tell you to take it down. But if you published it in a commercial publication, you could get sued." The contrast Berry draws here between academic and industry approaches to IP centers on "non-commercial" and "commercial" publication—the financial stake. (With the next ethical lens in this chapter, we discuss further study participants' attention to IP's role in economic systems.) He illustrated with a scenario where a major commercial publisher might print "six million issues in a given month"; thus, using "someone's image without getting credit" results in serious "financial penalty." But in academia publishers "target[] a very small audience" so work that "push[es] the envelope" regarding use of copyrighted text "tends not to get the same sort of attention that it would if it was in a major [commercial] publication." From this perspective, because academia and industry have different—and differently sized—audiences, treatment of IP differs.

In her interview Diane Kelly-Riley also shared a story framed by contrasting business and academic practices regarding IP. She discussed how IP worked differently for the "shop documents" she authored for administrative tasks, particularly regarding who claimed authorship (and ownership) of the texts. We quote her explanation at length:

> I've noticed interesting slippage related to intellectual property: I worked for many years for the Washington State writing program and there [were] the shop documents that you have, like where you get attributions for things. So there were lots of reports that I wrote to the provost that [. . .] —I think an accreditation review is one that I remember, in particular—were just wholesale cut and paste [in]to the document that was submitted. That was written by the provost. And that went down to differing levels as well to the entire program. So that was interesting in terms of . . . for people who are in tenure line positions; they really need to have specific things that they've done, that they have their names on, and the position I was in at Washington State, it was just an administrative position, so that wasn't as important. But there were definitely people in tenure line positions who would use things that I or my other colleagues would write—would claim them as their work. So that's interesting, too. And the administrative setup kind of facilitates that, but is nested within this broader intellectual property terrain where people really . . . their careers rise and fall on the things that they can count on their CV, which is part of the system we live in.

Here Kelly-Riley calls attention to how the stakes of IP decisions differ in different contexts, even within higher education. She sees singularly owned IP as crucial for tenure-line academics because "their careers rise and fall on the things that they can count on their CV"—that is, the texts they can claim to have written and to own. However, she situates such a notion of IP as less applicable, or at least less adopted, when the work "was [for] just an administrative position," even though "there were definitely people in tenure line positions who would use things that I or my other colleagues would write—would claim them as their work." She notes that as part of a business practice, for instance, writing accreditation reports, "wholesale cut and paste" was not uncommon. For her, then, the ethical lens of IP as part of business practice allows her to see certain treatments of text (e.g., copying and pasting) as conventional in certain contexts and for certain purposes (e.g., accreditation reports) but not in others.

That business practices regarding IP are different than those in academia was further underscored by Donna J. Kain. In discussing what she thinks students should leave writing courses knowing about IP, she noted, "If we're teaching students who need to go out into the workplace—here's another thing I think we have to deal with—we're teaching one set of ethics. When they get out into the workplace, they may face another set of ethics—or no ethics." In her interview she called attention to a need to make students aware of the different ethical lenses for IP that they may need to apply in their workplaces—and that they may need to recognize a need to apply ethical lenses as part of business practice in the first place.

Other interview participants applied this lens to situate protecting IP as an expected part of business activity. In her interview, for instance, Joyce Locke Carter related stories of both receiving and initiating cease-and-desist letters (letters sent to demand that certain IP stop being claimed or circulated or used). For the former, she shared how the Daedalus Group—a group of computers and writing scholars from the University of Texas Austin, including her, who incorporated in the 1980s—received a cease and desist letter for their product DISCourse. The letter was from an Israeli company "that had filed a sweeping global—not just Israeli, but global—trademark on all things education dealing with the word 'discourse.'" She recounted that, after checking with a lawyer and investigating the company, they concluded, "Alright, we don't have the funds to fight anything, and besides, they seem to be in the right." So they ceased using the name DISCourse. For the latter experience, she likewise described sending cease-and-desist letters as necessary for protecting IP. Her response is worth quoting at length:

> [T]here've been some design copyrights that I think I had to write a letter to send out. I mean, when you file a copyright or a trademark—or a patent, for that matter—I mean, you're cautioned to—no one's going to be looking out for your interests. You have to look out for your interests. So, I mean the patent office isn't going to, and no one else is going to. So if someone says, "Hey,

> this thing looks a lot like your thing," you say, "Wow, it really does." So you can't just let it lie there because the longer you let it lie, the stronger the claim by the other party that you're not tending your—you're supposed to protect, right? The word is "protect." You're supposed to protect your trademark, your copyright, your patent. You have to be vigilant, so even if you're not sure, you send off a cease and desist letter.

From Carter's perspective, protecting one's IP is an expected—and necessary—part of business practice, largely because "[y]ou have to look out for your interests." Creators are "supposed" to do this work—and do it in a timely manner. It is part of the responsibility of having a copyright, trademark, or patent.

In connecting her discussion of IP directly to her work as an academic, Carter does not draw the distinction between business practice and academic work that Kelly-Riley does. Rather she frames academic work as an extension of business practice. And from this perspective, academic work (in its multiple forms) is IP that requires vigilant protection. She explained,

> So I think that if you're going to develop intellectual property—in other words, you have to know how to get it, if you're working with universities, for example. But you also have to understand, and be clear—either on your own or working in conjunction with your office of commercialization, or whoever you're partnering with—who's going to be looking out and protecting this copyright or this trademark. If the university's got a really good intellectual property office, they'll help you with those things. They'll send those [trademark] and cease and desist letters out. And they'll get the permissions for . . . images and citations and paragraphs and that kind of stuff. But then, you know, they might not be. They really might just be into collecting royalties and equity. So that's another thing you need to figure out. Ask "When am I going to have the time, and how am I going to protect these things?" [Because if] I seek protection from the government in the form of trademarks—filing trademarks and patents and copyrights—I also have to be willing to spend the time to protect those.

For Carter, actively protecting one's IP—that is, being "willing to spend the time"—is a requisite part of having IP. She indicates that university IP offices can "help you with those things," but the ultimate responsibility for protecting them lies with the creator. Through an ethical lens seeing IP as part of business practice, being a creator of IP means necessarily being a protector of IP, including when that "business" is academic work.

Like Carter, Hugh Burns also discussed work with the Daedalus Group as part of his IP story and shared ways in which seeing IP as a business practice shaped his decisions. He explained how the Daedalus Group emerged from concerns over IP ownership, including the University of Texas Austin's refusal to grant IP permission to (at the time) its students:

> Fred [Kemp] received an invitation from Harcourt Brace Jovanovich to come to the 4Cs[6] and share a micro-version of invention programs. So Jerry [Bump] and I thought that it would be appropriate for Fred and Jerry to go over to the intellectual property office and get permission to show this program. Harcourt Brace Jovanovich, which was gonna pay $0.25 per disk at the 4Cs—hey, [we] were really [naïve]—they went and they came back, and the answer was no, Fred didn't own that intellectual property, and I said, "well, I don't own it" and Jerry says he doesn't own it. So at that moment we had a little talk and I said, "well, let's incorporate." And then we founded The Daedalus Group that moment. And Fred had his property—that version of the program—and we had our separate pieces of property as well within this umbrella called the Daedalus Group. So we became a corporation in Texas. And we headed over to Paul [Taylor]'s house and started making disks for Harcourt Brace and we looked for investors in the company and we needed not much money. We just needed Fred to have a computer that we would have off campus in his home, and so Fred's mother came through, and bought him the personal computer, and the rest is history. The Daedalus Group was founded with that. I think that story illustrates something that is much improved since the mid-80s, and that is that the relationship between universities, research labs sponsored by government, graduate students, professors, have to collaborate in order to understand—up front—what the technology transfer issues are going to be, what the copyright issues are going to be, and a plan, a program for managing intellectual property as it grows out of the university.

As Burns recounts, the Daedalus Group chose to do its work outside of the University without university resources—at Taylor's house with a computer purchased by Kemp's mother—so they could own the IP for their work. He describes this move as a business decision. If they wanted to be able to sell their software program to Harcourt Brace Jovanovich, they needed to create the infrastructural situation (i.e., to use non-university resources) that would allow them to do so. In this story, Burns calls attention to the need for clear agreements between students, faculty members, and universities regarding who owns IP created when university resources are used. As we learned from our nationwide survey, not all academics have this knowledge, particularly regarding pedagogical resources. In response to the survey question "Do you know who owns the copyright for teaching materials you create at your university?", forty-eight percent of respondents (126 of the 288 people who answered this question) answered no. This finding demonstrates a clear need to follow Burns's suggestion.

Moreover, Burns, like Carter, encouraged entrepreneurial work as part of academic work. In addition to recounting his work with the Daedalus Group, he shared his work as a consultant with Hugh Burns Associates, advising teachers at the K–12 level to start their own corporations to sell "their lessons and their worksheets in books"—to, in effect, make money from their IP. Indeed, he concluded his interview with Jim by suggesting that Jim incorporate as a step toward advising academics about IP based on the findings of this study. For Burns, seeing IP as part of business practice makes such entrepreneurial work natural for academics as they produce IP.

These stories from the lens of IP as part of business practice remind us that writing studies scholars (and education professionals more broadly) do work that is marketable. That is, they create IP that has economic value. Academics are often loathe to see higher education as a business, but these stories reinforce the value both of recognizing ways in which academic work is distinctive from "the business world" as well as ways in which academic work aligns with the business world.

IP as Part of Economic Systems

That IP is part of economic systems was a related lens used by participants in our study. For instance, in his interview Timothy R. Amidon explained the genesis of his interest in IP issues for his own research in terms of economics: He wanted to share his master's thesis freely under a CC license, and his advisor was not sure if that was possible. He continued,

> So, part of what we did is we used that thesis as a space to enact an argument for why I was allowed to do that. And I had to make arguments that were compelling to him and convince him and the rest of the committee that this was actually something that was viable and that I had a legal right to do. And that it wasn't just something legally I had the right to do. It was scholastically something that was ethically appropriate to do—was to share my work so that it wasn't behind the paywall, so that only ProQuest had the rights to it. Anyone could have the rights to it. And so, that was kind of the thing that really got me early on very motivated about the question of who owned my intellectual property—what I could do with that. I mean, I thought that if I'm investing all this labor in this thing, then I should kind of have a say in how it gets used, right? And it doesn't mean that all economies have to be open, right? I think there's value in the different types of economic systems. [. . .] if you're working in

> an institution that's public, and that's receiving public funds, I just think it's ethically responsible to share content with the citizens that surround that institution.

Here Amidon describes the ethics that drove his approach to his scholarship: If IP is a product of his labor in an economic system, then he has both a legal right and an ethical obligation to share that labor, particularly as a scholar at a public institution of higher education funded by public monies.

Writing studies practitioners we surveyed and interviewed also applied this lens in discussing the economic value of IP. Several addressed this economic value in terms of their own income from IP. One survey respondent noted, for example, "I am also the recipient of royalties on various publications, which leads me to appreciate IP" (Question 20, Response 134). Another responded, "Because I am an author, I am very sensitive to the issues of fair payment for creative work. It pains me to see teachers trying to 'open up' access to materials that have been laboriously and lovingly created by authors who are paid an excruciatingly small percentage of their books' cover price" (Question 20, Response 130). Such responses show practitioners to see the efforts of creating IP as appropriately rewarded through financial remuneration.

Others addressed this economic value in terms of cost to themselves or others.[7] Cruz Medina, for instance, connected concerns about copyright as arising from scholarship that becomes "monetized," or saleable for profit. He offered the hypothetical example of an author wanting to use an image in a book-length project but deciding not to because of the publisher's financial interest: "Okay, I started this project. I found these really good sites with analysis. They're well demonstrated in this image; however, I can't use this image in my book because the publisher's going to want to sell the book for a lot of money." He continued, "I think that just feels like a weird place that you find yourself in, where you have great imagery. You have things that really demonstrate what you want to, but then you know it's a question of the publisher telling you that it's completely your responsibility to get signed off on it, and that you're also to pay for or get funds for whatever you want to use." From this perspective, the use of particular IP becomes a function of an author's ability (and willingness) to pay for it. Medina explained that in this example the author consequently has fewer "resources available" to make desired arguments. In other words, seeing IP as a part of economic systems leads this author to shape what they can analyze to support claims, which affects the knowledge-making process (something we discuss further in Chapter 5). Medina noted adopting this lens for his own work. He explained that, though he did not encounter this problem of lacking funding to include desired images with his last book project, this lens would shape his "philosophy" of usage in the future: He would be mindful of what and how many images he would use.

This attention to IP as part of economic systems also characterized the stories of other participants who worked as editors and publishers. Mike Palmquist, for instance, in speaking from the perspective of a publisher, shared his experience directing the WAC Clearinghouse (a major writing studies website that hosts and publishes articles and books, as well as provides online resources for instructors, on writing-across-the-curriculum topics)[8] and negotiating with the Colorado State University Press:

> We've used print publication for the small number of readers who want things and then we make sure the revenue from any sales of those books goes back into publishing the next book, and we usually don't make a profit, in that sense, on any books. We never . . . I think maybe once or twice we've made enough from our books to fully fund the next book. But combining that with support from the university, and support from donations, from the people that support us, we've been able to form a way to make it work. So now we're going to be talking with University Press of Colorado; we're going to be talking with Utah State University Press and saying how do we make this work?

Here Palmquist reinforces that the publication of IP requires money, and this money, at least in many publishing structures, comes from the sale of print books. Yet IP published in the form of print may not be significantly profitable—not even enough to fully fund publication of the next book, as Palmquist notes.[9] He continued,

> We recently just entered into a relationship with West Virginia University Press, which is cool for Cheryl Ball's series, "#writing" [. . .]. So that book will be able to go to print, if someone wants to buy it that way. It'll be able to be submitted for tenure and promotion purposes for more conservative members of the academy. But we don't expect to make huge amounts of money off that book, even though we might. So, it's interesting and I think that the role that the publishers are going to play is starting to say, "Well, intellectual property: we have to be commercially viable. Can we be commercially viable and still have these kinds of discussions of open access, and still find ways to support the tenure and promotion process and the review process? How does this all get involved?" So I think that it'll be interesting to see the slow transformation of what I think is a very conservative industry into something that embraces what I think are critical issues in terms of providing access to materials.

In his narrative, Palmquist emphasizes that the economic value of IP is a significant component of what makes academic publishers "commercially viable"; indeed, the first association publishers make with IP is its commercial viability. Here and elsewhere in his interview, Palmquist noted, too, that there exist multiple possible revenue streams for funding academic publishers, including individual university support, publisher collaboratives (as with the Colorado State University, University of Colorado, Utah State University, and West Virginia University partnerships Palmquist describes), grants, and private donations—all of which entail what Palmquist calls "sweat-equity." Such stories emphasize that IP is part of an economic system that funds the circulation of the scholarly work of writing studies practitioners (and, of course, academics more broadly). The money generated from the sale of IP facilitates the publication of future IP.

Krista Kennedy addressed explicitly that the move to digital publishing is changing ways in which academic IP figures into such economic systems. She shared, "The fact of the matter is that broadly—and this touches every aspect of publishing—digital environments have changed things. It changed the speed. It changed the reach in direct terms. It changed the economics of publishing. And part of that is reaching readers with click-throughs, with advertising." She elaborated,

> So part of it is economics: being able to sell paper products at the cost of producing paper products. And part of it is simply the affordances of digital environments. You can put in an archival video, especially if you're reusing from the Internet Archive.[10] You can work with a variety of resources and licensing structures to develop rich content and then deliver that as long as your readers have access and broadband, and all the things they need to . . . and use that as a way to sell your product because you're providing a "richer" human experience and a more educational experience.

Kennedy notes that digital publishing requires decisions about access, use, and reuse that are bound up with economic considerations, including "licensing structures" and "advertising"—both aspects of the circulation of IP that writing studies may not consider without applying the ethical lens of IP as part of economic systems.

That the cost of producing and accessing IP is very real was mentioned by other participants as well, who addressed the multiple stakeholders in these economic systems. As Amidon put it,

> But we also have to look [at] what are the consequences of using certain economic systems. We might add quality and produce better quality and content, but then if it's a textbook, for instance, what's the cost going to be? How is that cost of that value going to be

> transferred onto students? Are there other ways to fund these projects and longer-term more sustainable ways instead of the edition model where every four years there's a new edition and it's worth $100 versus the older edition that's ostensibly—quite frankly—mostly the same as the new edition and it's $80 cheaper. That has . . . that's an economic consequence of how we operate these value systems. I think we need to do a better job of educating scholars about the underlying economies that impact how they do scholarship and what the consequences of those choices are when you want to publish with this scholar, or with this publisher or that publisher, or with this journal or that journal.

Amidon emphasizes here that the republishing of textbooks every few years in new editions that cost more money is "an economic consequence of how we operate these value systems." He expresses concern both that this cost, that is, this "economic consequence," gets passed on to students and that scholars are unaware of such economic consequences of their publication choices. In applying this lens, Amidon, like Palmquist, did not argue against for-profit publishing. He explained, "it isn't an either-or proposition that you do. Scholars need to be able to work with both [copyleft and for-profit publishing models] because there's different types of value economies and there's different types of labor that those value economies can support." He reinforced, however, that writing studies practitioners need to be more mindful of the economic consequences of their IP decisions, including who expends financial capital.

Amidon discussed another example of IP as part of economic systems—one connected to multimodal work in writing studies and the use of YouTube as a mechanism of storage and distribution of text. This case, *Lenz v. Universal Music Corporation,* involved demands to remove a video posted to YouTube because it used copyrighted material.[11] The video included a toddler dancing to a brief audio clip of a Prince song. In responding to the case, and the ultimate removal of the video, Amidon reinforced, "we['ve] got to build systems that are a little bit more ethical than that. If you [as a composer] put that labor in, I think you ultimately have to still have access to it." In making decisions about IP, he considers the perspective of "systems," particularly economic labor systems where labor expended to produce a text should be rewarded with continued access to that text. Taken together, in their stories Palmquist and Amidon draw attention to a tension that other study participants addressed as well: the tension between making IP freely available and earning money from IP.

Viewing IP as part of economic systems highlights not only that the circulation of scholarly work requires funding, but also that IP is the currency of academic knowledge-making and, more specifically, tenure and promotion. As Palmquist noted, books in the "#writing" series with the

WAC Clearinghouse will "be able to be submitted for tenure and promotion purposes for more conservative members of the academy." In other words, they can be exchanged for economic and cultural capital in the form of job security and higher academic rank. This framing of tenure and promotion as an IP-based economic system was reflected in Cynthia L. Selfe's interview as well. Selfe explained that "with print I was so used to giving away my material to presses. That giving away copyright, of my own copyright to a press, for example, was an accepted way of publishing books when I was coming up as a scholar. And so I think we saw that as a bit of a fair trade. We gave up our intellectual property rights to a print manuscript in exchange for something like tenure." In this description, Selfe frames academic work as bound up in an economic system that relies on scholars "giving away" to presses the copyright on their IP in exchange for tenure and promotion at the educational institutions where they work. Indeed, this system was (and perhaps still is) so naturalized that she "was so used" to this practice. When viewed through an economic lens, this system of exchange works when both parties are economically rewarded, for example, the press earns profit from book sales and the scholar receives a raise and job security for earning tenure. Thus, such transfer of copyright may seem reasonable. However, when this treatment of IP does not "pay off" (e.g., scholars do not receive tenure or get promoted, tenure and promotion do not come with commensurate salaries), then changes may seem to be warranted. Selfe continued,

> [I]t is a very fortunate thing, I consider, that my work is so little known that I haven't missed out on a great deal of money or royalties. I mean I've gotten royalties that I thought at the time were perfectly reasonable and adequate to the level of my labor and I was not loathe to give up my intellectual property rights. So I have never considered that an undue burden, but I think that that if there were world enough and time to fight those intellectual battles, I think that would be a good use of my time even in the early days. It's just that I was doing other things, fighting other battles. But I do think it's worth fighting over now. [. . .] Now I think younger scholars have seen that equation a bit differently. They're a little less likely to give up intellectual property rights, and I think they're probably correct about that. The battle for those rights I think is starting to be joined, and I think people are disgusted with the complexity of the legal system and also more cognizant of how few rights scholars have for themselves, and how much money is being made on the backs of scholars who are not fighting for their own intellectual property rights.

As Selfe reports here, she never considered giving up the copyright to her IP "an undue burden" because, through the lens of IP as part of economic systems, she did not lose out on royalties and felt that the royalties she did receive "were perfectly reasonable and adequate to the level of [her] labor." That is, the economic exchange was fulfilled. Yet, she acknowledged this situation is changing: "much money is being made on the backs of scholars," scholars have "few rights [. . .] for themselves," and they are "disgusted with the complexity of the legal system." That is, the economic exchange is not being fulfilled.

These reflections show the value of considering the costs—financial, cultural, and infrastructural—of creating, publishing, and disseminating IP. For writing studies practitioners in particular, these costs are inextricably bound up in labor structures of higher education (e.g., systems of tenure and promotion, adjunct and non-tenure track labor). Teacher-scholars, therefore, need to consider the goals of their work (whether scholarly, teaching, or editing) in making decisions about the acceptable costs of their IP.

IP as Fundamental to Democracy

Study participants advanced IP not only as part of economic systems, but also as fundamental to a functioning democracy. Amidon, for instance, explicitly connected IP to the workings of a democracy. He explained,

> I really see intellectual property as having a huge impact on my scholarly identity, on my teacherly identity, but also maybe just my identity as a citizen in the world in which we live. [. . .] I want the people I share this world with to have agency to communicate in the ways that [. . .] are meaningful and important to them. I mean, I think there are so many ways that folks around us are silenced in our everyday lives, and rhetoric to me is a tool for helping people understand how to make persuasive arguments or compelling arguments about how their realities might differ from someone in a different vantage point. And so, to me, that's where intellectual property really fits in; it becomes this tactic or this legal mechanism for impacting who has agency to enact a democratic voice.

From the outset, Amidon constructs IP as impacting his "identity as a citizen" as a member of a democratic society. He frames IP as fundamentally "this tactic or this legal mechanism for impacting who has agency to enact a democratic voice." Because of this ethical lens, Amidon expressed concerns about legislation under consideration by the US Congress at the time of his interview, particularly the Trans-Pacific Partnership.[12] He expressed concern not only about the content of this Bill, but also the way in which it was to be passed: "[T]here's a couple ways that I see that as really a cornerstone issue for what intellectual property might mean for not just the academy but for *democracy* and a *democratic* world . . . a *democratic* country" (emphasis added). Amidon mentions a version of the word *democracy* three times in this sentence, illustrating his sense that IP is inextricably connected to what it means to work and live in a democracy. And because IP is fundamental to a functioning democracy, he presents IP decisions as requiring reflection on what is good for that democracy—at the local, national, global, and conceptual levels.

Charles Lowe further applied this lens of IP as fundamental to democracy in connecting IP to its origin in the US Constitution. In his interview, he affirmed a need for teachers to think of IP in terms of its Constitutional roots:

> [I]f they [teachers] understood the basics of the idea in the Constitution that IP was supposed to be for a limited time to encourage progress, then they could all say, "So exactly how does this encourage someone to create a text by extending IP? It seems like they've got enough copyright protection to do that already. What's the actual benefit from this?" which is the big question to ask and the big question to hammer them on. We can talk about anything else related to copyright term extensions we want, but if you increase the terms, does that really encourage more progress? Or when you start looking at what happens when texts are available to be shared, isn't that what's going to encourage more progress? But we need teachers to engage with some of these ideas, and I'm not sure that they're all thinking about it very much. And I don't blame them because they have so many different issues to confront in the classroom, so many different things to work with, but intellectual property laws are an important consideration for the future.

In this response Lowe suggests that extending the term of copyright works against democratic ideals because it stifles progress, a reference to Article 1, Section 8 of the US Constitution, which presents the rationale for a fixed term of copyright as "To promote the Progress of Science and the useful Arts." He affirms that freely sharable IP is necessary to achieve this goal, that is, for a democracy to function. Therefore, he encourages teachers to consider how the work they assign in the classroom encourages such progress as well as to become involved in urging Congress to limit extensions on the term of copyright.

Taken together, these and other study participants' reflections told through this lens highlight the political nature of IP and situate it as instrumental to the growth of a democratic society. Such reflections suggest that writing studies practitioners consider the civic value of IP and make decisions that reflect ways in which IP can contribute to a larger public good and foster the progress of scientific and artistic advancement.

IP as Protecting Individual Expertise

Alongside this conception of IP as part of a democratic system is the conception of IP as protecting individual expertise. Michele Eodice, for instance, explained, "I think of intellectual property in a very broad way as the things that you think about, produce based on your experience and your expertise, but they're not necessarily . . . what's the word? . . . made into visible products sometimes." Here Eodice emphasizes IP as focused on the individual, as what someone creates based on their "experience" and "expertise"—that is, what they know and do, something that is unique to the individual person.

In her interview, she described how she applies this approach, and in this chapter, we recount two of her stories. In the first story, Eodice shared being asked by another university to provide all the handouts from a "Camp Completion" she ran starting in 2008–2009, her "spin" on and reformulation of the "Dissertation Boot Camp." She recounted hesitating before ultimately agreeing to share the materials and offered the following reflection on why:

> I have friends who will say to me—senior, very accomplished women scholars—"Don't give everything away!" And then other people will say, "What's the difference?" You just have to hope that people will acknowledge your contribution. I don't think there's a day that goes by that I don't try to acknowledge people, by name, in everything I'm doing. I feel that's an important practice.

Here Eodice associates IP with acknowledging—and protecting—a person's "contribution." As a result, ethical practice for her calls upon her both to "acknowledge people, by name, in everything" and to refrain from giving "everything away." The tension between these goals is part of what makes IP decisions so complex and part of what makes hearing from scholars like Eodice so important.

The second story that illustrates how Eodice applies this ethical lens involves an invitation from a book publisher to a dinner at a conference. She shared that during the dinner she was

> invited to dump my twenty-some years' experience as a writing center director onto someone they wanted to write a book on writing center work. And I thought . . . I wasn't thinking at the time, "intellectual property." I was humiliated that I had been kind of baited into that situation and ended up very flustered and thinking [. . .] it sounds like you want me to be a ghostwriter or something [. . .] So when I think of it now, I hadn't thought of it as intellectual property, but it's the kind of capacity that you build [. . .] and at some point in your career you just kind of realize "Wow! This is what I'm carrying

> around. This is what I understand pretty well. I can contribute this with confidence and credibility."

Eodice's conception of IP as something an expert "carr[ies] around" drove her ultimate refusal to consent to the publisher's invitation. For Eodice, IP is a "capacity" built over time—an expertise developed over the course of one's career. Thus, it requires respect and protection. Her IP choices, then, were based on what courses of action provide that respect and protection. She summarized her approach: "So I always say this Walt Whitman line. I'll probably mangle it, but it's 'What you don't know for yourself, you do not know.' I think that I'm at one end of the continuum around experiential learning. That fits with my orientation." Through this lens, IP protects what you "know for yourself."

Anne Ruggles Gere highlighted in her interview that this individual expertise carries over into multimodal texts. In explaining how she talks to students about attributing images, she shared, "it's something that I put in that general category of intellectual property: that people who are producing images, it's also their work just as text is, and we need to be attributing to those the same kind of citation that we do for the non-image—for the text." She explained how this approach manifests in her work at the University of Michigan: "Sweetland [Center for Writing] offers a minor in writing. And students are producing electronic portfolios, and in those electronic portfolios images play a very significant role. And so that's a space where there has to be a lot of conversation and talking about the importance of attributing for images as well as text." From this perspective that the expression of individual expertise extends beyond the written word to other modes of production, images deserve as much protection as other kinds of texts. For Gere, this protection starts with seeing images as requiring citation in the same way that "non-image" texts do. In other words, images can be the product of individual expertise as much as linguistic texts so merit the same treatment as legitimate IP.

Krista Kennedy shared a story about images that echoes this lens for IP. In her interview, Kennedy recounted the only time she received a takedown notice: when a photographer contacted her about a photo of Tennessee Williams in the French Quarter that she had posted to her blog. She shared that she mistakenly labeled the photo as "Photos by me" rather than "Photos by others," two labeling options directly next to each other in the categorization list, and when she explained this to the photographer they "ended up having a really rich conversation about IP, and about reuse of work, and about how he was devoted to sending a lot of takedowns out because he was very protective of his work." Kennedy, in relating this experience to her attendance at her first Conference on College Composition and Communication, explained that she learned from this "short epistolary correspondence" that "someone could be angry with you—legitimately angry—about a topic that you were trying to develop expertise in, and that actually a really rich dialogue could come out of that." From this perspective, protecting one's IP is a way to protect one's expertise. Someone can be "legitimately angry" about reuses of their work that do not acknowledge their expertise. Thus, as Carter and Eodice likewise attest, sending a takedown notice or declining to share one's materials, respectively, can be responsible practices to acknowledge and protect expressions of one's expertise.

IP as Part of Ethical Systems

While we frame all of the lenses we discuss in this chapter as ethical lenses, insofar as each represents an underlying value system that guides practice, several participants in our study explicitly situated the lenses they use for understanding IP as part of particular ethical systems. These include a technical and professional communication (TPC) disciplinary code of ethics, the Air Force honor code, and the Catholic Jesuit tradition. Ballentine offers an example of such a professional disciplinary ethical system as the Institute of Electrical and Electronics Engineers (IEEE) code of ethics, which he suggests writing instructors reference in the writing classroom as a way to help students learn to anchor their writing and IP approaches to an explicit ethical standard ("In Defense" 83). While no one else we surveyed or interviewed cited this particular IEEE code, study participants referenced disciplinary TPC ethical systems more generally. From our survey, for instance, one respondent indicated IP issues are "a central ethical concern" for TPC (Question 20, Response 91), and another echoed that "students in business & technical writing" courses require a "sense of IP and Creative Commons" (Question 18, Response 17). These responses position informed handling of IP as a part of ethical practice in TPC as a field.

Hugh Burns offered another ethical system example, addressing IP in terms of a larger military honor code. In response to the interview question, "What do you think is the most important thing that writing studies teacher-scholars need to know about intellectual property?", Burns responded, "I've been at The Air Force Academy three times—a total of about ten years off-and-on—and I think that honor—the honor code that we will not lie, steal, or cheat—that those kinds of ethical issues need to be taught really early." Burns discussed this honor code approach as particularly important given opportunities for multimodal composing, where writers can draw on evidence (i.e., IP) from a variety of modes, including video and audio, and the "rules" for source incorporation for these modes may be less clearly defined. He explained, "all these different means of persuasion are available to us, but the support, the evidence for our claims that we are calling on is developed by others. So we can borrow, but we need to borrow properly." In his article for the twentieth anniversary issue of *Computers and Composition*, "Four Dimensions of Significance: Tradition, Method, Theory, Originality," Burns explains his application of this approach, which he referred to in his interview as "TM^2." In the article, Burns suggested four topoi for assessing the significance of research in computers and writing, a subfield of writing studies: "[T]radition, method, theory, and originality." Important for our purposes in this chapter is that he offers originality as what makes tradition, method, and theory "significant," as, perhaps paradoxically, a way to "honor" the past. In his interview, he summarized the merits of this approach: "It's a wonderful, wonderful way to *honor* the history and the law and the ethics of producing a work for an original contribution" (emphasis added). Burns's experience in the Air Force led him to have a particular sense of honor, and this carried over into how he treats—and teaches others to treat—IP.

Burns presented this honor code as intertwined with the classical rhetorical tradition. He framed his response to what students should leave writing classes knowing about IP in terms of the Aristotelian notion of ethos:

> When young people are trying to find their identities—their true selves—they need to have developed a fine sense of integrity. And then we need to put them in hypothetical situations, cases where leaders have been challenged to not be truthful in the production of their own credibility, their own ethos. Once it is damaged, as a leader you cannot get it back. The reputation, the perceptions will be not good. So that deep sense of integrity and figuring out how to do that within the writing context would be the challenge I would see today.

In this way, Burns uses the rhetorical notion of ethos, in which one seeks to be (or at least present oneself as) credible and honorable, to guide IP decisions. For him, students who have a "deep sense of integrity"—that is, who seek to cultivate a strong and truthful ethos—approach writing decisions, including those involving IP, honorably. Part of the training Burns calls for from the perspective of this lens is asking students to make decisions in situations not governed by prescribed rules, to "put them in hypothetical situations" where they need to test out, develop, and protect their ethos.

In his interview, John Logie provided an example of such a case that illustrates the challenges to preserving one's ethos and being one's "true sel[f]" (Burns). He explained that when he was a doctoral student he was invited to contribute to a respected journal's special issue on IP. To include his article, which focused on "teaching Fair Use in the classroom," he was asked by the journal's managing editor to complete the copyright form to "sign away" his copyright to the publication. Surprised, he asked to review a copy of the form. Uncomfortable with its terms, he attempted to negotiate. He further explained, "at one point I remember saying very clearly, 'If you'd read my article, you would understand. This is an article where I'm arguing specifically about educating people to not sign contracts like this. And so it kind of undercuts my own ethos, for me to sign this.'" Logie reported feeling that he was acting in a way inconsistent with his true self, as author of an article asking writers not to sign contracts that cede their copyright, if he signed a contract that did just that. He framed this response in terms of his ethos: He would lose credibility as a scholar if he did not practice what he preached. He was told, however, that the decision to refuse to sign would "embarrass" the special issue editors and the journal editors because blank pages would need to be printed in place of the article. He recounted that, as a result, he "caved" and signed the form, though ironically it was made freely available online at a later date. Logie's decision here was likewise guided by ethos: He sought to protect the reputation of the journal and its editors, privileging them above himself. This story helps to illustrate that making IP decisions sometimes necessitates determining which aspect of one's ethos (i.e., one's "true self") gets to be privileged. Logie's decision might have been different were he to have privileged protecting his own ethos over that of the journal and special issue editors.

Bob Whipple discussed this lens of IP as part of an ethical system with respect to the religious mission of his university. Whipple explained,

> [A]t a Jesuit university there's a lot of emphasis on ethics, being intellectually ethical and doing the work that's required. I mean, a lot of it has to do with doing the work. And part of the work is making sure that you give credit, making sure that you know the work is a support rather than simply a cut and paste job, making sure that it's not a pastiche rather. Making sure that—I mean there's a certain honorable set of conventions—I think it's portrayed that way. And those conventions are to be followed because they are good to do, not because they are simply some roadblocks put up by an antagonistic teacher.

Whipple's framework for approaching IP is based on an "honorable set of conventions" founded in Jesuit beliefs that being "intellectually ethical" means "doing the work that's required," including clearly giving credit to sources referenced. He reinforced that, from the Jesuit perspective, IP conventions—which, in Whipple's discussion, include conventions regarding source use, integration, and citation—"are to be followed because they are good to do." That is, first and foremost, IP decisions are to be based on a sense of what is "good." And what is good is connected to representing accurately the work done in composing, of providing a true account of effort expended. Like Burns, Whipple frames students seeing IP as part of an ethical system as especially exigent regarding multimedia composing, where students may be less practiced in acknowledging incorporated material. For Whipple this means teaching students about Fair Use, CC, copyright, and copyleft "for at least one class period" in all writing courses he teaches—that is, making attention to IP part of writing instruction at all levels. For him, teaching at a Jesuit institution of higher education where training students to be "good" and "intellectually ethical" is part of the mission makes IP instruction at every level necessary.

What these stories help illustrate is that IP is inevitably imbricated in ways of thinking and being in the world. In addition to their potential economic and democratic value, IP decisions can have personal, ethical value for writing studies practitioners in their construction of personhood and establishment of ethos. Their authority and reputation as teachers, scholars, professionals, and members of the discipline can be affected by the honorability of their IP choices.

IP as Collective Development of a Culture

This sense of what is "good to do," what it means to be honorable is, of course, connected to particular cultural ideals. And the ideals we have discussed thus far have, at least to some extent, been based in US or Western traditions and ideas. Several participants, however, offered ethical lenses for IP that reflect non-Western views. In the questionnaire, respondents did so by foregrounding their national or non-US affiliation. For instance, the first three responses for Question 17, which asked respondents to indicate their knowledge of particular aspects of IP (e.g., determining Fair Use, securing copyright, responding to takedown notices), highlighted that Fair Use is "more relevant in [the] US" (Response 3), and practices may differ elsewhere, including in Iceland (Response 1) and Europe (Response 2). Another respondent prefaced an answer to the survey's final open-ended question, "I think here in Colombia, Latin America, we have not opened this discussion yet, though I believe it is really important for us. Intel[l]ectual property concerns raise when legal issues raise, most of the time. I think this is not an appropriate approach to these issues" (Question 20, Response 36). This respondent notes not only that approaches to IP differ internationally, but also that IP needs to be discussed beyond the law (precisely what we seek to do in this book).

In interviews, participants likewise called for thinking of IP beyond US legal code. In her interview, for instance, Ellen Cushman, a member of the Cherokee nation, noted early on, "I'm going to talk about intellectual property from a slightly different perspective than I think that you might be using it." Throughout the interview, Cushman emphasized that the very notion of property does not apply or make sense as a way of describing her tribe's approach to IP. McKee and Porter offer the case of *Milpurrurru v. Indofurn Pty Ltd.*, in which Aboriginal artwork was reprinted without permission on carpets sold internationally, to illustrate this idea: "[T]he Australian court recognized that the Yolngu Clan did not hold to a Western view of property and, in fact, did not even view these images as 'property' per se but rather as part of their heritage and subject to an entirely different set of legal standards—that is, they were afforded a higher level of protection than is customary for intellectual property" (*Ethics* 62).

Cushman noted, moreover, that for the members of her tribe not only does the notion of property not necessarily apply but IP is also about the collective rather than the individual. In their book chapter "The Ethics of Assemblage," Kristin L. Arola and Adam Arola illustrate an application of this IP lens to a related IP context, assemblage composing: "We suggest that keeping both the idea of *peoples* and *culturing* in mind when working with the rhetorical potential of assemblages encourages a richer understanding of both purpose and audience. That is, if one chooses to compose an assemblage, a leading question should be 'Why, and whom does this benefit?' There is, then, a collective ethical obligation" (210, emphasis in original). Here, Arola and Arola explicitly frame assemblage composing as an ethical practice. To make explicit the belief about IP underlying their claim, we might add to the penultimate sentence of this quotation the following italicized section "if one chooses to compose an assemblage *seeing IP as the collective development of a culture*, a leading question should be 'Why, and whom does this benefit?'" In other words, for Cushman, as well as Arola and Arola, questions about IP must start with discussions of the collective (i.e., the group) rather than the individual. This starting place is different than the Anglo-American and Continental traditions we discuss in Chapter 2 that have produced the US's current legal approach to IP.

In discussing cultural artifacts she studies as part of her research, manuscripts written in Cherokee and wampum belts, Cushman offered an example of considering, to use Arola and Arola's phrase, the "collective ethical obligation" (210). She noted that these manuscripts and belts "could not be translated or shared or sold" because of beliefs of the tribe. She explained, "It's something that's actually really quite important to our tribe to think of it as collectively understood within our nation but not to be shared with others outside of our nation." She continued, noting that such decisions are "both exclusionary but also protecting it as the property of our tribe—as a collective [. . .] [I]t is seen as something that is part of intellectual heritage, our cultural heritage and linguistic heritage, but it's not seen as property per se." Here she describes tribal creations as "collectively understood" within the Cherokee community as part of its "heritage." Thus, they require a different kind of protection than those that motivate prevailing US IP law. This alternative protection includes rules that certain materials cannot be shared outside the tribal community and cannot be profited from or sold. When approached from the lens of IP as the collective development of a culture, IP protection is not motivated by a desire to protect individual financial interests. It is not to ensure the commercial viability of a product.

This approach is in tension with Western ways of thinking. Such an ethical lens opposes US copyright law where, for instance, a criterion to determine Fair Use is the "effect of the use upon the commercial value of the copyrighted work" (17 USC § 107). In other words, using a textual artifact is not "Fair Use" if doing so impinges on the ability of the author (or copyright holder) to make money from that textual artifact. As Cushman shared, from a Cherokee perspective, however, commercial impact is not valued or desirable: "[W]ith Cherokees at least the understanding is that it makes no sense to sell language materials." So this "commercial value" criterion for Fair Use is not applicable. More broadly, conforming to US IP law asks members of the Cherokee nation (as well as members of other indigenous and non-Western groups or cultures) to privilege ways of being and thinking that can oppose tribal epistemologies. Cushman made this point explicitly in her interview: When asked what she felt is particularly important for writing studies teacher-scholars in the field, as a whole, to know about IP, she responded, "it would be how incredibly imperialist it is and how it flies in the face of so many different epistemologies and [the] world's understanding."

Damián Baca echoed this sentiment. In his interview, he addressed at length how IP is a construction of Western cultures and how Latino cultures, particularly indigenous Latino cultures, hold different views.[13] In discussing his research, which he characterized as exploring "how dominant Western practices of knowledge-making can contribute to the dis-authorization of non-Western people, of non-Western cultures, non-Western rhetorical production, non-Western ways of knowing and being in the world [and . . .] the reactivation or restitution or reclamation of indigenous and Latino, pre-Hispanic forms of knowing in rhetorical production," he explained,

> [I]f we're agreeing that there is a potential false universalization with the idea that intellectual property is something that just exists in the natural world and applies equally to all cultures, and all peoples on the planet understand it in the same way and practice it in the same way—if we can remove that, is there a way to better understand intellectual property, its cultural roots, the ways in which it's grounded in particular cultural assumptions, and also, historically, in particular pockets of the world? So, in other words, there's a geopolitics to intellectual property. So that's how I get around to thinking about it. Intellectual property is an importation largely; it's the idea that we have is: it's imported from the West, from Western civilization, from North Atlantic, first world civilization. So

now, what do we do with it? And what do I do with it as a researcher in my own work?

Like Cushman, Baca calls attention to IP as a uniquely Western idea, "an importation" steeped in the views and traditions of "particular pockets of the world." Therefore, his first step in considering IP for his professional work is to recall this situatedness, especially to consider who it privileges and who it marginalizes. He went on to explain this approach as akin to code switching: "I do happen to see observances and practices of intellectual property as a kind of code switching." Baca noted his definition of "code switching" comes from Chicana feminism, particularly the work of Gloria Anzaldúa, and might also be called "trans-languaging" or "code meshing." He explained that such code switching entails "switching from one cultural practice to another. Sometimes it could mean using one language and then using a different language. And sometimes it means conjoining those in collaborative and sometimes subversive ways." He grounded this code switching approach to IP in awareness of relationships to audiences and the "meaningful ways" of communicating with those audiences—noting that not all audiences have the same needs.

Cushman's and Baca's reflections suggest that decisions about IP cannot (and should not) take a one-size-fits-all approach—precisely because of the sociocultural views privileged in and marginalized by IP laws. Context matters. Writing studies practitioners must not assume that legislative and institutional positions on IP fully and equally represent the beliefs about property and knowledge-making—or even what constitutes "the Progress of Science and the useful Arts" (USC, Article I, § 8, Clause 8)—of the entire US or world populations. Decisions about IP are not neutral. Just as they privilege certain elements in the balance among authors, distributors, and audiences, as we discuss in Chapter 2, they privilege ideas about who can own property and for what ends—and whether property can be owned in the first place. This realization need not mean ignoring or disavowing current US law, but it should mean, as in *Milpurrurru v. Indofurn Pty Ltd.*, recognizing who that law favors and the contexts in which that law may not apply.

IP as About Disciplinary Relationships

This attention to relationships was also reflected in another ethical lens applied by our study participants. In survey responses and interviews we found study participants to frame IP as part of cultivating relationships that form the basis of disciplinary knowledge-making practices. One survey respondent, for instance, noted that IP issues "have made me more aware of what it means to be an author, and what are the relationships of business, ownership, and knowledge-building in the world" (Question 20, Response 87). In particular, several of our interview participants who work(ed) as editors made IP decisions based on what stances were likely to build the most productive relationships among members of the writing studies disciplinary community, as well as relationships with the texts created by members of that community. For example, Kristine L. Blair, editor of *Computers and Composition* and *Computers and Composition Online*, explained that *Computers and Composition Online* "relies on a Creative Commons sort of process as opposed to any form of copyright" because "people need to be able to feel as if [. . .] they have ownership over their own work but that that ownership in the 21st century is a very intertextual process." She elaborated, "I think that we've always had that sort of understanding that there's no such thing as an original idea, which is sort of a sad state for people who are dissertators: 'I want to be so original' and then, guess what? You owe your ideas to so many other people." Blair's application of the lens of IP as about disciplinary relationships is encapsulated in her professed belief that "[y]ou owe your ideas to so many other people." From this perspective, treatment of IP is based in a sense of indebtedness to others, including those whose work is referenced and those who are members of the disciplinary community.

Blair shared two stories that illustrate her application of this ethical lens. In the first, she recounted an experience as a department chair with "an electronic thesis and dissertation requirement":

> [W]hen we were implementing that, for example, all of the rhetoric and writing faculty thought that would be a great idea, that students' work is out there. It's not embargoed necessarily, though students certainly choose to embargo their work. But some faculty, for example, creative writing, are very vehement against their students having their work out there online because the publication processes in some literary magazines really do rely on first publication rights in both print and electronic form. So I think that it's a very complicated issue that has discipline specific ideologies attached to them. And I think within rhetoric and writing, within computers and writing, over the years—we see this with *Kairos*, for example, as well, and other journals—that this idea of making work accessible, shareable, usable, and immediate is a key goal of the field and one that I certainly want to embrace as a teacher-scholar.

Blair's conclusion that decisions regarding IP have "discipline specific ideologies attached to them" reinforces that scholars use IP to create knowledge in particular disciplinary contexts. And these contexts are based on relationships between people in time and space, which can vary. Thus, what seemed natural and exciting for rhetoric and writing faculty at her institution, an electronic thesis and dissertation requirement that shares students' work and makes it more widely accessible, was not natural and exciting for creative writing faculty because they believed students would later be unable to publish from their thesis or dissertation. In both cases, even though their ultimate decisions differed, faculty were concerned with cultivating relationships that would serve students in their future careers: giving rhetoric and writing students opportunities to benefit from circulating their work freely online and giving creative writing students opportunities to benefit from publishing their work for the first time in commercial venues. Blair explained the tension these differing positions posed for her:

> [H]ere I was as a faculty member who advocated open access, who advocated that notion of the dissemination of online research as something that makes research more immediate and accessible. Yet, at the same time, I had a group of faculty who were deeply concerned that the standards in their own sub-discipline of the field would find this type of model very punitive for practicing, publishing artists. And so [. . .] we worked out a negotiation with the graduate college [. . .] to have an exception for those students.

She went on to explain that the exception was to require creative writing students only to publish an abstract of their work. This negotiation ultimately made sense to her, even though she "advocated OA," because of approaching it through the lens of IP as about disciplinary relationships.

In the second story, Blair shared an experience as a journal editor. Blair recounted paying out of her pocket the $250 fee for an award-winning *Computers and Composition* article to be reprinted in an edited collection from another press: "I would call that the most current challenge I faced as an editor: seeing a piece, wanting to see it rewarded, wanting to see it get published, and realizing the only way out of this impasse—you know, the editor of the current press not willing to pay a fee, Elsevier not willing to make it free—was for just two hundred and fifty dollars. I just basically resolved that problem." Viewing IP as about disciplinary relationships made possible this generosity. Blair's story highlights that the belief that interpersonal relationships form the foundation of IP means making decisions that protect those relationships, even potentially at personal financial cost.

Writing studies practitioners we interviewed and surveyed also applied this lens in terms of institutional relationships. Naomi Silver, for instance, discussed teaching students in an introductory course for writing minors about Fair Use not only in terms of their relationship with the material they use, but also their relationship with the University of Michigan (U of M):

> [W]e talk about Fair Use at the university and basically how the work that they do in the course falls under the Fair Use law [. . .] U of M is a very strong defender of Fair Use and so that's one thing that

> I reassure them of, that, you know, you may be making a mashup in this video, you may be [. . .] using these materials in different ways, but if you're crediting them properly, if you're showing where they came from, acknowledging them when you can, finding Creative Commons things that you can use—images, for instance—if you're using pieces of a music video that you're using clips of it and not the entire video [it's Fair Use]. So it's just helping them to understand some of the parameters of Fair Use. I'm sharing with them that their work will generally be protected by the university and the university is very supportive of that and sees that within the context of their learning.

Silver emphasized that she reassures students that they have the support of the university in pursuing remix or mashup compositions. That is, their relationship with the university allows them to pursue certain kinds of composing and scholarly work.

She further explained how this university support facilitated certain kinds of composing in reflecting on her work as an editor with the Sweetland Center's Digital Rhetoric Collaborative (DRC), which is partnered with the University of Michigan Press. Silver discussed the DRC's relationship with the University of Michigan Press as essential in pursuing a book project "drawing on lots of copyrighted video":

> [S]o it was very important to us to get reassurance from the press that they would be supporters of that work and that wherever . . . basically wherever the author can get permission, he should [. . .] but that if the author can't get permission and it falls within a typically defined Fair Use use, that that would be supported by the press because it is supported by the university and that the university really believes in backing people's abilities to make the kinds of arguments that they need to make within a pretty broad interpretation of the law.

The DRC editors' decision to pursue this project was based in institutional relationships that support certain kinds of disciplinary knowledge-making—in this case, university press support for Fair Use activities that allow authors "to make the kinds of arguments that they need to make within a pretty broad interpretation of the law."

Interview participants also told stories that reflect applications of this lens to authorial relationships, in particular collaborative authorship. In response to a question about what she teaches graduate students about IP, Anne Ruggles Gere, for instance, explained a series of workshop "modules" offered to graduate students at the University of Michigan that are "designed to prepare them to be ethical in their research writ large—to basically be ethical professionals." Gere herself ran a workshop "about collaborative authorship and the kinds of issues and questions that you have to think about when you're working with other people in terms of who's going to get credit for what, down to who is going to be first, second, third author—how you handle issues of people who are and are not contributing the same amounts and that kind of thing." She focuses here on ways in which IP decisions are imbricated in relationships with co-authors, determining fair allocations of work and crediting colleagues for their contributions. Gere highlights that the decision of how to list authors on a publication is, at the core, an IP decision.

Writing studies practitioners we interviewed also discussed relationships with and among publishers—or, said another way, different models of academic publishing. For instance, at the opening of his interview, Mike Palmquist framed his IP story as fundamentally about such relationships:

> [O]ne [part] is the work we've done with the WAC Clearinghouse and open-access publishing, and the other part has been the flipside of that, the work I've been doing with [commercial] textbooks. They sort of go back and forth, and it's . . . I don't know quite how to describe the *relationship*, but it's complicated. On the one hand, I'm thinking about how do we put out new open-access teaching and learning materials? How do we get textbooks out there? Do we start a new site called textbooks-dot-whatever? And you compare that with the work that I'm doing with Macmillan, and Bedford St. Martin's, in particular, that I've been working with for almost twenty years now, and that doesn't quite line up. And sometimes very good friends at Macmillan will say, "So tell us more about what you're doing with open-access textbooks." So it's complicated and it's interesting, and *you have to tease out some of the relationships*, and some of the reasons why, on the one hand, I go out and support a site like the WAC Clearinghouse, and on the other, I engage in work with publishers who sell textbooks. So it's just kind of an interesting *relationship* there.
> (emphasis added)

Here Palmquist couches his IP story in terms of relationships, both with different publishing models (OA and for profit) and with "very good friends" who are editors. He advises, "you have to tease out some of the relationships." Rather than choose only OA or for-profit publishing, his application of the lens of IP as about disciplinary relationships allows him to negotiate a "back and forth" where he maintains a strong presence in both systems: He is a prolific for-profit textbook author as well as the major force behind one of the main OA instructional resources in the discipline, the WAC Clearinghouse.

Applications of this lens of IP as about disciplinary relationships reinforce the importance of recognizing, attending to, and cultivating interpersonal, intertextual, and institutional relationships as part of IP decisions. Study participants' reflections in this section affirm that writing studies practitioners do well to recognize that IP is in some sense fundamentally about relationships—between creators and their work, between texts and other texts, between scholars and educational institutions, between practitioners and other members of the discipline, between writers and readers, between teachers and students, between authors and co-authors, among others. Indeed, this book project depended upon considering such relationships: We (Karen and Jim) needed to work together as co-authors, and we needed to interview and survey members of the writing studies community, without whose generosity in sharing their reflections this project would not have been possible. We believe practitioners' reflections are such a compelling and necessary means for teaching and learning about IP precisely because they can highlight relationships that might otherwise be invisible or naturalized. In the next chapter, we discuss ways in which actors in these relationships can serve as sponsors, particularly gatekeepers, that mediate IP decisions.

We end with this lens of IP as about disciplinary relationships because it highlights something we saw across all the lenses study participants applied: Approaches to IP are intimately tied to practitioners' identities as writing studies professionals, which are intertwined with their identities as entrepreneurs, Native Americans, citizens of a democracy, and so forth. Participants, in other words, saw IP as part of business practice, IP as protecting individual expertise, IP as part of ethical systems, and so on because of the ways in which they negotiated the multiple facets of their identities as practitioners in the field. Thus, disciplinary ways of thinking cannot help but suggest certain approaches to IP.

Conclusion

In this chapter, we analyzed how respondents articulated their stances towards IP, and we described a range of ethical frameworks that individuals drew upon when wrestling with IP issues. We argued that these ethical lenses arose from and reflected participants' understandings of themselves qua academics in writing studies. An IP decision is inflected by a participant's goals for a specific project, commitments to an overarching academic agenda, and ideologies that encompass not only writing studies as a discipline but also academia and US culture writ large. We noted that an individual's responses may shift depending on which role is being foregrounded and negotiated over at any moment: Is the participant considering an IP issue as a creator, a distributor, and/or as an audience member? Even more, an individual may sustain multiple, even contradictory, ethical lenses simultaneously. By paying attention to these ethical lenses, we suggest that IP decisions are not as isolated or episodic as they often have been presented in the IP literature. They are part of the fabric of an academic's lifetime. That writing studies practitioners use a range of ethical lenses when making decisions regarding IP is perhaps not surprising. We would argue, however, that we (as a field and as individual practitioners) have not paid attention to this variety of perspectives, and it is worthwhile to consider what it would mean to do so more systematically.

The list of ethical lenses we address in this chapter—IP as part of business practice, IP as part of economic systems, IP as fundamental to democracy, IP as protecting individual expertise, IP as part of ethical systems, IP as collective development of a culture, and IP as about disciplinary relationships—is not exhaustive. Study participants used others. However, we hope the lenses we discuss here provide readers with ways of thinking about the ethical stances they can adopt in their own IP decision-making and their considerations of others' IP decision-making. Being mindful of these lenses can help writing studies practitioners both better prepare for and reflect on their own IP decisions. This mindfulness can allow practitioners to recognize the perspectives from which they make their own IP decisions as well as to consider alternate ethical lenses when IP decisions do not yield desired results, giving them more agency in navigating the complex IP landscape. Such agency can allow writing studies practitioners to make choices that correspond with their desired theoretical approaches to writing and knowledge-making.

Increased awareness of this range of ethical lenses can also help writing studies practitioners recognize the ethics of prevailing US approaches (both the law and stories about the law) and what beliefs might motivate the decisions of others. As one survey respondent put it, "IP laws articulate well-established ethics and conventions" (Question 20, Response 151). We think it is important to recognize, for example, that these laws in the US seem to privilege ethical stances that see IP as part of business practice, as part of economic systems, and as protecting individual expertise. Academics must decide what it means to abide by (or not) the laws that reflect these perspectives.

Part of making such informed responses and proactive choices is recognizing the people, institutions, and technologies that intervene at particular IP decision points. Thus, the next chapter turns to the sponsors that mediate the application of these ethical lenses and the relationships among stakeholders involved in IP decisions.

Notes

1. See Appendix B for the interview questions and transcription conventions; see Appendix C for the position titles and affiliations of interview participants from at the time of their interviews.
2. The Office for Human Research Protections flowchart has since been revised (and somewhat simplified) from the version McKee and Porter (*Ethics*) discuss, but we believe their larger point still holds.

3. Our participants, as writing studies scholars and rhetoricians, were well aware that they were telling stories to us as an invested audience, and their responses were undoubtedly shaped by this fact. Some participants even explicitly commented on this situation with answer prefaces like "you're more expert in this than I am" and "you might do this in another way." This awareness also led some participants to express desire for us to share the correct way to handle IP situations based on our study.
4. In the chapter we do not provide raw counts of instances of ethical lens use. We found that quantitative approach not to make sense since, in many cases, we would be double or triple counting. For our purposes, we found it more helpful to provide examples of ways in which writing studies practitioners discussed and applied these lenses.
5. Certainly this literature mentions IP and copyright, but IP issues and decisions are not its primarily focus.
6. "4Cs" is an abbreviation for the Conference on College Composition and Communication, the annual flagship academic conference for writing studies professionals.
7. We address further in Chapter 5 what we learned about how much writing studies practitioners report paying for copyright permissions.
8. See https://wac.colostate.edu for more information on the WAC Clearinghouse.
9. Such profit is more likely to come from other forms of IP, such as patents, trademarks, or proprietary knowledge (see Newfield *Great*; Rooksby *Branding*). Furthermore, such profit is more likely in STEM fields outside writing studies, first-year writing textbook publishing notwithstanding.
10. The Internet Archive (https://archive.org/) is a free digital library of books, film, software, and, through its Wayback Machine, previous versions of websites.
11. The case Amidon referenced, *Lenz v. Universal Music Corporation*, was resolved in 2018, after a more than ten-year legal battle. The case centered around a 29-second video Stephanie Lenz posted to YouTube of her then toddler son dancing to Prince's "Let's Go Crazy." Universal Music Corporation claimed that the video was a copyright violation under the Digital Millennium Copyright Act (DMCA) and demanded that YouTube remove it. YouTube did. In turn, the Electronic Frontier Foundation sued Universal on behalf of Lenz, arguing that the video was clearly an example of Fair Use, which Universal did not take into account. The US Court of Appeals for the Ninth Circuit ruled that copyright holders must consider Fair Use in seeking to protect copyright under the DMCA. In 2017 the Supreme Court declined to hear the case, upholding this ruling. Lenz and Universal settled out of court in 2018, with Universal agreeing to a more "fair" process of issuing takedown notices ("Lenz"; Farivar; McSherry).
12. The Trans-Pacific Partnership was a trade agreement between twelve nations, including the United States, that was signed on February 4, 2016. It sought to decrease tariffs and non-tariff impediments to trade among the member countries. However, it was not ratified so did not take effect. US President Donald Trump withdrew the US from participation in January 2017.
13. We take up Baca's account at length in Chapter 5.

4 Sponsors That Mediate Academic Intellectual Property Decisions

> *[I]n writing a textbook for a publisher, [I] needed to acquire permissions myself for 30 items to be included in it. Doing the permissions requests was an arduous process, especially since I had to figure it all out myself, and pay the permissions fees up front to the authors/entities who held the copyrights, with the theory that the publisher would pay me back after I did them all. This was not a fly-by-night publisher, either; it was Pearson!*
>
> (*Question 20, Response 94*)

Introduction

In the previous chapter, we focus on ways in which participants articulated their own complex, ethical stances towards IP. We share survey and interview responses that show writing studies practitioners making IP decisions that position IP as part of business practice, IP as part of economic systems, IP as fundamental to democracy, IP as protecting individual expertise, IP as part of ethical systems, IP as collective development of a culture, and IP as about disciplinary relationships. We explain that the application of the lenses is contextual and, at times, even oppositional. We affirm that writing studies practitioners apply different ethical lenses based upon the roles and relationships that they privilege in particular rhetorical situations. The chapter ultimately argues that an awareness of this range of ethical lenses prepares writing studies practitioners to make IP decisions more aligned with their value systems and to understand the value systems behind others' choices and US law.

In this chapter, we turn to the larger professional networks that participants inhabit, as they interact with other sponsors (a term we adapt from Deborah Brandt and define later in the chapter) to make IP decisions. Participants in our surveys and interviews identified a wide array of sponsors—human, institutional, and technological—that mediated their choices about IP. Sometimes such interventions were viewed positively, as in the case of campus librarians who assisted in determining the IP status of research or instructional materials. Often, though, sponsors were described in more ambiguous or negative terms, ranging from time-consuming hoops to be jumped through to project-sapping hindrances to be deferred to or, with luck, outwitted. In many cases, then, study participants perceived IP sponsors to be gatekeepers, agents denying access or permissions to use IP. For instance, 44 percent of survey respondents decided not to include desired material in a publication because of perceived issues with IP that were suggested or reinforced by sponsors. Although some IP sponsors have been explicitly recognized in previous literature about IP (e.g., Crews, *Copyright*; Galin "Own"), our study suggests that even though academics live within environments saturated by IP, the array of IP sponsors is much broader than previously documented. We further argue that the day-to-day impact of these sponsors on academics' research, teaching, and editing activities has not been adequately analyzed. Indeed, we profess that IP sponsors are often invisible precisely because academics are so deeply enculturated in IP-steeped systems.

In this chapter, then, we turn to identifying the sponsors that shape academics' expectations and decisions regarding IP. We analyze these processes of enculturation by adapting Deborah Brandt's concept of *literacy sponsors*. As she explains in *Literacy in American Lives*,

> Sponsors, as I have come to think of them, are any agents, local or distant, concrete or abstract, who enable, support, teach, model, as well as recruit, regulate, suppress, or withhold literacy—and gain advantage by it in some way. [. . .] Although the interests of the sponsor and the sponsored do not have to converge (and, in fact, may conflict), sponsors nevertheless set the terms for access to literacy and wield powerful incentives for compliance and loyalty. Sponsors are delivery systems for the economies of literacy, the means by which these forces present themselves to—and through—individual learners.
>
> (19)

Although we are not focused on the development of knowledge about alphabetic script per se, we share Brandt's interest in how literate activities are embedded within complex systems that mediate economic rewards and cultural capital. Indeed, in *The Rise of Writing*, Brandt notes how copyright laws influence understandings of "authorship" for non-academic participants who write for hire (21–31) and how notions of copyright shape attitudes towards distributing texts for non-academic participants who aspire to publish fiction (101–4). We amplify Brandt's work when we claim that knowledge about IP is a specialized aspect of literacy, one that foregrounds explicitly questions of ownership and potential profit, possibilities of censorship, and legal responsibility for fixed utterances. Important for our purposes in this chapter, then, is our claim that IP sponsors "set the terms for access" and "wield powerful incentives for compliance," and they do so because they represent, quite literally, the "delivery systems for the economies of literacy." Moreover, as Brandt suggests, "the interests of the sponsor and the sponsored do not have to converge (and, in fact, may conflict)." This conflict was especially resonant in our participants' responses: The terms in which they discussed IP sponsors—whether as relatively benign or downright obstructive—frequently referenced a sense that other entities exerted more or less control over individual academic products. Thus, we argue that it is important for academics to pay critical attention to the full array of IP literacy sponsors that influence them. Without such critical attention, their IP decisions and practices can become normalized in automatic and unreflective ways.

Before turning to the sponsors that participants mentioned in their questionnaire and interview responses, to illustrate this normalization and to highlight the need for critical attention to IP sponsors in academia, we first identify one influential IP sponsor participants did not specifically mention: the Copyright Clearance Center (CCC). The CCC, which was founded in 1978 as a not-for-profit organization by negotiations associated with the US Copyright Act of 1976, is now a company located in Danvers, Massachusetts whose not-for-profit status is ambiguous. CCC provides copyright licensing services for academics as well as corporate entities (Armstrong). In other words, if an academic needs to secure permission to use a copyrighted text, that request likely goes through the CCC, although most academics rarely think about the process. Even the six survey responses noting that their campus bookstore or copy center handles permissions for course packets did not mention that they do so through the CCC. We suggest that, because the bookstore or copy center mediates requests for permissions, the CCC is one step removed from attention and thus is overlooked. In other words, we argue the absence of discussion of the CCC signals it has become so normalized as part of academic practice that academics have forgotten about it. Indeed, we had difficulty finding scholarship written in writing studies about the CCC, another absence which further supports that it has become invisible as part of academic writing practice. We think it should not be. In her 2018 article "Copyright Clearance Center at 40," Corilee Christou explains that "35,000 companies, hundreds of academic institutions, and 12,000 publishers use CCC products and services," providing evidence of its wide influence. In a reflective component of her article "Media Convergence: *Grand Theft Audio*" with Dànielle Nicole DeVoss, Suzanne Webb provides a telling example: "It seemed as if all the Internet searches I did took me to copyright.com [the website for CCC] which—for a fee—helps educators (and, of course, the business world) gain permission to use varied works" (94).

CCC embraces a particular stance toward copyright protection. In the About Us section of its website, CCC explains that it "advocates for copyright through [. . .] our collaboration with publisher, author and collective management organizations." That is, it is motivated to serve the interest of publishers. In fact, in response to the 1982 case *Copyright Clearance Center, Inc v. Commissioner*, CCC's not-for-profit tax-exempt status was revoked.[1] The judge ruled that rather than serving public interests, its "activities support a business purpose serving publishers and copyright owners" through "furthering [its] economic interest" (*Copyright Clearance Center, Inc. v. Commissioner*). Christou provides evidence of the success of this endeavor, indicating that "In 2015, [CCC] distributed more than $206 million in royalties to publishers and earned more than $305 million." As described by Zick Rubin in a *Chronicle of Higher Education* article, CCC is a "broker of licenses" that earns a 15 percent commission on the copyright fees it collects. Rubin indicates that the "annual 'Request for Permission' form" he receives from CCC "offers blanks to check for 'fee for page,' 'fee per copy,' and 'flat fee,' but not for 'no fee.'" The lack of such an option reinforces CCC's goal (understandable as a for-profit corporation) to make money from enforcing copyright.

That CCC has a clear agenda regarding copyright protection is illustrated by its role in the Georgia State case, *Cambridge University Press et al. v. Patton et al.*, which challenged Georgia State University's argument that posting sections of copyrighted texts in its library e-reserves system was Fair Use. (We discuss this case at greater length in Chapter 2.) According to a *Library Journal* article on the case, the court "infer[red]" that CCC, together with the American Association of Publishers, "recruited" Oxford University Press, Cambridge University Press, and Sage Publications to sue Georgia State University (Schwartz). Rubin explains that the case was "paid for in part by the Copyright Clearance Center itself." CCC has economic interests to enforce publishers' copyright claims. Such economic motivation need not be inherently negative, of course, as it can allow writers to profit from their work and incentivize them to publish. However, we suggest writing specialists in particular should not forget the CCC's transformation from a congressionally sponsored nonprofit to a (potentially) for-profit organization, nor overlook its current legal activities, and thus, without reflection, assume that the CCC is a neutral organization. The CCC has had a significant impact on academics' (and their students') access to materials, and its role in managing copyright permissions should not be left unexamined. For us, the lack of discussion of the CCC in our survey and interviews—and in the published scholarship—serves as a cautionary tale of how academics may not be paying sufficient attention to ways in which IP sponsors mediate their academic work.

Horror Stories and (Non)Human IP Sponsors

As we began our study, we anticipated that we would hear examples of another type of cautionary tale. We anticipated that study participants would tell us about certain, highly obstructive sponsors, as, in our previous experiences (particularly as chairs of the Conference on College Composition and Communication Intellectual Property Caucus), we had heard frustrated scholars share accounts of how these sponsors had disrupted their academic work. We had heard, for instance, conference lore about certain author estates refusing scholars permissions to reproduce passages or images, and we had heard other detailed scenarios upon which the vignettes in Chapter 1 are based.

Beyond these academic horror stories told to conference attendees circled around dinner tables, we were aware of published anecdotes. For example, Steve Westbrook reports on a single, disruptive, IP episode: He was not allowed to reproduce in *College English* a text that his student, Sara, had created. Sara's text was a multimedia parody of a Maybelline cosmetics advertisement. Even though Westbrook had Sara's permission to share her work with *College English* readers, he did not have the permissions from L'Oréal (the parent company for Maybelline) to reproduce what could be considered a derivative work of their original advertising image ("Visual" 472–73; see also Westbrook "Introduction" 2). The fact that the student's text was a parody might have provided sufficient argument for Fair Use, but this claim could be costly to argue in court. It did not suffice to allow Sara's creation to be included in Westbrook's published essay. Throughout his *College English* essay, Westbrook calls attention to the absence of Sara's text to underscore the legal and pedagogical implications for academic work if copyright holders use IP law to practice censorship. In this case Westbrook recounts, the main sponsors are L'Oréal (who refused to grant permission to publish Sara's parody of its advertisement); Sara (who gave Westbrook permission to reprint her work but was not given permission by L'Oréal to publish her parody); and, less directly, the National Council of Teachers of English (NCTE, the publisher of *College English* which did not publish images of Sara's text).

One early motivation for our study was to gauge to what extent other writing studies scholars encountered similar challenges to their academic work, and, if so, to document those events officially. To avoid skewing responses, we did not ask participants specifically about ways in which IP sponsors disrupted them (though some of our survey questions certainly suggest possibilities for disruption; see Appendix A for our list of survey questions). We simply asked participants to share their IP stories. But stories of disruption were common. In fact, in both the survey and the interviews, participants shared accounts of IP challenges presented by different sponsors, as well as accounts that comment on the impact of recent, disruptive IP legislation and the OA movement. We analyze some of these reported challenges in this and in the next chapter.

Our intention to document horror stories was soon complicated, however. As we coded both the survey responses and the interview transcripts, we discovered that participants did not solely dwell on isolated IP episodes. Rather, their survey and interview responses reflected on the IP norms they encountered (and fostered) as academics. That is, as participants discussed how IP was incorporated into their academic routines, they readily identified IP sponsors who were active in different domains. These sponsors include humans, institutions, and technologies and exist on a spectrum rather than in a dichotomy. For instance, institutions can have human interfaces with which people interact. And technologies can have human representatives (e.g., CEOs, copyright trolls) as well as click-through licenses written by humans. But these three categories serve to represent the main groups of sponsors study participants identified. In the next section we provide some specific examples of references to them.

As interested as we initially were in documenting the disruptive IP cases that academics have experienced in order to document the full extent of these disruptive influences, the data from both our survey and interviews suggest that it is even more important to make visible the subtle influences that IP sponsors have. Doing so allows us to examine the processes of enculturation through which IP decisions are shaped by, facilitated by, and/or offloaded to sponsors. Because IP decisions are guided—if not, by default, made by—such sponsors, they can become gatekeepers that exert legal, economic, and cultural control over academics' creative materials. When sponsors act as gatekeepers, they end up enforcing legal decisions that may not be correct. And we argue the work of gatekeeping sponsors can be subtle, not just horror stories but daily effects. Moreover, an individual sponsor can serve both to gate-keep and to facilitate, depending upon the context and the perspective of the actors. Copyright law or a Creative Commons (CC) license, for example, can thwart professionals in some situations and enable them in others. As a result, we did not code sponsors as simply gatekeepers or facilitators.

To illustrate the subtle influences of sponsors, we first offer examples of participants' survey responses that show them reflecting on the influence of sponsors—both in isolation and in concert with other sponsors. Then we turn to more extended examples from our interviews. We trace a common thread across our interviews: references to archives/repositories that illustrate a wide array of IP sponsors (often in their roles as gatekeepers). We then focus on a single interview from Cruz Medina that illustrates how such gatekeepers become accepted and invisible, as Medina reflects on multiple gatekeepers that affect IP decisions throughout his teaching and research activities, particularly in regard to remix culture.

Survey Responses: Range of IP Literacy Sponsors

Human Sponsors

Throughout participants' survey responses were references to representatives and colleagues whom participants saw as being assigned

Table 4.1 Human Sponsors Mentioned More than Ten Times in Survey Responses

Sponsor	*Total #*
Professor/Teacher/Instructor/Faculty Member	179
Writer/Author	116
Editor	68
Student	43
Scholar/Researcher	23
Colleague	16
Copyright holder	16
Attorney/Lawyer	14

responsibility for assisting with IP issues. The top two sponsors (across all categories) that survey respondents mentioned were people: Professor /teacher/instructor/faculty member[2] and writer/author. Table 4.1, which lists the human sponsors that questionnaire respondents identified more than ten times in their responses, shows that editor, student, and scholar/researcher round out the top five. As we outline in the Layers of Sponsors section later on, survey respondents both encountered others and themselves served as sponsors in these roles. Wittingly or not, they were often the professors and editors others consulted as sponsors.

Survey respondents often (179 times) identified a teacher as a sponsor, either themselves or others. For respondents these teachers acted as sponsors both in shaping what their students could (or were required to) do through the assignments or guidance they gave and in modeling practices of making IP decisions for students. One respondent, for instance, explained,

> Students understand the duplicity at work when professors who threaten expulsion for inadvertent plagiarism or incomplete citation also distribute to their students stacks of photocopied articles whose distribution in that manner clearly violates both the letter and the intention of copyright and fair use (despite the professors' assertions that their distribution of copyright protected work in such a manner constitutes "academic fair use"). My teaching and policy work has been strongly informed by students' experiences with the many inconsistencies they experience when it comes to the academy's relationship to IP and to our specific "IP-control" policies.
>
> (Question 20, Response 98)

This example reinforces that students learn directly from their teachers ways in which to approach IP. For this respondent, students learn to disrespect IP when they see professors crack down on what they characterize as students' plagiarism but in turn "distribute to their students stacks of photocopied articles whose distribution in that manner clearly violates both the letter and intention of copyright and fair use." That is, according to this respondent, when professors themselves violate copyright law, they teach students to do the same—or at least to feel the system disadvantages them as students with respect to their IP. The result for this respondent is students who experience "many inconsistencies" in their encounters with IP.

Another survey respondent expressed concern about another IP decision of teachers. In particular, this respondent decried the role teachers who favor open access (OA) can play in limiting textbook production and distribution. The comments read,

> Because I am an author, I am very sensitive to the issues of fair payment for creative work. It pains me to see teachers trying to "open up" access to materials that have been laboriously and lovingly created by authors who are paid an excruciatingly small percentage of their books' cover price. I agree that textbooks are priced unfairly, but that is not because of the authors. One thing I fear is that content experts will cease to sign textbook contracts because the advances and royalties are so pathetic, while thousands of teachers and students across the country (world!) continue to openly attempt to use these materials without paying for the privilege of access.
>
> (Question 20, Response 130)

For this respondent, teachers who use and openly share with students copyrighted textbooks create financial loss for textbook authors. They[3] also fear that, in acting as a sponsor in this way, teachers will dissuade "content experts" from signing textbook contracts. For this respondent, free access to instructional materials must be weighed against financial incentive and compensation for authors to produce quality instructional materials in the first place.

Another respondent echoed this concern for respecting copyright holders, positioning them as the major sponsor in making decisions:

> I've come to regard these concerns with care and try to respect the rights of copyright holders and authors. As an author myself, I have seen my work sold by second-hand sellers and circulated even in my own program without regard for copyright restrictions and it's discouraging.
>
> (Question 20, Response 71)

Because this respondent identifies as an author and has experienced what they characterize as misuse of their copyrighted materials, they act to protect and respect the copyright of other authors.

Throughout the questionnaire, respondents expressed confusion about what to do when the authors or copyright holders of materials cannot be contacted (because their identity is unknown, because they cannot be tracked down, or for other reasons). One respondent illustrated this concern, positioning students as a sponsor:

> I am a retired instructor of writing. When I wanted to use selections from students (in a publication), I was concerned as to when we have the right to use them, even if all identifying material is deleted. Sometimes the material is old and/or the author is unknown or unreachable. What should one do in such cases?
>
> (Question 20, Response 27)

Here, the respondent reports wanting to respect students' copyright but is not sure how to proceed with securing permissions for reuse—or even if such permissions are required for old or anonymous material. Such consideration of interpersonal relationships ran throughout answers to the survey, reinforcing that IP decisions are in many cases also decisions about relationships, for example, between teacher and student, among colleagues, between editor and author, and so forth. (This emphasis on relationships is consistent with the ethical lens, IP as about disciplinary relationships, which we discuss in Chapter 3.)

Institutional Sponsors

Coding participants' survey responses allowed us also to identify a large range of nonhuman institutional sponsors that mediate IP decisions. As shown in Table 4.2, these nonhuman sponsors include everything from Fair Use guidelines to cost to copyright law to CC licenses. Because

Table 4.2 Institutional Sponsors Mentioned More than Ten Times in Survey Responses

Sponsor	*Total #*
Fair Use guidelines	99
Creative Commons (CC)/CC license	72
Publisher/Press	57
Cost	51
IRB/IP office	38
School/University/Institution	29
Open Access/Open source	23
Journal	16
Copyright law	14
Time	13
Hassle/Work	12

these sponsors are often less visible than human sponsors, identifying and being aware of them is especially important. Moreover, in addition to Brandt's work, recognition of nonhuman sponsors as rhetorical and agentive in IP decisions is consistent with writing studies' recent embrace of work in actor network theory and materialist rhetorics.

Participants in our study reported that inanimate sponsors such as cost, hassle, and time often determined whether they would pursue or drop a certain IP issue, and these sponsors shaped participants' perceptions of their projects. The respondent quoted at the beginning of this chapter, for instance, sums up a typical, exasperated reaction to the amount of effort that clearing copyright permissions can take: "[I] needed to acquire permissions myself for 30 items to be included in it [my textbook]. Doing the permissions requests was an arduous process, especially since I had to figure it all out myself, and pay the permissions fees up front to the authors/entities who held the copyrights" (Question 20, Response 94). This experience reinforces Steve Westbrook and James Ryan's claim that "the vast majority of scholarly publishers require their authors to bear the brunt of the raw cost—but also [. . .] the time and labor required to navigate the permissions process" (94). In such instances, effort and cost serve as gatekeeping sponsors.

Because cost, time, and hassle are addressed in the following chapter on the effects of IP on the academic knowledge-making cycle, we concentrate in this chapter on examples of other institutional sponsors that survey participants reported: IP/IRB offices, CC licenses, Fair Use, and copyright law.

Thirty-eight questionnaire participants identified as a sponsor a campus resource responsible for assisting with legal aspects of filing IP claims, such as a Technology Transfer Office, IP office, or IRB. For instance, one respondent noted, "Because various research projects include student work, our IRB requires us to address students' rights to their own work" (Question 16, Response 26). Another commented, "Having IRB asking to account for students' copyrights seems pretty standard these days" (Question 16, Response 27). For these respondents, IP decisions based on documenting and preserving student copyright of studied texts was part of receiving IRB approval, a conflation of human subjects ethics and IP legal practices that speaks to the entanglement of IP concerns in academics' work (in this case, particularly their research).

Another popular institutional sponsor, with 72 mentions, was CC licenses. Respondents indicated using, instructing, and/or even requiring their students to use CC licenses (or other sources with CC licenses). For instance, one respondent noted, "I now only use materials with CC licences" (Question 18, Response 2). Another similarly shared, "I often use CC licensed images in teaching materials and professional presentations. I license some of my own work that way as well" (Question 18, Response 7). Still another echoed, "I license all of my teaching materials through CC" (Question 18, Response 19). This connection of CC licenses to teaching materials was more common than to scholarly publications. Not all respondents, though, considered such licenses for teaching publications. One, for instance, noted, "I regularly give (and ask students to give) C[C] licensing to new media projects like video and audio essays. However, I have never thought to give my teaching materials a C[C] license. Interesting!" (Question 18, Response 40). Such responses illustrate that CC licenses serve as sponsors in shaping which materials some writing studies practitioners use in their teaching and research as well as ways in which they choose to publish the products of their teaching and research.

The most popular institutional sponsor survey respondents referenced, with 99 mentions, was Fair Use guidelines. One respondent indicated, "I OFTEN invoke Fair Use for using limited quotations from other texts or visual materials etc in my publications" (Question 10, Response 31). Another respondent was even more emphatic: "I've never attempted to use materials in amounts or ways that would fall outside of fair use." For such respondents, adherence to Fair Use guidelines becomes a shaping force in research and teaching decisions.

Study participants, however, reported frustration with the contextual nature of Fair Use. For instance, respondents explained that acceptance of Fair Use as a rationale for publishing, teaching, or editing decisions varied. One respondent shared,

> I tried to publish an article about non-profit advocacy organizations; the organization refused to give me permission to include either images or text (the publishing company dismissed my claim that this was fair use, and also required me to get permissions for both text and images). I finally pulled the publication and published it elsewhere with a publisher who knew it was fair use.
>
> (Question 10, Response 16)

Here the respondent was compelled to change publication venues because the initial publisher did not accept their Fair Use argument, even though they made the same argument to both publishers.

Another respondent likewise explained, in a response we quote at length, the challenge of applying Fair Use guidelines to their scholarly work:

> I've invoked fair use multiple times in audio-based scholarship. Each time, I relied on the four-factor test,[4] explaining that my use of brief audio clips (usually music) were fair because they were an integral part of my criticism, I used so little, and I wasn't profiting. However, that line is sometimes tricky to find. Generally, when I'm looking

> for just nice background music, I'm careful to find CC [Creative Commons]-licensed music, reserving my use of copyrighted works to when I'm discussing them directly.

To illustrate, this respondent reflected on a co-authored "audio book review" that "talks about the music production techniques" of several popular bands.[5] The respondent explained, "we played brief examples of those copyrighted works to illustrate our discussion, even though most of the background music in the piece was CC-licensed music from Jamendo.[6]" This respondent continued, focusing on "one illustrative moment in the review" in which they discuss the inhabitants of an island and chose music from a popular TV show as the background music. In reflecting on the thought process of this choice, the respondent explained,

> We don't use that musical clip as an object of analysis or even mention [the TV show] in the narration. We just like the way the music sounds there, and we like the way it adds a subtle suggestion of meaning for those who recognize the music. That effect was so cool that we kept it, even though we felt we were walking closer to the line of "unfair"—a clip that could be portrayed as failing the [four] factor test. If we hadn't had to worry about fair use, all the musical selections would have been so much easier—no endless browsing of Jamendo looking for CC-licensed music, instead relying on the music we already knew and loved. So while I can't think of a specific track I've avoided out of intellectual property concerns, that's a regular thought in my mind while doing audio scholarship (and my podcast, which walks the same line).
>
> (Question 10, Response 41)

This respondent notes that determining a use to be fair, even when applying the "four-factor test," is "tricky" and not straightforward. They and a co-author writing an audio book review decided to include background music from the TV show even though that music was copyrighted and not an object of analysis (and, therefore, seemingly would fail the four-factor test). Though this respondent's general rule was to use only CC-licensed music in the background, "reserving my use of copyrighted works to when I'm discussing them directly," the suitability and "cool"-ness of the music in this context led this respondent and their co-author to proceed differently. They willingly "walk[ed] closer to the line of 'unfair'" for a desired effect in their multimodal composition.

That copyright law beyond the Fair Use exemption was mentioned only 14 times in the survey suggests that the interpretation of, stories about, and reflections on the law offered by other sponsors were more powerful (or at least more visible) in shaping participants' IP decisions and practices.

This finding illustrates Rife's quote with which we open this book and reinforces the need to recognize a wider range of sponsors beyond the law as well as to realize that what we have come to understand about IP law may be filtered through and reflect the interests of other sponsors rather than the law itself. The law, of course, is inevitably subject to interpretation and itself does not necessarily provide clear guidance for making decisions, but writing studies practitioners need to take care to consider to what extent what they know of the law reflects the actual law.

Technological Sponsors

In addition to human and institutional sponsors, participants also reported on entrenched, albeit evolving, technological systems that could enable or discourage IP choices. As shown in Table 4.3, references to technological sponsors were generally less frequent than to human and institutional sponsors. We posit that this lower frequency suggests that these sponsors are less visible to writing studies professionals (rather than that they function less as IP sponsors). This lesser visibility, together with the power of respondents' examples of technological sponsors, reinforces the vital need to attend particularly to technologies as sponsors. In the past two decades, debates over which interests will control entrenched IP infrastructures have become especially potent at moments when new computer and information technologies have been introduced. For example, peer-to-peer file sharing disrupted traditional ways of distributing and purchasing music and film, leading to intense arguments over the criminality or collegiality of those who participated in file sharing. Subsequently, new legislation, including the DMCA,[7] was passed in the US (DeVoss and Porter; Logie; Reyman *Rhetoric*). Scholars have likewise raised concerns over frequently overlooked restrictions to students' IP rights that are embedded within the learning management systems and other pedagogical platforms that instructors require students to use (Amidon, Hutchinson, Herrington, and Reyman). Most

Table 4.3 Technological Sponsors Mentioned More than Once in Survey Responses

Sponsor	*Total #*
YouTube	21
CMS/LMS/Blackboard/WordPress	13
Wikipedia/Wikimedia Commons	7
Google/Google Maps	4
Facebook	3
Vimeo	2
WikiHow	2

recently, two opposing visions of the Internet have developed: At the same time that governments have legislated that results of research funded by the government be made OA, they have also allowed the emergence of copyright trolls and bots to police the use of online materials, often to the point of producing "chilling effects" on free speech (*Chilling*, Schaffner). Much of our interest in this chapter, then, centers on ways in which academics are negotiating the evolution of a culture that is saturated with technologies used to argue over and establish new IP practices. In particular, we are interested in the offloading of IP decisions to technological infrastructures that have become so normalized that they have become invisible.

For example, thirteen survey participants reported mixed experiences regarding how using campus-provided course management systems (CMSs) (would) affect the copyrights of their instructional materials. Some study participants reported that they were less likely to post material to a campus CMS because of concern that universities (who licensed the CMSs) would assume copyright of their materials, while others felt confident that they retain their copyright even if they use these technologies. Mention of CMSs was not always explicit, however, as some respondents simply noted that "teaching online" compelled their IP decisions. For instance, one respondent shared,

> When I began teaching online, a question again arose about whether my own pedagogical material would be my or the university's property, and fortunately, the union to which I belonged also was concerned about this question and made a determination about this, incorporating their response into that year's union contract. It wasn't only my issue, of course, that prompted their attention to IP and online teacher-created material, but the time frame in which most other higher ed institutions in that state system were also beginning to launch online courses as well.
>
> (Question 20, Response 94)

Here the broad category of "online" technology plays a significant role in this respondent—and in the faculty union at their university—seeking clarity on who owns teaching materials used and delivered for online courses. That the CMS was not overtly named signals potential obfuscation of the role of an influential sponsor.

Beyond campus CMSs, we highlight references to three technological sponsors built into infrastructures that are common facets of the everyday work of writing studies practitioners (and academics more broadly): YouTube, Google, and Wikipedia. Video-hosting services such as YouTube were identified as sponsors that silently enact IP decisions on behalf of (often to the detriment of) their users, such as by automatically removing a video flagged as having a copyright violation. Some participants reported resisting those IP choices, whereas others incorporated them as a routine part of doing business with the service.

YouTube itself was the technological sponsor identified as having the most influence on IP decisions. At 21 mentions, it was most frequently referenced by survey respondents. In response to the survey question "Have you or students in any of your classes encountered problems publishing course projects in online venues because of intellectual property issues?" (Question 19), one respondent recounted experiences with YouTube:

> I have been erring on the side of caution with students, urging them to keep school-based blogs private in case they have made any copyright errors, thus keeping them out of external circulation. I consider these spaces practice for not only IP issues, but writing overall, and they can be kind of messy learning spaces. One student team produced an award-winning promotional video, posted it to YouTube, and I raised some questions to them about their use of a full song in the soundtrack. They attributed it, but did not seek permissions. They opted to keep it posted. Another student reported having his videos removed from YouTube because of ambient music that he hadn't scripted in, just was there during his recording.
>
> (Question 19, Response 32)

This respondent recounts shaping their publication advice to students at least in part based on YouTube's (potential) actions regarding posted or linked content, "urging them to keep school-based blogs private." Thus, the potential visibility and circulation of students' texts are shaped by the possibility of "copyright errors," or more precisely, YouTube's response to (perceived) copyright violations. The respondent expresses concern that the "award-winning promotional video" students created includes a full song and so presumably might be removed by YouTube—exactly what occurred in the second example this respondent shares: A student reported having YouTube videos removed because of songs playing in the background. In both of this respondent's examples, students chose to post to YouTube despite potential video takedowns. In one case, the video remained; in the other, videos were removed. The instructor grants students the agency to make their own decisions about posting to YouTube. However, these experiences cause this respondent to "err" on "the side of caution with students" and discourage students from publishing course projects publicly. In turn, this respondent's pedagogy—at least in terms of discussion of textual circulation and delivery—is shaped by YouTube as an IP sponsor. In her chapter in *Cultures of Copyright,* Angela M. Shetler shares a similar example of the power of YouTube as a sponsor: "While I would have liked to distribute my remix under a Creative Commons CC BY license, which allows for further remix and reuse with attribution, YouTube only allows this licensing for works consisting entirely of content owned by the uploader, other CC BY licensed videos, or videos in the public domain" (249–50). Several interviewees, including Cruz Medina, whose interview we analyze later in this chapter as a more extended example of the shaping influence of IP sponsors, mentioned YouTube as well. Medina's interview includes multiple references to YouTube as a powerful IP sponsor.

Though less frequently referenced, Google is another technology sponsor respondents discussed. One survey respondent, for instance, explained Google as shaping what images could be included in a book project. The respondent shared,

> In a recent book manuscript, I wanted to include a geographic map of a city in which I had conducted community work to show the distance between the college campus and our community partners. It would have been easiest and most professional looking to use Google Maps, but I couldn't due to proprietary laws. I tried to reconstruct the map using open access mapping tools, but the end result didn't look professional enough to use in a scholarly publication, so my co-author and I just cut the map idea. It would have been valuable for our readers to see the map to get a better sense of space and place, but the map I built just didn't look professional and wouldn't have reproduced well in print.
>
> (Question 10, Response 36)

While this respondent mentions "proprietary laws" as restricting use, the respondent does not elaborate on which laws, placing agency with Google as the sponsor of the decision not to use Google's version of the map. Trying to use "open access mapping tools" to create a version as close to what Google produced proved unsuccessful, so this respondent chose not to include the map—even though including such a map "would have been valuable" for readers.

Wikipedia was also referenced a handful of times by survey respondents. Also in response to Question 19, a respondent mentioned Wikipedia alongside YouTube as an IP sponsor:

> I put a song that I didn't have the right to use in a private video (it's shared privately on the site too). It is the only warning I have received from YouTube, so it's not a big deal. . . . I have a couple strikes left before they send a take down notice, but there is a red flag next to that video. Similar things have occurred in work that my students have created for courses, notably on YouTube and Wikipedia. It seems that Blogs aren't policed as much because my students and I regularly post images that could be considered outside of the scope of fair use. . . . Folks on Wikipedia and Wikitravel have

> removed images that students have uploaded to these sites because they weren't properly uploaded (e.g. the students didn't note that they owned the copyright or that it was an image from the public domain). YouTube tends to use algorithms to identify music predominately. Perhaps as image recognition improves film and video may raise more red-flags on a wider variety of sites.
>
> (Question 19, Response 44)

Here, the respondent contrasts different IP sponsors (blogs, YouTube, and Wikipedia) and different modes of copyrightable texts (video, image, and audio). According to this respondent, even though students' blogs "regularly" include "images that could be considered outside of the scope of fair use," these blogs are a safer venue for publishing student work. This respondent offers two reasons: 1) blogs are not "policed as much" and 2) images are harder to machine read. This respondent indicates that texts posted to YouTube and Wikipedia are more likely to be flagged for copyright violation. In particular, this respondent notes that Wikipedia removes images for which the copyright status is unclear, stipulating that the "proper" way for images to be uploaded to Wikipedia is for their copyright to be identified explicitly: either owned by the uploader or in the public domain. Thus, a best practice for authoring a Wikipedia article with images is to designate clearly that the copyright of the image is held by the author or that the image exists in the public domain. Otherwise, according to this example, the image can be removed, even if uploading the image does not constitute a copyright violation and falls under Fair Use. In this way, Wikipedia, like YouTube, is framed as an IP gatekeeper: It makes decisions about the suitability of included material based on (perceived) copyright designation and may fail to allow for Fair Use arguments.

This respondent also reinforces that the (lack of) sophistication of machine reading facilitates the work Wikipedia and other technological gatekeepers can do. The respondent explains that the flagging of videos is more automatic in YouTube because it can "use algorithms to identify music." That is, the respondent connects the ease with which multimodal texts can be deemed to violate copyright to the mode used: Sound can be targeted more easily than film or video. This respondent, however, suggests that as "image recognition improves" this flagging of posted content will expand. This response suggests that they expect that technologies like YouTube and Wikipedia will continue to act as IP gatekeepers, determining what texts can be posted to them based on their integration and use (or lack of use) of copyrighted material.

Layers of Sponsors

As this last example shows, discussion of IP sponsors together was common in participant responses. Our study supports that IP sponsors often work in concert rather than in isolation. Thus, IP decisions are frequently about positioning, navigating, and privileging sometimes opposing sponsors alongside one's individual ethical lenses (see Chapter 3). Brandt's notion of literacy sponsor is again useful here. In addition to arguing that both animate and inanimate sponsors might act as literacy sponsors, Brandt demonstrates that they form a "deeply textured history that lies within the literacy practices of institutions and within any individual's literacy experiences. Accumulated layers of sponsoring influences—in families, workplaces, schools, memory—carry forms of literacy that have been shaped out of the ideological and economic struggles of the past" (*Literacy* 56). In one case, for example, Brandt illustrates how the means and uptake of literacy sponsorship evolved as one man learned the conventions, language, and genres needed to become a union organizer. Dwayne Lowery's story is one of escalation, as both his government employers and his union sought to control which literate practices would be needed to negotiate over contracts. At first, Lowery attended union-provided training workshops to learn how to organize his fellow public employees and to argue effectively with the government officials who hired them. Over time, however, the government hired university-trained attorneys to conduct the negotiations, and, although Lowery countered by attending union-sponsored training and education to match them, he was eventually displaced by a new, younger union member with a master's degree. In other words, some changes in necessary literate practices might be perceived by participants as sudden, as when a new type of information technology is introduced to the home or workplace. But, as Lowery's story illustrates, consequential changes in literate practices for individuals and communities are both more subtle and cumulative. They are the product of engagement with literacy sponsors over time. In this section, we provide four further examples that illustrate this subtle and cumulative layering of sponsors.

In the final open-ended survey question, one respondent offered an illustration of this layering. In recounting an experience with litigation against Google (presumably connected to *Authors Guild, Inc. v. Google*, in which some publishers sued Google for digitizing books as part of the Google Books project[8]), this respondent shared,

> I am in the lawsuit against [G]oogle; after they basically stole my copyright, I really saw no point in pursuing publication. Publishing got me tenure, but [G]oogle's actions (and my publisher's nonresponse) took away my desire to publish and probably made me more careless about using the work of others in classes (I do attribute sources, but not in 'page and paragraph precision'; I am likely to just give a general reference).
>
> (Question 20, Response 24)

Here, at least three IP gatekeepers are at work: Google, the publisher, and the respondent. This respondent indicates that, directly because of Google's treatment of their published work and their publisher's lack of adequate (in their eyes) response, they made two significant changes in research activities: 1) This respondent no longer publishes and 2) this respondent no longer follows best practice conventions for citing sources. As IP sponsors, Google and the publisher made the respondent feel that IP is both less respected (i.e., protected by copyright) and less respectable (i.e., no longer requires the same accepted attribution practices). The respondent, in turn, became their own IP sponsor, refusing to circulate their own IP and to follow prescribed rules of practice. Their faith in the system of IP recognition and reward was lost.

This survey response illustrates, then, that sponsors can serve as IP gatekeepers through both what they do and what they do not do. Being a gatekeeper does not require visible action, which can contribute to making gatekeepers harder to identify. For this respondent, Google and the publisher serve as gatekeepers through action and inaction, respectively. Google "stole [the respondent's] copyright," seemingly by including the respondent's book in the Google Books project, and the publisher did nothing to counter. In both cases, the respondent felt their copyright was not adequately protected and made subsequent changes to their behavior as a result.

In another (less dire) example, a survey respondent discussed the multiple IP sponsors that influenced their teaching (as opposed to research) behaviors. This respondent explained,

> Students created videos for which they were required to remix and reuse existing material to make a new argument. Students were asked to perform a fair use analysis for each use of assets to which others' owned the copyright. One student's video was removed from YouTube per their policy regarding any use of copyrighted materials, even though I thought the student had a strong claim for fair use. Other students chose to use Vimeo to host videos rather than YouTube because they did not want their projects removed by YouTube for similar reasons.
>
> (Question 19, Response 29)

Here, the respondent acts as a sponsor for their students in assigning them a remix project that requires them to "reuse existing material to make a new argument" and to "perform a fair use analysis" for each of the components used. This respondent asks students to create with IP (through remix) and to reflect on that use (through Fair Use justifications) in prescribed ways. In turn, the Fair Use guidelines act as a sponsor, stipulating the criteria with which students must justify their creations—and that their projects must meet Fair Use standards (Fair

Use protects only certain uses of copyrighted materials; see Chapter 2 for further discussion of these criteria).

We venture that most instructors who assign similar projects do not think of themselves as IP sponsors. Yet we think it is important for instructors to recognize when—and that—their teaching practices, including the texts they ask their students to create, ask students to assume certain stances toward IP. While this sponsor role may seem more obvious when instructors directly invoke concepts like Fair Use, we venture this sponsor role also comes into play when IP issues are less (or not) explicitly referenced, for example, when instructors require that students publish their materials to a course CMS or when they require students to contribute to a Wikipedia article for a course assignment or when they mandate that students upload their papers to a plagiarism detection service like Turnitin. When writing instructors are more mindful of the ways in which such decisions communicate (even if subtly) certain stances toward IP, we believe (and hope) that they can in turn use these as "teachable moments" for students—and that they might even rethink their own decisions if they realize they communicate stances toward IP with which they may be uncomfortable (Chapter 6 provides some heuristic questions instructors might use to reflect on these teaching decisions).

This respondent's example includes other sponsors as well. The respondent reports that students encountered other IP sponsors in their attempts to publish their remix projects: YouTube and Vimeo. YouTube acts as a gatekeeper for one student in removing a posted video "per their policy regarding any use of copyrighted materials." Consequently, other students selected Vimeo as a publication venue. According to the respondent, they made this decision explicitly because "they did not want their projects removed by YouTube." Students' text circulation choices were the direct result of how YouTube deals with (or how students perceived YouTube as dealing with) previously published materials—that is, YouTube's stance on copyright. This example reinforces the subtle, shaping role that digital technologies have as IP gatekeepers, especially regarding delivery, circulation, and archiving decisions.

Another example further highlights the role of IP sponsors in writing studies practitioners' teaching and scholarship decisions, particularly how relationships with particular sponsors cut across the pedagogical and scholarly facets of academic work. A respondent to the final open-ended question shared,

> I teach about Fair Use and IP. I ask students to use free, Creative Commons licensed images and other media in their work, and I ask the same of the graduate students I supervise. I also publish a lot of work in webtexts, and although I don't take a lot of my own photographs, I make sure those photographs have a Creative Commons license.
>
> (Question 20, Response 115)

As in the previous example, this respondent acts as a sponsor for their students, asking them to engage with IP in a particular way—in this case, through the use of CC-licensed materials. For this respondent, this consideration of CC-licensed material extends to their own scholarship. When this respondent does not take their own photographs for webtext publications, this respondent "make[s] sure" the photos they use "have a Creative Commons license." Decisions for creating multimodal texts are based explicitly in a stance toward copyright. Though less directly, CC also comes to serve as a sponsor here as its licenses grant certain kinds of uses without permission. The respondent (and their students) must comply with those stipulations to fulfill the CC license (e.g., they cannot seek to profit from publications, if the CC license so stipulates; they cannot change or remix incorporated materials, if the CC license so stipulates).

A final example in response to the survey's closing open-ended question shows human, institutional, and technological sponsors all at work in a survey respondent's decision not to teach online courses for their university. The respondent explained, in a response we quote at length,

> It became a concern when the university where I was teaching online courses focused on this issue—for online courses. Librarians were appointed to develop policies and procedures; my colleagues and I felt that the librarians were overly cautious in their interpretation of the copyright law. It seemed to us that they ruled out any "fair use" argument and assumed copyright infringement until we faculty could document permissions for material—or document that the copyright holder had informed us in writing that permission to use their material was not required. At the same time, the university wanted faculty developing online courses to sign contracts protecting the university against any potential claims regarding copyright infringement and assigning copyright for the faculty-developed components of the online course material to the university. The university would only award release time and/or course-development fees if the faculty member signed such a contract. Like some of my colleagues, I turned down the release time/extra compensation opportunity rather than give the university rights to materials I had developed.
>
> (Question 20, Response 50)

At least six sponsors are at work in this respondent's decision. Human sponsors include librarians, who the respondent felt were being too restrictive in developing institutional policies for (re)use of copyrighted material; other instructors, who reportedly agreed with the respondent's assessment that these policies were overly stringent; and copyright holders, who were required to grant permission for reuse under these new policies. Institutional sponsors include the university, which "wanted faculty developing online courses to sign contracts protecting the university against any potential claims regarding copyright infringement and assigning copyright for the faculty-developed components of the online course material to the university"; and Fair Use guidelines, which for this respondent should support different, less stringent policies than what the university developed. Technological sponsors include the online technologies that precipitated the discussion of course material ownership. In this instance, it was possibilities and opportunities to teach via online technologies that occasioned the conversation regarding who owned teaching materials created for online delivery. Ultimately, for this respondent, these sponsors together worked to convince them not to accept release time or additional compensation from the university so a "work-for-hire" argument could not be made that the university owned their teaching materials. For this respondent, this choice about teaching classes online was fundamentally an IP decision: They want to retain copyright ownership over their teaching materials, and they want to ensure there is no possibility their copyright ownership over these teaching materials can be questioned.

These individual examples show that writing studies practitioners are guided—or compelled—to make teaching and research decisions based on their interactions with people, policies, and technologies that act as IP sponsors. At times, they are mindful of these sponsors. For instance, they become frustrated when these sponsors act as gatekeepers to them or their students publishing videos on YouTube or become energized when they are enabled to use photos that are assigned a CC license. At other times, they seem less aware of the shaping force of these sponsors—for instance, when they themselves act as sponsors in assigning students projects that ask them to adopt certain approaches to IP. Being mindful of these sponsors can be particularly challenging when (and because) their influences and guidance are often layered, connected, and even opposed.

An Extended Example: Archives/Repositories

As can be seen from this analysis of survey responses, participants were concerned with an array of human, institutional, and technological IP sponsors in association with a wide variety of teaching, research, and editorial contexts. When we turned to the interviews, we likewise identified an array of IP sponsors among different contexts. We were especially struck by how nearly all interviewees reflected on, in some fashion, one particular context: Ways in which the material conditions of archives/repositories are changing and, concomitantly, ways in which the roles of IP sponsors and strategies for dealing with these archives/repositories are also changing.

Open Access

As might be expected, 22 of the 28 interviewees expressed interest in issues of OA publishing and in creating OA repositories of published materials. Self-professed OA advocate Charles Lowe[9] illustrates:

> [A]s an open access advocate, I think one of the best things we could do is to make people more aware of the reasons why they should want to publish in an open access manner, and to try to resist some of the current paradigm of "Hey, I'm gonna send it to that journal because this particular journal has this great reputation, oh, but they're not gonna publish as open access." Well, that does benefit you maybe in terms of your career, but you also have to balance this with two other important considerations: 1) Who's gonna then read your work if it's behind a locked gate, through a database? and 2) when you start to think about it that way, how do we . . . how does our work propagate? Are people going to be using it in K–12 if you [produce] a particularly good study? Because they're not going to have access to that database. So, when we start to think about those things, we need to ask ourselves, so we maybe want to try and publish in a journal that has open access, or at the very least, do we want to push for more access than the journal publisher might normally get us because, as we know as a discipline, often if you ask for more rights, you'll get some of your rights back.

In his comments, Lowe identifies human, institutional, and technological IP sponsors associated with OA. He challenges researchers in writing studies to be more thoughtful about how they participate in the current, often unexamined assumption that academic authors should sign over all of their copyrights to established publishers "because this journal has this great reputation." Doing so, Lowe and other OA advocates (e.g., Joseph "Open"; Lessig *Free, Remix*; Suber; Willinsky) have argued, means that publications are closed, and therefore substantive and potentially impactful research may be hidden "behind a locked gate, through a database." For them, researchers, as humans involved in knowledge generation, need to be more mindful of their own power over IP decisions and their impact on a discipline by choosing to challenge established publication institutions. One way to do so is to publish in OA journals, or "at the very least," to ask, "do we want to push for more access than the journal publisher might normally get us." Otherwise, as Lowe presents it in this excerpt, the publisher's online database becomes embedded and empowered as a defacto gatekeeper, imagined as keeping out K–12 teachers who are "not going to have access to that database."

We acknowledge the importance of OA publishing for our participants and writing specialists at large (including ourselves; see Chapter 2 and Chapter 6; see also, Lunsford). Productive commentary on OA publishing is readily available in the field's scholarship (e.g., Bazerman et al.; Lowe "Brief," "Considerations"; Logie; Ratliff). Here, rather than concentrate on OA, we seek to make more visible a conversation that has not had as much attention, the impact of IP sponsors not on the archives of final (or near-final) scholarly publications, but on archives that curate primary resources, collated research data, and/or datasets associated with publications. Nearly all interviewees reflected on doing (or needing or wanting to do) archival work. This work included accessing (or needing access to) archived materials for instructional or scholarly projects, and/or needing permissions to reproduce those archival materials. In several cases, the participants themselves were constructing archives for curating materials, and thus they were thinking through the IP implications both for protecting their own contributors and for allowing other researchers to employ the archived materials.

IP Sponsors that Mediate Accessing and Curating Archives

To be sure, there is a rich history of scholarship on archival methods in writing studies, particularly regarding the ethical collection and use of archival materials (e.g., Enoch and Bessette; Kirsch and Rohan; McKee and Porter "Archival"; Ramsey, et al.; Powell; Theimer) and the need for libraries to secure IP rights before accepting materials into their archives (Oral History Association "Principles"). Yet, we argue, reflections specifically regarding IP rights and their connections to archives deserve to be discussed more extensively in the writing studies literature, for digital archival work is critical for the future of our discipline. Because digital technologies make it easier for every researcher and teacher to become an archivist—intentionally, by setting up databases, or unintentionally, through using technological platforms such as learning management systems or social media—we need more extensive analysis not just of the law, but also of how writing specialists think about these IP decisions.

Fortunately, our interviewees provide examples. Ellen Cushman extends concerns raised by several scholars (e.g., McKee and Porter, "Archival"; Powell) regarding archives of indigenous materials when she speaks of her experience with Cherokee "manuscripts [that] are in libraries and archives around the country." Referring to the perspective of her own "tribe in Oklahoma," she explains,

> [S]ome of those manuscripts [remain] sensitive and contain cultural information that many of the translators I am working with are not interested in imparting to others. And so they have steadfastly refused to translate those documents and to open those documents up to a larger public, which tends [. . .] to fly in the face a little bit of how people understand intellectual property.

As Cushman notes, at issue here is a different approach to ownership and access than is proffered in Western copyright, one that "fl[ies] in the face a little bit of how people understand intellectual property." Of concern is one of the specific rights bundled within copyright: the right to distribute materials. In this case, the translators act as IP gatekeepers on behalf of Cushman's tribe, protecting sensitive information by controlling access to translations of the manuscripts. Cushman's case challenges the notion that curated IP is necessarily meant to be accessed, or that the goal should always be to make IP accessible and distribute it. Her example demonstrates how data archives can present difficult ethical challenges that are deeply intertwined with both legal and commonly circulated notions of IP. Her comments remind writing specialists to be sensitive to histories of and fears for future exploitation of IP.[10]

Similarly, in speaking of her experiences with accessing historical materials preserved and curated by the women's societies and groups she researched, Anne Ruggles Gere noted how she addressed fears of exploitation by negotiating with IP gatekeepers. Her account amplifies the importance of human sponsors, as she focused on how IP issues (again, distribution and access) are mediated through building a relationship between a researcher and those who control the archives. Gere explained how and why she carefully negotiated with the group's executive board: "Women were, I think, rightly very protective of their materials, and I would often have to write a letter to the executive committee. In one case I had to go meet them and explain in some detail about what I was doing and why I wanted to see their materials." She reported that sometimes it was clear that the relationship remained quite formal, with institutional procedures put into place to protect access to materials:

> And in one case I was assigned a watcher. And I sat at a table not much bigger than this and they would bring me a box at a time and I could sit and look through it and there was somebody sitting about as close to me as you are right now, watching everything that I did to make sure that I—I guess—didn't put things in my bag.

Here the concern with protecting materials extends quite literally to stealing. The women's groups do not want a researcher to walk away with their items. Such a reflection is a reminder that while a concern with copyright violation centers on stealing credit or profit, another concern is intertwined with protecting physical property itself.

Along these lines, Gere suggested ways that materials could be better preserved by professional institutions. She explained, "And in several cases I was able to persuade people of the value of this material and say there's the historical society, there's the library—some local place that would take care of these materials and preserve them." While these issues are ostensibly more about preservation than copyright (in many cases, these are materials whose copyright has expired), they are components of larger concerns surrounding IP. Gere went on to make this direct connection:

> But I understood very clearly why they even hesitated at [giving materials to libraries to preserve], because, as a group, women's clubs have been often laughed at or criticized, and they were very protective of themselves as an entity, and of course weren't protected by intellectual property rights. And so they felt that they had to do this for themselves, which is again sort of a flip side of the questions that you're interested in, but I think it's related in that some materials are privileged by intellectual property regulations and some are left completely outside and are therefore vulnerable, and that's what they were feeling.

Here Gere explains that it is the historical legacy of ridicule, and of being outside traditional legal protections, that makes the women's groups cautious about their IP—including being cautious about granting a researcher access to their physical archives. These women's groups were acutely aware that IP policies did not (and perhaps were not intended) to protect their work. To mediate this disconnect, as Gere suggests, often requires human contact between a researcher and archive curators.

Other interviewees suggested additional approaches to mediating these concerns. In response to such potential exploitation of human creators, we heard several accounts where participants pointed to institutional mechanisms as a means to mediate IP concerns—for both good and ill. Joonna Smitherman Trapp, for instance, shared her experience of being "part of a group of scholars who participated in the first NEH seminar on [Flannery] O'Connor" and finding a "wonderful cache of tapes of her public speaking appearances." She shared frustration with ultimately being unable to use these archival materials because of gatekeeping sponsors:

> I did substantial research on them, and later discovered that I had to write to the family to get permission to talk about them [. . .] So, I did write to the family on two occasions and have since discovered that they are very uncooperative, and I have never heard back from the lawyer. I have worked with Georgia College and State University to try to see if they'd had any help because they have a lawyer there that's worked with the family, and they've had nothing but problems, too. So I have a substantial amount of research with . . . I can't do anything with it. I presented it at a conference and I had to, at many times, say, "And this is something I can't share with you," which is frustrating.

While Trapp was able to listen to the recordings of O'Connor's "public speaking appearances"—that is, she had access to the physical archive—she did not have permission to discuss this IP publicly. She conducted a "substantial amount of research" that she ultimately does not have permission to use because of IP gatekeepers (in this case, O'Connor's family and lawyer). In turn, her academic knowledge-making about O'Connor was significantly shaped (one might say thwarted). Trapp's story reinforces that accessing and collecting research materials is necessary but not sufficient for academic knowledge-making.

Her difficulties in negotiating with the O'Connor archive gatekeepers, who ultimately denied access, had her wishing for an institutional solution:

> So, Institutional Review Boards are requiring people to do this [formal review] at the beginning of projects with human subjects. Maybe they also need to think about having some kind of a review that would help you when you're working on non-human subjects—you're doing work in a library with material that might be protected by IP rules—and have some kind of training and require university approval so that you don't invest tons and tons of work on something that you can't do nothin' with.

Here Trapp casts academic institutions such as IRBs as having some responsibility (and oversight) to protect researchers from wasting their time pursuing scholarly projects that will ultimately be unable to bear fruit because of IP issues, such as lack of access to archives or lack of permission to reprint archival materials.

Patrick W. Berry echoed this caution for researchers. In particular, he warned new researchers to be conscious of the potential difficulties of acquiring permissions to do archival work and the impact this challenge can have on their scholarship. He told us of a graduate student who

> ended up finding a piece that was very very difficult to identify the copyright author [i.e., was an orphan work]. And we ended up going through lots of different channels before she was able to get permissions for doing that. So, I think that for graduate students sometimes working with archival material is also just trying to understand where things are available. Sometimes I think that understanding availability becomes so central before you even submit something for publication to understand you can't get the rights to use them.

Like Trapp, Berry suggests that knowing what and whether IP permissions are possible is a critical part of scholarly work. He intimates that having confidence that materials will be available for reuse is (or should be) a key component of publication decisions, particularly for early career scholars like graduate students.

Other interviewees noted that institutional IP sponsors may serve more as gatekeepers than as facilitators. Christa J. Olson, for example, shared her concerns with trying to do international research, as her university attempted to mediate the issue of paying for permissions to copy archival materials. She explained that, like many universities, the University of Wisconsin

> sees payments for image permissions or image use as royalties. And because it treats them as royalties, the holder of the image permission, in order to receive payment from the university for those permissions, has to have filled out a W-8-Ben, or if they're a corporation, a Ben-E US tax form. And unless they are identified with a US identification number as a tax-exempt organization, the university will withhold 30 percent of the payment for taxes, which is a terrible method. So, you also cannot get reimbursed for paying for permissions; if I paid somebody, the University wouldn't reimburse me.

Olson's experience illustrates that how IP work (in this case, paying for permissions to use copyrighted images) is institutionally classified (in this case, as royalties) directly affects the work writing studies scholars can do. She went on to explain ways in which this requirement for certain tax forms and identification numbers tangles up the request in bureaucratic layers: "And so this became a particularly complicated issue for me because I was working with the Danish Royal Library, and as you can imagine, the Danish Royal Library doesn't have [a] US tax identification number, and didn't particularly want to pursue one." Her scholarship, then, to some extent hinges on the Royal Danish Library's decision whether to conform to US and University of Wisconsin IP permissions procedures. The result for Olson is that the permissions remain "in limbo." The result for writing studies practitioners more broadly is that IP decisions can be inextricably bound with institutional—and national—policies beyond their immediate control.

These issues of potential exploitation and institutional complication can be exacerbated or mitigated with the introduction of digital technologies. Krista Kennedy, whose research compares the development of the early print collective Chambers's *Cyclopœdia* with the digital collective Wikipedia, provided commentary on how collective projects are perceived. She emphasized the vulnerability of creators in light of new types of archives:

> For instance, when I was growing up, you could be a freelance photographer and make—you would[n't] become incredibly wealthy in most cases—but you could do this work alongside some freelance journalism and you could make a living. My mother did that for years.

> And I think that the launching of licensing like Creative Commons, the development of environments like Flickr, which had many, many years ago started incorporating those licensing structures into their system, has been a wonderful thing. But it's also driven a devaluation of creative work—particularly photography. [. . .] the fact that more and more creative people are asked to contribute their work for exposure, for purposes of circulation, and to consider that to be their compensation for that labor as opposed to actually getting paid. And as a result, a lot of venues don't have a budget anymore that's dedicated to, for instance, acquiring images.

Here Kennedy notes a possible unintended consequence of the establishment of digital OA commons spaces (like Flickr), where artists', particularly photographers', work is freely available: not only the loss of a line of work (i.e., the freelance photographer), but also a "devaluation of creative work." Part of what is at issue here is the ease of circulating images to large audiences through digital technologies like Flickr, something not as easily possible with analog technologies like print photographs. The mechanisms for storing, circulating, and accessing IP are now different—and these differences change ways in which IP is treated and valued.

Yet her reflection also points to issues of labor and knowledge. For her, when artists (like photographers) cease getting paid for their contributions—that is, for their IP—their work is devalued. Kennedy reinforces that compensation for IP not only makes certain occupations possible, but also substantiates certain kinds of expertise. She reinforces that sponsors who promote and protect the financial benefits of IP also promote and protect the value of certain kinds of textual creation. She thereby provides a reflection that balances perspectives that promote OA as an unquestioned good—a view that dovetails with Cushman's experience with translators who refused to translate Cherokee materials deemed inappropriate for certain audiences to access.[11]

Similarly, academic archival projects require researchers to think through the implications of how materials may be preserved, exploited, and/or newly valued, as institutions are charged with mediating IP issues. In her interview, Kathleen Blake Yancey commented on her department's collaborative research project to preserve examples of an ephemeral, everyday writing practice—postcards—by creating a digital, publicly accessible data archive curated by her university. As collaborators Michael Neal, Katherine Bridgman, and Stephen McElroy explain in "Making Meaning at the Intersections," the Florida State University (FSU) Card Archive aims to draw upon connections with the Tallahassee community where FSU is located, inviting both casual and professional researchers to analyze the rich collections of postcards the digital system makes available, searchable, and visible. As the "About" page of the archive notes, these collections include "postcards and stereocards from the late 19th to the early 21st centuries." The page further argues that the inclusion of cards published after 1923 constitutes Fair Use.

In her interview, Yancey reflected on different scenarios inspired by the FSU Card Archive in response to her own ventriloquized question:

> And in fact that actually just came up—somebody just asked me that as a matter of fact—and the question was, if you own the postcard, could you publish it? [. . .] We have a digital postcard archive as you know at Florida State. We have a lot—thousands of postcards at this point. Now, there are billions in the world so thousands isn't even a drop in the bucket. But we have a lot. We bought them all; we own them. So, in that sense they're our property. But I might have a harder time with a postcard that was just published today. That it had no writing on it and I choose to circulate that. I can imagine the manufacturer being very unhappy about that.

Yancey's responses to the question illustrate that, even with FSU mediating some IP issues associated with the digitized postcards, the IP issues surrounding the use of these data remain complex. That complexity centers on figuring out who the IP sponsors are. Initially, it might appear that the FSU department may claim ownership over the cards and thus should be considered the sole IP sponsor: "We bought them all; we own them. So, in that sense they're our property." In other words, at first it may seem that the physical acquisition of a postcard may justify any reuse, just as FSU's ownership of the postcard collections justifies the use of their digitized counterparts. Yet, as Yancey knows, that is not how copyright works. What may seem straightforward quickly becomes complicated along the lines of medium and modality. She "might have a harder time [advising republication] with a postcard that was just published today," since a copyright holder might be present to exert copyright claims, as opposed to those artifacts published prior to 1923, or those whose copyright holders no longer exist or are unknown (i.e., orphan works). Moreover, a postcard with additional writing might have a different IP status than one that "had no writing on it." In short, there may be layers of competing IP sponsors at play for any artifact, particularly those held in an archive. Yancey's reflection highlights that figuring out who or what the IP sponsors might be, deciding which are still relevant, and determining whether Fair Use guidelines are the IP sponsor that overrides others are all potential challenges facing today's scholars working in and assembling digital archives.

IP Sponsors and the Digital Archive of Literacy Narratives

These IP concerns especially influenced a cluster of six interviewees who commented on the development of the Digital Archive of Literacy Narratives (DALN). The DALN "is an open public resource made up of stories from people [. . .] about their experiences learning to read, write, and generally communicate with the world around them" ("Home"). Although we did not deliberately seek out DALN members or commentary, our interviewees happened to include one of the DALN founders, Cynthia L. Selfe, as well as Ben McCorkle, who was an early collaborator on the DALN project and, at the time of this interview, a co-director. As technology innovators and archive curators, Selfe and McCorkle reflected in their interviews on how they worked with different institutional infrastructures to create a digital archive that would, they hoped, forestall certain IP issues both for contributors to and researchers of the archive. We end this section by sharing and analyzing their experiences because, as with the FSU Postcard Archive, the substantial work of building and curating effective digital archives deserves to be made more visible, especially with regard to how IP decisions made by humans and mediated by institutions become operationalized and embedded within digital technologies.

Before we discuss the DALN itself and interviewees' discussions of it, we first consider its contents pertinent to our study. That is, we analyze the literacy narratives included, as of March 2019, that address IP. There are few. This dearth further supports the need for our project to gather and document the reflections of writing studies practitioners that explicitly address IP and its effects on their academic work. In the entire corpus of 7,500 narratives (Comer et al.), two narratives are explicitly framed as about IP. The first, "Little Dear and Intellectual Property," contributor Elkie Burnside glosses as "An early lesson about stealing other ideas and claiming them as your own" and shares Burnside's experience as an eight- to ten-year-old writing her first book. This "writing" entailed copying a book from the *Little Dear* series and changing only the character names. Burnside recounts that her mother explained to her that doing so is stealing, and this event impressed on her "that you can't take someone else's ideas." She explains the experience was an early lesson in IP and taught her the value of originality and doing something differently than the way everyone else does it. In the second, "Teaching IP Literacy Narrative," E.D. Woodworth shares, "A literacy narrative about teaching IP in a writing class—my IP literacy/writing story." Woodworth explains her new approach to teaching first-year writing "using the lenses of Intellectual Property, Copyright, Copyleft, Open, Attribution, Remix and Mash-up" to help students realize "knowledge—theirs and others' (and the knowledge they were trying to get at the university)—was a giant mash-up and that we might be giants standing on the shoulders of giants standing on the shoulders of giants." A few other DALN narratives touch on issues connected to IP. One mentions OA, and seven discuss plagiarism. But the DALN remains an unrealized resource for documenting the impact of IP on writing studies practitioners. Though current contributions about IP issues are few, the DALN provides an excellent potential site for continuing to gather such stories.

Reflections on the DALN's own story of creation highlight important IP issues encountered by writing studies practitioners and other scholars who create and use archives. To begin this story, we turn to published reports and scholarship on the DALN. As H. Lewis Ulman (another DALN founder) explains in his "A Brief Introduction" to the DALN, the project was the brainchild of Selfe, who, in 2005, convinced The Ohio State University (OSU) to be the initial institutional sponsor of the archive. As Ulman comments further, the motivations behind the archive were many:

> Unlike previous projects that collected literacy narratives primarily to conduct and publish research on the narratives—the original records remaining in scholars' files—the archive Professor Selfe proposed to her colleagues at several universities would be online, multi-format (e.g., text, audio, and video), preserved for the long term by an institutional host, and publicly available to multiple audiences for multiple purposes including but not limited to research. At a time when literacy practices and values are changing in response to new digital modes of composition and communication, we hoped that the Digital Archive of Literacy Narratives, as the archive came to be called, would create an invaluable historical record of a period of rapid change. We also realized that the DALN would require a "big humanities" model similar to "big science" projects: it would have to attract external funding, would require wide collaboration by people with very different skill sets, and would require extensive institutional infrastructure.

At the time of the DALN's founding, " 'big science' projects" were being established worldwide because of legislative trends that mandated that governmentally funded science projects must make provisions for data sharing. Reflecting this trend, this "big humanities" project garnered a large coalition of supporters, including facilitators who continue to help individuals at conferences and other venues record and upload their literacy narratives. As of January 2019, the DALN "collected approximately 7500 unique contributions of people's literacy experiences from across the globe and from a variety of backgrounds" (Comer et al.). As of the time of this writing, the archive is institutionally co-sponsored by The Ohio State University and Georgia State University, and it has gained a substantive reputation within the disciplines of literacy studies and writing studies.

Indeed, the purposes and values of the DALN, as stated by Ulman, were echoed in comments by our study's participants. In particular, interviewees recognized the DALN's potential to model a new approach to humanities research and to model ways to reconceive how archives deal with IP, particularly when the curated data are crowd-sourced and digitally diverse. For example, Hugh Burns[12] echoed the DALN's purpose in modeling a means of preserving ephemeral practices and digital media, in this case, authentic teachers' reflections:

> So when I came back to Texas Woman's University [as] a part of our honors scholars program, I started producing videos of our students and really authentic assessments of what they'd learned in the class. I did video final exams, and I was just doing a lot. [. . .] So I tried to do a little mini version of that in the DALN at Texas Woman's University when I got back.

In Burns's view, the DALN inspires "mini versions" of being "proactive" about recording materials that future researchers could value and so serves as a model for big humanities projects.

Similarly, Kristine L. Blair emphasized the DALN's capacity to preserve a variety of rapidly evolving media formats and modes, as Ulman's introduction mentions. She further noted the benefit to other researchers to have such materials in a centralized database: "The Digital Archive of Literacy Narratives is a great type of place to look for various types of media that might be used in [. . .] literacy research because that is what we do." Blair especially praised the DALN because it means researchers "don't necessarily have to reinvent the wheel to use those artifacts, especially in terms of them representing an existing dataset." By working with this "existing dataset," researchers "don't necessarily have to reinvent the wheel to use those artifacts" because they have already been collected and, Blair implies, their permissions have already been cleared. Patrick W. Berry's comments align with Blair's. He likewise reflected on the DALN's benefits for future researchers:

> One of the things that I find really valuable is I'm seeing a trend in the field where people are sharing the research that they produce with others. [. . .] I'm really interested in the work that's taking place with the Digital Archive of Literacy Narratives. And the idea that perhaps there could be this database of research that others might be able to draw on as well.

For Berry, the DALN enacts and embodies a new set of research values, and, he implies, a new collaborative approach to sharing IP, the "trend in the field where people are sharing the research that they produce with others." Ellen Cushman similarly highlights this benefit of the DALN, as she explained that the database resonates, if imperfectly, with the non-Western, collective approaches to research and IP that she has been advocating for the discipline:

> I think that there's a sense of collective property and collective understanding that would be really, really helpful for us [. . .] as a

> field to work with and in. And to some extent I think the DALN was trying to do just that and to help us understand students and that, it, it's not without its problems, the DALN [corrected from DLAN], but still, it was trying to tackle some of those thorny problems of intellectual property along the way as it was doing its work.

Cushman's last point is particularly significant: Decisions about IP were deliberately integrated into the construction of the DALN technology. The technology was designed to solve some of "those thorny problems of intellectual property," so that future researchers would be less encumbered by the need to seek IP permissions for reusing the data. Contributors to the DALN must designate those permissions up front, as a condition of uploading their work to the archive.

As Selfe and McCorkle explained in their interviews, the human designers of the DALN thought carefully about IP issues on behalf of both contributors to and users of the digital archive. The specific institutional sponsor driving some of these discussions was the OSU's IRB, as the research project underwent human subjects review. We recall here Joonna Smitherman Trapp's wish that an institutional review might help scholars avoid wasting time on research endeavors that might be blocked by IP concerns. In this case, the institutional review led to a technological IP sponsor. Whenever a contributor chooses to upload a literacy narrative file (whether written, audio, video, or some combination of these formats), that individual must first fill out a digital informed consent form. As Selfe detailed, in addition to collecting contact information and informing the contributor about their rights as human subjects, this digital interface also addresses their choices regarding IP:

> So part of the process that we go through when we go through the Digital Archive of Literacy Narratives interview process is informing participants about their—what we're trying to do, and also asking them to release—to give their intellectual property to the Digital Archive of Literacy Narratives, understanding that they can download and use their intellectual property in any way that they choose and license with the digital archive.

The DALN's digital informed consent form at the time of this writing calls attention to these IP choices. It appears on a separate page and its title, "Consent To Participate & Release of Materials," appears in boldface. The sections regarding IP permissions constitute about half of the form. Such clarity is important to Selfe and other interviewees who commented on the DALN, as they repeatedly remarked on how the DALN is an asset to people who are inexperienced with research and inexperienced with the implications of submitting materials to a public archive. By explaining IP rights to potential contributors, the DALN consent form acts as a de facto IP sponsor, a sponsor that privileges accessibility of its contents for researchers. Through its consent form, the DALN makes clear what contributors are giving away—something other websites that are arguably archives, such as Twitter or Facebook, do not do. In other words, what is unique about the DALN, in terms of how it treats IP, is that it is an archive that operates more as a commons, typically privileging researchers—those who would use the archive—over those who upload to it. This approach contrasts with Gere's and Trapp's experiences, which we discuss earlier in this chapter. For Gere, the women's social group archives she visited were intended to protect IP (and perhaps for good reason), not make it openly accessible to researchers. For Trapp, the contents of the O'Connor archives could be accessed but not subsequently referenced or shared; a researcher's needs were not privileged.

This decision to combine a human subjects protocol with an IP protocol has precedence, but, in keeping with its stance towards modeling new research approaches, the DALN offers an innovative alternative. As McCorkle explained, the DALN consent form offers contributors not one, but two, options for designating the IP status of their literacy narratives:

> The two big options with the DALN [are] either deed of gift—you give it over to the archive for us to do with as we will—or you designate a Creative Commons license for it. And so we try to be explicit about what those different options mean, even though practically [. . .] there's not a lot of difference between. But there is a retention of rights, if you choose a Creative Commons option.

As McCorkle suggests, a "deed of gift" is a legal protocol, a signed document that transfers the ownership of an item from a donor to a recipient, in this case, from a research participant to an institutional archive (see also the explanation by the Society of American Archivists). As with many legal means of transferring property, the deed of gift comprises a specified bundle of rights, each of which can be negotiated separately. Through a deed of gift, a donor might transfer the physical ownership of materials to an archive, but retain the copyright over those materials (as, presumably, has occurred in the example that Joonna Smitherman Trapp relates, where the university has physical ownership of the Flannery O'Connor tapes, but the family estate retains control over the copyright). Most archives, though, prefer that researchers design a deed of gift so that it includes a complete transfer of IP rights, an approach considered to be a best practice among oral historians who plan to curate their audio and video recordings in library archives (Oral History Association "Best"). A deed of gift that transfers all IP rights allows the archive owner to grant permissions to reproduce materials, so that future researchers do not have to track down and contact the creator or copyright holder to secure permissions for reuse. It also avoids the problem of orphan works, where the copyright owner cannot be located or has died. In the DALN informed consent interface, all of these potential concerns are addressed within a few sentences that describe the deed of gift option, embedding the work in the interface of making a decision about IP.

Likewise, the informed consent interface teaches participants about the second option for their IP, a CC license. McCorkle explained, in contrast with the more established deed of gift, the CC license was unexpected, as it was just becoming popular as the DALN was being designed: "[C]oncurrent with that conversation [about the deed of gift], Creative Commons emerged. So [. . .] there was a convergence or a confluence of factors that made us think, 'Oh, let's offer this option as well.'" Although McCorkle's comment suggests that offering the CC license choice was somewhat of an afterthought ("'Oh, let's offer this option as well'"), the option is significant. As he mentioned earlier in the interview, "there's not a lot of difference" between a deed of gift and a CC license, "but there is a retention of rights, if you choose a Creative Commons option." In other words, like the deed of gift, the CC license allows future researchers to reuse the materials, but, unlike the deed of gift, it allows the contributor to retain the copyright and to determine the conditions of that reuse. Like a deed of gift, then, the CC license comprises a bundle of rights that can be individually identified and negotiated. Importantly, a CC license can allow the reuse of materials with the provision that they not be reproduced for commercial purposes. The informed consent interface thus also mediates between the contributor and a different interpretation of IP regulations, one based on licensing options in place of full ownership. Again, the informed consent interface operationalizes a complex IP system.

Yet, a technological sponsor cannot completely operationalize and resolve IP issues. Human sponsors play a significant role. The DALN consent interface enacts an attempt to navigate different configurations of IP rights, and to continue to open up new, more humane, IP possibilities. For example, as McCorkle explained, protecting participants' rights as human subjects remains a priority, and those rights have a direct bearing on IP:

> But again the practical side of that: our working philosophy at the DALN—and I've inherited this from Cindy [Selfe] and Lewis [Ulman]—if we get a takedown request and it's a deed of gift kind of thing, you know we have no problems taking it down. I guess technically we don't have to, but if someone says something about his or her grandmother and then they thought differently about it down the road, I'm perfectly fine expunging the record.

In other words, McCorkle is pointing here to one of the "thorny problems of IP" that Cushman references. Historically and recently, owners of archives and archival researchers have been criticized for ignoring the wishes of certain human donors and their communities. A deed of gift may "technically" mean that the archive retains ownership and copyright over an artifact, but that legal right, according to McCorkle's understanding of the DALN's mandates, does not override the rights of human participants. The human sponsors of the archive have an obligation to respond to a "takedown request" and to be "perfectly fine expunging the record," if a participant changes their mind. In essence, the DALN's human subjects permissions reassert one of the "moral rights" that Continental approaches to copyright automatically preserve and the US approach excludes: the right of retraction. As McCorkle's comments suggest, then, the DALN's informed consent interface exemplifies the layering of IP sponsors and their different values. These comments also reinforce that human sponsors are sometimes called upon to interpret or override the decisions of technological sponsors.

At the same time that the DALN and its curators pursue their purpose, in Ulman's words, to "create an invaluable historical record of a period of rapid change," the traces of that rapid change can be found in the interface's layered approaches to IP. Integrated within the consent interface are an older and a newer option that reflect different tactics for securing IP permissions from donors: the deed of gift and the CC license. Both IP tactics may be overridden by a participant's takedown request, because the consent interface is not just a means to secure IP permissions but also a human subjects form, and, as interpreted by the DALN directors, the rights guaranteed by an IRB forbid researchers from collecting materials from unwilling or unaware participants (as historically has been done, for example, with materials from indigenous cultures).

Selfe expanded further on this point. When asked what resources should be developed by the NCTE or CCCC for teachers and researchers in regard to IP, she commented that she desires both certainty and experimentation:

> I tell you what I would like, personally, as a teacher, I'd like somebody to call up, like my friend who's an intellectual property attorney, just to reassure me that I'm on the right track. [. . .] So I think that in particular would help me, having somebody to confer with about these issues that might help straighten [things] out, if I get on the wrong track or identify a different approach. And I guess that's another thing; there're a lot of creative approaches now out there—that arrangement with Utah State University, for instance, and Computers and Composition Digital Press—so that authors always have access to and can use their own materials [. . .] or the Digital Archive

> of Literacy Narratives where participants can attach a Creative Commons license or a deed of gift to their narrative.

Selfe's comments name an array of possible IP sponsors. Her first request is for NCTE or CCCC as an institution to provide a direct human IP sponsor "like my friend who's an intellectual property attorney" to advise teachers and researchers on potential IP issues. Even more, she wants that sponsor to be able "to identify a different approach" to IP. She then notes the different IP approaches that she, as a founder of the CCDP and the DALN, has implemented. Selfe went on to further detail her point: "[I]f teachers and scholars know the different kinds of arrangements that can be made, then they have more choices when they're doing a project and they feel a little bit more comfortable." She explained her philosophy as an IP sponsor herself who created such choices:

> So I almost think that we have to get a little bit more adventurous in trying new things and pushing the boundaries a little bit so that we're not disciplining ourselves into compliance with an imagined set of restrictions. I would like to—I'm just a bit of a rebel on that [. . .] I'd like to push a little bit and see if we can discover new ways that would allow us to use intellectual property and not abuse the rights of original authors and creators.

As we will detail in the next chapter, Selfe's concern that writing studies scholars should "push[] the boundaries a little bit so that we're not disciplining ourselves into compliance with an imagined set of restrictions" is substantiated by our survey data (where respondents reported doing this disciplining of themselves). In being "a little bit more adventurous in trying new things," the DALN offers one such alternative to approaching IP.

In analyzing these accounts of curating and using archives, we are reminded that archives (whether analog or digital) are components of the IP triangle of creators, distributors, and audience members that we discuss in Chapter 2. IP legislation has come about in different cultures to formalize assumptions about ways in which the relative rights of these creators, distributors, and audience members should be defined. Archives enact specific institutional protocols to mediate among creators/participants and researchers, as they define and control access to the IP of an artifact. We are also reminded, though, that IP and its various protocols are moving targets, as our own participants' comments remind us through their reflections on (potentially) changing or competing attitudes towards IP. These reflections raise important questions:

- Who is allowed to hold IP rights? (e.g., women, indigenous people)
- How should those rights be perceived? (e.g., is property an appropriate metaphor?)

- Which rights should be asserted within which contexts, and which should have priority? (e.g., moral rights? human subjects? contracts?)
- What mechanisms ought to be used to articulate them? (e.g., permission from a governing board? a deed of gift? an online interface?)
- Who and what have responsibility for educating others about those rights? (e.g., a researcher? a form?)
- How might researchers set up archival projects to continue to address these questions for the long term?
- What solutions become automatic, operationalized, entrenched, enculturated?

An Extended Example: Sponsor Layering in Teaching Remix

In the previous section we examined a trend across interviews and focused on a site of analysis illustrative of this trend. We turn now to a more extended single example of a subtle, cumulative change in IP practices drawn from our interview with Cruz Medina. We focus on Medina's reflections on his teaching both because they are representative of other teaching stories we heard (e.g., Amidon, Blair) and because they make visible ways in which IP practices and teaching practices coevolve as different literacy sponsors come into play—and how attempts to resolve the tension between educational and entertainment interests get codified into practices that can obscure the shaping roles of IP sponsors.

In this series of excerpts from his interview, Medina first responds directly to a question about whether his students have ever received takedown or cease-and-desist notices for their online materials:

> I think it was probably in either the second go around of having done these [assignments] where I was having students upload their completed projects to YouTube just so they could then share that link with me and I didn't have to worry about receiving these large files sent to me online. As a part of that, though, too, we were watching videos in class so it would happen that I'd find the video of a student, hit play, and we'd be watching the images go by, but there would be no audio. That was where you know you sort of find out like "ok, I think your video's been flagged for copyright infringement." Although that's one of those funny situations, too, where there could be another video also using copyrighted material and it plays just fine. And so [. . .] I think it was part of that growing process [. . . ,] even the evolution of just how they [services like YouTube] detect things.

Medina's comments highlight the intricate relationships between on-campus pedagogy and the broader culture of (often commercial) digital products. In this example, YouTube acts as a convenient literacy sponsor because Medina's available means of communication cannot handle the large video files his students produce, and YouTube allows him to share students' work with the class in ways that individual submission to a teacher does not. However, YouTube functions as more than a convenient platform for sharing materials. Under pressure from the film, music, and television industries, YouTube has become an IP gatekeeper. At the time Medina is reflecting on, YouTube did not consistently alert uploaders to potential IP violations, in part because the platform's software could not reliably identify the appropriate metadata to flag. As a result, YouTube served as a "funny," to use Medina's term, adjudicator of IP violations for two reasons. First, the uploading student, the other class members, and the teacher needed to guess, for example, why the audio was removed. Medina needed to explain to his students, "I think your video's been flagged for copyright infringement." Second, YouTube was capricious. Medina explained, "there could be another video also using copyrighted material and it plays just fine." So YouTube's mechanism for and rationale behind flagging certain videos was unclear, which made it a frustrating sponsor. As a result of these awkward disruptions, the technology and its potentially incorrect adjudication of IP remained visible and open to question. In a chapter in *Cultures of Copyright*, McCorkle reinforces this point in his analysis of Kickstarter co-founder Andy Baio's discussion of "the utter confusion that YouTube users exhibit when it comes to copyright concerns." He explains, "According to Baio, this confusion is to be expected, especially since the new normal of digital production for so many younger users is at odds with current interpretations of copyright law." McCorkle concludes, "I'd wager the vast majority of people under 25 see nothing wrong with non-commercial sharing and remixing, or think it's legal already" (61). In this sense, prevailing practice is at odds with what YouTube allows as an IP sponsor.

Yet, as Medina pointed out, the cultural environment he and his students inhabit continues to evolve. He continued his commentary by reflecting on the coevolution of technology, teaching, and broader disciplinary practices in writing studies around IP:

> I think that was probably I would say five years ago, and that was even in the field of rhetoric and composition. At CCCC[13] I think we had that conference theme of "The Remix." It was this very seductive idea of "yeah, we're remixing constantly," you know, "Writing is remixing." And that's where, I think, once again [. . .] we unaccounted for the fact that YouTube wasn't always going to be that sort of [wild] west, the third space where we could put all of these user-generated remix videos—some other things. It was going to be eventually corporatized, monetized, and part of that process meant that publishing there was going to be like publishing in a lot of situations. So I think it tends

> to be one of those more reactive things where students learn about it from having [the question], "Why is my video not working?" Then [they] have to work backwards from, "Ok, what did it have?"

An IP sponsor himself to his students, Medina articulates how he is negotiating between opposing, large-scale IP sponsors that are attempting to frame the (then) new technological innovation of YouTube. On one hand, he identifies a collective, abstract sponsor of the field of writing studies, with its disciplinary concepts of authorship and ownership reflected in a more concrete, more proximate instantiation of an IP sponsor, the specific Conference on College Composition and Communication devoted to the theme of "The Remix." He wryly comments on how people who accept the values of "Writing is remixing" and creating a "third space" might lose track of how a range of sponsors can frame a new technology: "[W]e unaccounted for the fact that YouTube wasn't always going to be that sort of [wild] west." Again, the impact of the technology is visible here because it shifts from being unregulated to regulated. The YouTube platform, according to Medina's interpretation, "was going to be eventually corporatized, monetized," and, as a result, instead of being an IP agent that sponsored OA, Fair Use, and the public domain, YouTube was "going to be like publishing in a lot of situations."

In Medina's example, a significant impact of YouTube's evolution as an IP sponsor is that students learn to be reactive instead of proactive. They adopt a mindset of asking forgiveness for using materials instead of asking permission to use them. When confronted by YouTube removing their materials ("Why is my video not working?"), students "then have to work backwards" to determine what metadata triggered the automatic takedown because the platform makes hidden decisions about what will be removed and what will stand. In this way, students offload the decision-making about IP to this (then new) technology. That said, since YouTube comes across as capricious and oppositional to these users' values of remix, third spaces, and authorship, they resist this IP gatekeeper by not seeking out IP issues until forced to do so. That is, they only consider whether their use of copyrighted sources is appropriate (e.g., constitutes Fair Use) when confronted with a takedown or removal. Doing so positions them on the defensive.

Medina continued his reflection by thinking about how his own responses to IP sponsors as a teacher have continued to evolve. The change is remarkable with regard to who and what have agency in making IP decisions:

> [T]hat was more like 2010 and then more of the projects I'm working on now [in 2015] [. . .] are viewing any kind of project [. . . as] multimodal composition where they're going to be composing [. . . with] video or using images and sound. I'm starting off at the very

> beginning talking about [. . .] at the very least attribution, finding those open access sources, images on Google or going to websites like freemusicarchive.org, where you can [find] music that has all levels of attribution, which, usually, if you're using it for educational, not commercial, [purposes] they're usually fine with you using it. So I definitely push students in that direction from the get go.

Here Medina indicates changes in abstract writing studies concepts (e.g., multimodality, OA, attribution) that serve as potential frames for the technologies he references, like freemusicarchive.org, which includes content with CC licenses, and thus serve as IP sponsors. Instead of focusing on the freedom of remix and associated challenges to the ideas of authorship and ownership, he focuses on questions of attribution, CC licensing, and OA. In reflecting on his changed approach in 2015, he sets up slightly different disciplinary ideals that act as IP sponsors: no longer the wild, wild west, but a more codified approach towards maintaining the availability of materials to reuse. Such codified approaches, for example, rely on online clearinghouses of images and music with CC licenses, offer "safe" versions of Fair Use—or, at least, not as labor-intensive versions of Fair Use as users need not search the Web for materials that they have permission to reuse. These materials have already been compiled for them. The CC licenses that distinguish among different types of use (e.g., granting permission for educational but not for commercial use) explicitly highlight the education versus commerce divide about which so many of our participants expressed concern. As we address in Chapter 3, different participants applied different ethical lenses when making IP decisions, including IP as part of economic systems and IP as fundamental to democracy. As Medina puts it, "if you're using it for educational, not commercial [purposes], they're usually fine with you using it."

This example of how Medina shifted his teaching practices in concert with student experiences with YouTube highlights the need to pay attention to ways in which technology platforms have stepped in as IP gatekeepers. He advocates a proactive instead of reactive approach to IP decisions: "I'm starting off at the very beginning talking to them about [. . .] at the very least attribution." He also shifts the main IP decision to where students can go for materials that are sanctioned for reuse: He indicates he directs students to specific "open access sources," such as Google images, and certain music-distribution sites, such as freemusicarchive.org. For both students and teachers, these sources offer a workaround for the clash between educational and entertainment IP systems: They provide already approved materials for students (and teachers) to use in compositions. Including materials from such sources lessens the risk of texts published online being flagged or removed.

However, this workaround and associated ease of use have several potential consequences (as Medina and some other professionals we interviewed and surveyed are themselves aware). One implication is that the question of determining IP status and Fair Use is offloaded to technological platforms, and this offloading becomes part of a routine, normalized pedagogical practice. Medina was not the only study participant who mentioned routinely sending students to OA, CC resources as a solution to finding usable materials (e.g., Berry, Selfe, and Silver did, too). A second implication is a narrowed conceptualization of Fair Use. In other words, in automatically using such resource clearinghouses as a solution to thorny IP decisions, it can be easy for teachers, students, and the public to equate Fair Use with the resources located on such sites. In fact, however, Fair Use means more than finding images and audio that have CC licenses. The public domain comprises more than the materials available through these websites.

A third, and related, implication is that, by using materials from these resources as a shortcut, busy teachers, students, and other creators become enculturated into specific composing practices but not necessarily a full view of IP. For instance, as we note previously, CC licenses are not homogeneous as they do not all permit reuse in the same way (e.g., some allow for remix while others do not). To encourage creators to visit websites with clearinghouses of CC materials as a quick solution to IP dilemmas potentially minimizes these differences because composers do not need to reflect on their choices. Indeed, with this approach the role of IP in composing decisions can become backgrounded to more immediate needs, such as a desire for multimodal creativity in a course on multimodal composing or a need to finish a project by a deadline. Certainly, these Web clearinghouses can be helpful resources. We are not arguing against using them. However, we are arguing that, as writing studies specialists, we need to be especially conscious of and cautious about this unreflective backgrounding of IP in composing decisions.

For us, this extended example supports that writing studies practitioners also need to be aware of—and participate in rather than shy away from—the negotiation of multiple sponsors' perspectives that making informed IP decisions entails. After talking about the normalized practice of directing students to Web resources with clearinghouses of CC-licensed images, Medina talked through shifts in approaching still-in-doubt IP practices. He explained that for a course he teaches in digital publication he starts off talking about how composers write for the Internet and the expectations of online environments, including reminding students to make sure that the images they use are not copyrighted. But he recognizes this advice is not entirely straightforward or without exception, particularly regarding memes. To illustrate his negotiation of and reflection on multiple sponsors, we again quote him at length:

> But that becomes this weird thing with the area of Fair Use and online memes, right? Because memes kind of continue to be that sort of genre or that form of communication that [. . .] lives in the

> public sphere. It's one of those things that's out there, so you don't want to tell students, "never—I don't ever want you to have a meme in your blog . . ." because oftentimes there's some kind [of] echo to some argument. And you might even make the case that memes [are] fine if they have the work for mimesis.

Medina went on to explain that memes

> tend to have this sort of enthymeme in them where there's this assumption that's embedded, so it's not even a complete syllogism, right? [. . .] We try to unpack it a little bit, so it's not just, "That was a good use of the meme . . ." Once again it becomes sort of this weird thing of like "Ok, that isn't probably Fair Use because everybody's using it."

Here, Medina talks through different ways of conceptualizing—and teaching students to conceptualize—meme use. Rather than simply classify meme use as Fair Use or not Fair Use, he models thinking through the IP elements of this composing situation. He reflects on how meme use could be considered Fair Use if memes are used for educational purposes, for instance, an "echo to some argument" or do the "work for mimesis" on a student's blog. Yet he also considers that meme use likely is not fair just because it is widespread—that is, when a meme appears everywhere (which, of course, is the definition of a meme). Thus, with memes there is a tension inherent in the genre itself: For a text to be a meme, it must circulate in ways that would necessarily seem to preclude Fair Use. Medina is acutely aware that memes thereby pose an IP conundrum.

Medina then went on to share how this IP conundrum connects to economic interests:

> That's the nature of memes; they're easily replicable or they're familiar to everybody. So then why would I maybe say not to use something that has a Getty images logo on it, right? Because then Getty images has their own sort of site where you can buy access to Getty images and that when you're teaching in the context of class, you don't want to necessarily say, "Well, it's a part of your lab fees; you pay for Getty images." I guess you could do that [. . .] if you were going to talk to your students, maybe like in education [or] in an entrepreneurial class where you're going to know that at the end you want to monetize your blog or have some sort of money-generating thing and you want to be sort of covered by having images that you have access to. But that could be a little bit more once again that weird grey area where you can say, "Ok, this is for the most part [an] educational blog."

In outlining ways in which the educational clashes with the "entrepreneurial," Medina illustrates the negotiation of different frameworks for considering IP. Medina notes that, from an economic perspective, encouraging (or permitting) students to use the Getty images they find online without permission can represent a financial loss to Getty: "Getty images has their own sort of site where you can buy access to Getty images."[14] And this financial "loss" might be recuperated (or explained) by justifying such use by taking recourse to the fees students pay, for instance, their "lab fees." By reflecting on the nature of memes, Medina realizes that this solution is not adequate. In part, the problem is that traditional IP and copyright have no way of enforcing either attribution or payment for a meme that goes viral quickly. Even though the original image might have been "stolen," it is not likely the original can or will be tracked down.

From a rhetorical standpoint, for Medina, it is crucial that students be allowed to incorporate memes into their websites and blogs because memes represent a new, digital form of argument whose conventions are evolving. They may provide an "echo to some argument," serve as mimesis, or have an "enthymeme in them where there's this assumption that's embedded so it's not even a complete syllogism." Thus, for him, memes can serve rhetorical functions as part of argumentation, and it is therefore important for students to be able to interpret and produce them, even if doing so is not (yet) technically Fair Use.

Ultimately, then, Medina privileges composing possibilities with memes over the entrepreneurial possibilities of monetizing them. In this example, Medina privileges the writing studies disciplinary interests in audience, context, and the metacognitive work needed to recognize the conventions required by the particular communities of practice. He repeats that he directs the students in this second course to the OA resources (as he discussed doing in the previous example). However, here Medina indicates that he is aware that this is not an easy answer because of the genre conventions of memes: "But that becomes this weird thing with the area of Fair Use and online memes, right? Because memes kind of continue to be that sort of genre or that form of communication that [. . .] lives in the public sphere." For memes, the IP conventions regarding ownership are trumped because the genre exists, in its best sense, as viral replication—with or without the sanction of materials belonging to the public domain. Part of its defining quality is its free circulation. As Medina says, "it becomes sort of this weird thing of like "Ok that isn't probably Fair Use [simply] because everybody's using it. That's the nature of memes; they're easily replicable or they're familiar to everybody." In terms of IP, memes are as yet unregulatable.

By the end of his interview, Medina collapsed the distinction he made earlier in the interview between the educational and the entrepreneurial. He returned to where he began in discussing these new textual forms as unregulatable: The use of meme images, as was previously the case with the use of video and music, is flying under the radar until and unless someone comes along to call it out.

Medina concluded this reflection by considering the role of audience in making such an IP decision. He reflected,

> You're talking about something more or less related to writing studies, so not a lot of people are going to find it, not unless they're usually in the field and then if you're using some image that might be copyrighted, chances are I don't know if someone or the person who owns it is going to click on it or come to your website and be like, "Oh, you're making millions of dollars from this; give me money."

In other words, he frames the texts he, his students, and seemingly other scholars and students create as unlikely to generate large enough of an audience to be profitable.

In these excerpts from Medina's interview, we see an evolution of what remix could have been, the ideal that it was, and the practical problems that following the ideal caused because students were not taught to be proactive about IP decisions and instead were reactive to external IP interventions (e.g., YouTube ordering a video to be taken down). In essence, students were remixing until they were forced to stop. Medina (and others we interviewed) noted there are safe harbors on the Internet, such as CC archives for images and music, and these safe harbors embrace the disciplinary ideal in writing studies that composers should value attribution in place of ownership in order to better circulate multimodal texts. But even this solution can cause problems. Instead of deciding for themselves what counts as Fair Use, users are now going to an already determined set of resources (e.g., CC clearinghouses) that have been set aside as usable. In other words, the IP decision process has been offloaded to these technologies.

This offloading of decision-making responsibility is not limited to repositories of CC licenses images or music. Multiple interviewees talked through such shifts regarding other practices. What this example from Medina highlights, however, is the larger theme we saw at work when reviewing the interviews as a whole: Technological sponsors are being afforded increasing agency in making IP decisions.

Conclusion

Our interviews and survey reveal that human, institutional, and technological sponsors mediate the IP decisions of writing studies practitioners. The sheer range of sponsors is impressive and includes agents that members of the discipline (and academics more broadly) may not consider. We hazard that many of our readers will be as surprised by this gamut as we were. Many forces played into writing studies practitioners' choices regarding IP, and individual decisions were affected by multiple IP sponsors. For example, a colleague, a librarian, university policies, content management software, and Fair Use guidelines may all play a role in sponsoring a decision not to teach (or to agree to teach) online courses. This layering of sponsors can make the influence of particular sponsors less visible (or invisible), which we argue can have negative effects, such as a reactive rather than a proactive stance toward IP decisions or a lack of awareness of where particular positions or possibilities (can) come from.

Moreover, many of the sponsors participants identified extended beyond the law. Indeed, while copyright law and Fair Use guidelines were sponsors participants mentioned, other sponsors were mentioned more frequently. The three most referenced sponsors in the survey, for instance, were people. We argue, then, that discussions of forces shaping IP decisions need to account for the law but also extend beyond it. Such discussions also need to look beyond people to account for the power of nonhuman sponsors—for instance, technologies like YouTube and CMSs—and the role of non-academic institutions—for instance, CC licenses and publishers—in shaping IP decisions. Preparing writing studies practitioners to reflect on and trace out the multiple IP sponsors shaping their teaching, research, and editorial decisions is a crucial step in preparing them to intervene in policy conversations at their educational institutions and in discussions of IP legislation more broadly.

Our study also reveals that participants often gave sponsors the agency to make their IP decisions for them. For example, they relied on online repositories of images with CC licenses as necessarily safe for reuse (for themselves and/or their students). Sometimes they did so consciously; other times they seemed unaware of the power they afforded these sponsors. This off-loading of decisions can serve practical purposes. It takes time to sort out all of the sponsors that (can) guide IP decisions, and it is sometimes simply more efficient to take these sponsors at their word and accept their advice. Yet our study reinforces that sponsors can facilitate or gate-keep (and sometimes the same sponsor can facilitate in one context and gate-keep in another). While trusting sponsors might enable the work of writing studies professionals, it might also thwart it. Just as writing studies teachers (should) counsel their students to avail themselves of library databases and Google Scholar to find scholarly sources for academic research-based writing tasks but not to trust their results blindly, we likewise argue that the guidance of IP sponsors, while sometimes helpful, should not be trusted blindly. A first step in moving beyond that unquestioning trust is to recognize what human, institutional, and technological agents can serve as sponsors and consider the interests and values that might motivate their advice.

Just as writing studies practitioners (and the audiences of their work) sometimes do not recognize the full range of IP sponsors shaping their decisions, sometimes they do not recognize the multiple ways and moments when IP decisions figure into their work. In the next chapter, we turn to the effects of IP decisions on work throughout the academic knowledge-making cycle. The next chapter illustrates that IP choices play a foundational role in processes as well as products and in inventional as well as delivery decisions.

Notes

1. Despite the 1982 case, which suggests CCC may be a for-profit company, in a 2005 article, Tracey Armstrong, the then-vice president of transactional services and now CEO and president (since 2007) of CCC, identifies CCC as a nonprofit.
2. We included all of these references (professor, teacher, instructor, etc.) in a single category because respondents referred to educators using all of these terms.
3. As we note in Chapter 1, we use *they* as an inclusive pronoun (rather than using *he, she, or ze*).
4. See Chapter 2 for where we identify the four factors stipulated in Section 107 of the Copyright Act of 1976 to be used in determining whether a use of copyrighted material constitutes Fair Use.
5. We removed specific cultural references in this response to protect the identity of this respondent.
6. Jamendo (www.jamendo.com/) is a website that provides free music streaming and downloads licensed for reuse.
7. See Chapter 1 for discussion of the DMCA, or Digital Millennium Copyright Act.
8. In *Authors Guild, Inc. v. Google* the Second Circuit court found that Google's digitization of entire books, garnered from libraries without permission or payment, for the Google Books project was transformative and thereby constitutes Fair Use.
9. See Appendix B for the interview questions and transcription conventions; see Appendix C for the position titles and affiliations of interview participants from at the time of their interviews.
10. Other writing studies scholars offer similar recommendations for (re)use of IP, especially the IP of indigenous populations: Jennifer Sano-Franchini, Robyn Tasaka, and Lehua Ledbetter call for a "reflexive approach to remix" (238–42), and Kristin L. Arola and Adam Arola call for an "ethics of assemblage" (204ff.). For an anthropological perspective on ways in which the concerns of indigenous populations complicate, oppose, and are unaccounted for in Western notions of IP, see also Haidy Geismar's *Treasured Possessions.*
11. In this way, Kennedy's reflection provides an interesting counterpoint to John Willinsky's admonition in *The Access Principle* that scholars publish OA because they gain, and are subsequently rewarded with tenure and promotion for, scholarly "research reputation" (6).
12. At the time of these interviews, an edited book about the DALN was in press with the Computers and Composition Digital Press (CCDP), founded by Cynthia L. Selfe and Gail E. Hawisher. CCDP provides a publishing platform

for longform, multimedia scholarly texts. As they mentioned in their interviews, both Hugh Burns (an advisory board member) and Patrick W. Berry (an editor) were aware of the DALN in part because of their associations with CCDP.

13. CCCC is the abbreviation for the Conference on College Composition and Communication, the major annual conference for writing studies professionals.
14. While Getty images are "royalty free," users must pay to download and use them ("Plans and Pricing"). Westbrook and Ryan contend that Getty Images follows the now "widespread" practice among art museums and organizations of incorrectly claiming to own copyright over reproductions of public domain images (99).

5 Effects of Intellectual Property on the Academic Knowledge-Making Cycle

> *IP issues are often a deterrent to using anything where the IP status is unclear. Removing the images from my dissertation certainly made the text less usable and intelligible; the IP work I would have to do to get that dissertation portion to become an article is a deterrent to publishing the work.*
>
> —(*Question 20, Response 101*)

Introduction

In the previous chapter, we discuss the sponsors that mediate writing studies practitioners' application of ethical lenses in making IP decisions. In particular, we call out gatekeepers, those sponsors that thwart rather than enable professionals' ability to achieve desired teaching, research, or editing goals (because most study participants framed their references to sponsors in this way). Through analysis of survey data, we argue that sponsors can take human, institutional, and technological forms and exist both inside and outside academia. We then turn to analysis of a trend across interviews—the changing material conditions of archives/repositories and resultant changes in IP sponsors that mediate interaction with those archives/repositories—and a more extended single example of a subtle, cumulative change in IP practices in response to the mediating roles of IP sponsors as reported by one interviewee, Cruz Medina. The chapter contends that writing studies professionals often offload their IP decisions to sponsors and that an awareness of the range of sponsors highlights the key role of relationships (with other people, institutions, and technologies) in navigating IP dilemmas. In this chapter, we turn to the moments at which writing studies practitioners make IP decisions in their professional activities—that is, the times when they reported encountering sponsors while applying ethical lenses to make IP decisions. Our study reveals that these moments occur throughout aspects of what we call the *knowledge-making cycle* and that IP's influence is systemic, pervasive, and even sometimes insidious.

After reviewing our data, we determined that the best way to represent the knowledge-making activities that study participants referenced was to turn to a description of recursive processes identified in inquiry-based learning called the "inquiry cycle": asking questions, investigating, creating, discussing, and reflecting (Bruce et al.). The inquiry cycle is itself based on John Dewey's ideas regarding effective learning, particularly the idea that disciplinary knowledge is continually in a process of creation rather than a static thing that is discovered. We modified this inquiry cycle schema according to the recursive stages that participants in our study associated explicitly with IP practices. These spanned from invention to delivery, for both teaching and research. Based on our coding of survey and interview responses, the five parts of the academic knowledge-making cycle we identified include:

1. Choosing topics and texts to study and teach
   e.g., Should I write about cartoons produced by the Disney Company? Should I teach this entire book or only selected chapters?
2. Collecting data and materials
   e.g., Will this archive charge too much for permissions? Can I access the research databases that I need?
3. Negotiating procedures and products for publication
   e.g., Can I argue that it is Fair Use to publish this image? Who will pay the fee to secure permissions for this material?
4. Disseminating and storing texts
   e.g., Will this journal allow me to publish an open access (OA) copy of my article in my institutional repository? Is it okay for students to share their remix videos on YouTube?
5. Employing materials and technologies in face-to-face and digital classes
   e.g., May I legally post a PDF copy of that article into my course management system? Do I want to post my assignments online for other instructors to use?

There are many ways to represent the cycle of knowledge production. We are not arguing that this is the only way to represent this process, but it is a way that captures the themes that emerged from our analysis and represents the moments highlighted by our study participants.

From this knowledge-making cycle perspective, we argue that our study reveals that writing studies professionals' authority; access to information; and understanding of what it means to write, teach writing, and produce knowledge are all influenced by IP. IP, in other words, is not only a concern for published end products but a fundamental concern infused throughout academic work. From our survey, for instance, we learned that scholars often make decisions about what to research and teach based on the perceived ease and cost of securing permissions to access or replicate research or teaching materials. They report that they know about, as well as teach their students about, IP, including Fair Use and Creative Commons (CC) licenses; nonetheless, they do not frequently take recourse to these themselves in their own scholarship. In sum, IP concerns play a foundational role in determining scholars' teaching and research agendas.

For this chapter, we open our discussion by drawing heavily on survey data to provide quantitative evidence to support our claim about IP's far-reaching influence throughout knowledge-making work in writing studies. In particular, responses to the survey's final open-ended question, completed by 201 respondents, frequently in a paragraph or more, reveal the significant and wide-ranging influence of IP on writing studies professionals. Most notably, nearly all respondents acknowledged explicitly that IP issues shape their academic work. Ninety-two percent of Question 20 respondents (183 of 199[1]) indicated that IP concerns have influenced them. Of the 10 percent of respondents (19 of 199) who said it did not, three (16 percent) then went on to explain the ways in which IP issues in fact affected them and one (5 percent) indicated learning more about IP and related issues. Thus, this percentage might be calculated to be even higher than 92 percent.

In addition to these quantitative results, though, we include extended quotations from free response answers in the survey, as well as from the interviews. Part of our purpose with this book is to document the IP experiences of writing studies scholars, and including the words of our study participants is crucial for achieving that end. Moreover, for most of the survey questions, the qualitative responses crucially inform the interpretation of the quantitative results. The numbers do not tell the whole story. We provide in this chapter examples of the IP decisions, events, and concerns that study participants encountered during each aspect of the knowledge-making cycle. We conclude the chapter with in-depth analyses of interview transcriptions from two study participants, Damián Baca and Cheryl E. Ball,[2] as these serve as cases of individual practitioners being influenced by and making decisions regarding IP at all of these stages of academic knowledge-making.

Choosing Topics and Texts to Study and Teach

Survey and interview responses illustrate that IP concerns influenced participants' selection of topics and texts to research and teach. For instance, one survey respondent noted, "I'm sure that early in my decision making process, as I plan the beginning steps of my research and teaching, IP issues probably influence my strategies because I'm already thinking about ways to accomplish my goals without running into IP problems" (Question 20, Response 82). The overt mentions of "early in my decision making process" and "I'm already thinking" illustrate that IP exerts influence in the invention stage for writing studies practitioners, even before they embark on research or teaching endeavors.

More specifically, survey responses reveal that IP both thwarted and motivated study participants' choice of research topics. For example, one respondent noted, "Intellectual property concerns have prevented me from researching certain topics where I knew I would have to obtain certain permissions" (Question 20, Response 111). For this respondent, the prospect of obtaining permissions to use IP squelched particular research pursuits. Another respondent framed the influence of IP on a research agenda more positively: "[S]everal years ago, I refocused my research agenda so that I could better address IP concerns that I found affected me on a daily basis. Since then, I have edited a book collection on the subject, collaborated with peers on special issues of journals devoted to IP, and authored articles on the connections between censorship, IP, and students' writing" (Question 20, Response 125). For this respondent, IP encounters compelled a shift in research pursuits to study IP, which resulted in numerous publications.

Responses show this early influence extended to participants' choice of topics and texts to teach. Participants chose certain readings and not others precisely because of copyright issues—both an inability to secure permissions to reproduce texts and the desire to teach students about the role copyright plays in publication and delivery. For instance, one survey respondent shared, "I have had to change course reading lists due to copyright issues, because on several occasions the university bookstore, which prints course materials, could not secure rights to particular texts (poems, short stories, journal articles. . .) " (Question 20, Response 67). This respondent had to change the texts assigned to students because of the inability to secure IP permissions. Another respondent offered, "For courses on writing for digital media, where technological measures are often taken to prevent ANY use of copyrighted materials—even fair uses, copyright is a necessary topic to be addressed in class" (Question 20, Response 113). For this respondent, the course topic, writing for digital media, makes necessary choosing texts that address IP because of the roadblocks authors can face in digital writing.

Overall, survey respondents' answers show that IP motivates many writing studies professionals to make teaching and research decisions with caution. Sixty-four percent of respondents (128 of 199) indicated that IP concerns have caused them to think carefully about their choices (e.g., to avoid situations that could cause conflict, to use CC licenses). In characterizing their reaction to IP influences, respondents most commonly used the terms *care* or *careful* (17 times) and *caution* or *cautious* (14 times). This cautious approach is notable given that several respondents explicitly indicated that IP affected *all* of their academic work. One such response is as follows: "I see IP related issues as inherently fused into the core of our work—what is it to write, [. . .] the role of originality, authorship, etc. Although my experience with the legalistic side of IP is (thankfully) limited, I cannot overstate the importance of such issues" to writing studies (Question 20, Response 13). From this perspective, where "IP related issues" are "inherently fused into the core of our work," a cautious approach pervades the teaching, research, and professional activities of members of the writing studies community.

Such responses highlight IP as a particularly crucial concern for writing studies as a discipline. That is, as we note in Chapter 1, writing studies professionals are an especially important population to study not only because they encounter issues faced by academics writ large (e.g., what readings to select for a course, whether to teach online, to what journals to submit their work), but also because they study and teach the production of knowledge through writing. Part of what our study revealed is that IP issues are—and perhaps should consciously be more so—a fundamental component of this work. Academic knowledge-making cannot happen without IP decisions.

Some study participants framed the early and far-reaching influence of IP positively. For example, one survey participant responded, "As a teacher, scholar, and editor, I feel that IP concerns have been ever-present, but that's in a good way. The notion of IP seems central to understanding literacy—its genesis, its consequences, its activities—and thus central to all of my work" (Question 20, Response 159). This response highlights that some respondents saw attention to IP as a positive (even welcome) aspect of being a writing studies professional. Yet the cautiousness which study participants reported as characterizing their decisions regarding IP, together with this early and wide influence of IP, suggests writing studies practitioners may be (unduly) limiting their work.

This limitation is perhaps most visible in the survey data regarding cost. Participants reported paying less than we anticipated for permissions to use copyrighted materials; however, this finding seems to be largely because they chose to avoid asking for permissions altogether. Referring to publications other than textbooks, 88 of 390 participants (23 percent) indicated that they or affiliated funding sources (their universities, a granting agency, or a publisher) paid to secure permissions to include materials in a publication. Of these, 40 estimated that their out-of-pocket expenses for permissions (a career total) amounted to $1–$250. Referring to textbooks, 44 of 362 respondents (15 percent) indicated that they or affiliated funding sources paid for permissions. Most of these costs were covered by publishers and/or deducted from royalties, with responses ranging from $1–$35,000 (for career totals). At the high end of the range for textbooks, two respondents indicated that grants had covered career totals of over $50,000, and two more respondents indicated that the publisher and/or royalties had covered totals over $50,000. Perhaps unsurprisingly, the most common materials that required permission fees for both scholarship and textbooks were images, readings or reprints, and quotations, in that order. (For more details on the fees survey respondents reported paying, please see Appendix E: Reported Costs for Publication Fees and Appendix F: Reported Costs for Open-Access Fees.)

These reported career expenses for publication fees, especially for non-textbook publications, are unexpectedly low; however, the explanatory comments suggest important caveats. For the nine survey questions addressing costs, the quantitative results are tempered by voluntary qualitative comments participants provided in the "please explain" fields. Responding about non-textbook publications, three participants (of the seven who provided explanations) volunteered explicitly that their overall estimated costs were low because they had chosen to abandon desired materials rather than pay the permission fees. Of the nine respondents who offered explanatory comments regarding permissions for textbooks, three indicated that students were directly charged for the permission fees (through a rental service or for course packs), and six indicated that they were unsure of the amounts because some part of the process was invisible to them, stating, for example, "They've never shared that information with me" (Question 6, Response 5). Both of these themes—a decision not to use desired materials and a sense that publication processes involving IP are opaque—were borne out in later survey questions and interviews.

These themes, for instance, appeared in responses to three survey questions about OA fees. When asked whether they or an affiliated entity had paid OA fees for scholarship or textbooks, 346 participants responded as follows: Yes: 21 (6 percent); No: 263 (76 percent); I was offered the option, but declined: 37 (11 percent); and I am not certain: 25 (7 percent). In other words, the minority of participants (6 percent) who paid these fees were outnumbered both by those who explicitly declined (11 percent) and those who were not certain (7 percent). It is possible that participants were uncertain whether OA fees were included in subventions or permissions fees. This uncertainty, though, supports our claim that IP decisions are often invisible. Likewise, the explicit choice to decline payment for OA fees indicates that respondents are opting out, potentially shaping other researchers' choices about what texts to study based on IP concerns.

Collecting Data and Materials

Other responses highlight that IP influenced a second aspect of the knowledge-making cycle, participants' collection of data and evidence. In the survey, such responses include, "when using an archive, I begin with the permissions questions" (Question 20, Response 49) and "as an academic at a non-research university, we have much more limited access to academic journal databases. This inhibits my research and keeping current with recent scholarship. Given the overwhelming amount of scholarly monographs and edited collections that are not published OA, this similarly limits me and my colleagues in the field" (Question 20, Response 114). This latter response in particular highlights the differential support offered scholars at different types of institutions, supporting that those in vulnerable, non-tenure track, or non-research oriented positions may have the least IP support, be that in the form of legal representation or access to copyrighted materials.

Stories from the interviews similarly support IP's role in writing studies scholars' collection of data. Here we share two responses; we analyze other examples elsewhere in Chapter 4 in our discussion of IP sponsors and the Digital Archive of Literacy Narratives (DALN). Patrick W. Berry, for instance, shared a story of working with a graduate student who had a challenging time finding the copyright owner of "old Syracuse publications." He explained, "So I think that for graduate students sometimes working with archival material is also just trying to understand where things are available. Sometimes I think that understanding availability becomes so central before you even submit something for publication to understand you can't get the rights to use them." Here Berry emphasizes that part of the process of becoming a writing studies researcher is not only learning how to access desired research materials, but also figuring out how to determine what materials are permissible to use in the first place.

This concern for knowing what materials are ultimately permissible to be collected and used was echoed by Jeffrey R. Galin. He offered a series of examples to illustrate his point that "I think awareness of what intellectual property is, and Fair Use is, is extremely important in our research so that we're not prevented from publishing works of critical analysis that [. . .] clearly fit within Fair Use for critical analysis for higher education." Echoing Joonna Smitherman Trapp's account of being prevented from using Flannery O'Connor's audiotapes, which we discuss in Chapter 4, he first pointed to other famous literary authors who have rigorously protected their IP, including J.D. Salinger and the estate of James Joyce. Galin then shared an account that he was then researching, an incident in which, he explained,

> A women's studies professor who spent 5 . . . 7 years giving lectures on what she called, "The pornography of everyday life," which is the use of women's bodies in advertisements, in particular, but in magazines, and how they're cropped, and how they're forced into submission and positions of submission, etc. She started giving lectures, and someone approached her to do a documentary on her work. She started doing the documentary and got it completed only to have the publisher tell her, "Oh, I can't publish this. You don't have permission for these things, for these excerpts."

In his opinion, Galin commented, many of these materials ought to have been allowed under Fair Use exclusions, but the result was that "she didn't publish for years because she was completely shut down by intellectual property policy, intellectual property claims by the publisher." After seeking permissions, ultimately, "she ended up excluding a range of things [. . .] from her documentary that she wanted to include because she didn't have the expertise she needed to be able to fight . . . to argue for her inclusions. But even if she had, [. . .] she wasn't in a position to take on a lawsuit." In other words, regardless of what might be allowed by copyright law, the mere threat of a lawsuit was sufficient to stymie the project.

In fact, Galin continued, "The only person who's been really successfully able to [proceed with a Fair Use lawsuit] is Sut Jhally, who was basically told to shut down his documentary work on *MTV*, and he set up a whole corporation as a communications professor—I don't remember what university—but he set up this whole corporation to fight this claim and he won in court." Galin expressed his concern that academics need to know more about "ways to push back" against such overreaching IP claims, and that they need to have informed campus lawyers inclined to protect Fair Use rights rather than to be "conservative" over copyright challenges. He concluded, "[I]f we're making decisions about our research that limit our ability to do the research the way we want to, because of misuse of Fair Use, that's when [. . .] we're really facing serious problems." As Galin's examples illustrate, the legalities of Fair Use and copyright are complex, and they require time and resources to resolve; however, the price of inaction is an academic culture of self-censorship. We contend such concerns are often invisible in the training of novice members of the discipline, and writing studies professionals (and academics more broadly) would do well to be aware of and to consider explicitly such issues when they collect data and materials for scholarly pursuits.

Negotiating Procedures and Products for Publication

Responses to Question 20 of the survey (the open-ended question asking participants to reflect overall on their IP experiences) further reveal that not only are the topics and evidence of writing studies' scholars work influenced by IP, but the venues and frequency of publication, and what those publications include, are as well. Participants shared that they decided where and how often to publish based on their views of copyright. For example, one survey participant expressed a clear desire "to maintain copyright on my publications whenever possible" and elaborated "[I] have decided not to contribute to projects because of the copyright provisions in the contract" (Response 5). On the other hand, another respondent shared conceding copyright in order to meet publication expectations: "I need to publish, so I often sign away the copyright" (Response 92). Another shared that the process and cost of securing copyright permissions resulted in a less robust research profile:

> I've published much less than I should have because of inability to either obtain or AFFORD permissions to reuse existing images. Often, I know the illustrators, but they signed off on permissions in order to get paid by a publisher; then the publisher won't allow reuse, or they want too much money, or they won't reply to requests for info. It's a really problematic system and one that is keeping people in our fields from advancing and making names for ourselves because we can't publish our work.
>
> (Response 90)

Taken together, such responses evidence the significant influence IP, particularly copyright, exerts on publication decisions and ways it can directly affect scholars' research productivity.

Survey respondents' answers show copyright permissions play a role in determining publication decisions for not only authors but also editors. For instance, one respondent offered,

> I was on a journal review board and once found a submission that was rehashed from a previous journal she had published in, almost verbatim. I told the managing editor and they turned down the submission and pointed out that the author had plagiarized herself (saying it in a very nice/professional way). That was an eye-opener for me, and if I hadn't caught that, our journal would have published it and it would have reflected poorly on us at the very least.
>
> (Response 109)

For this editor, the reputation of the journal was intimately tied to its handling of IP issues, particularly not getting caught republishing material that had already been published elsewhere. Another editor shared concern about having to track down the ownership of images, indicating a possible need to forego use of particular images and charts "just to save time and money" (Response 62). Such answers show that the discipline's editors are faced with potentially sensitive interpersonal and time-intensive work on account of IP issues.

A significant number of survey respondents indicated having changed their publications due to IP concerns. In responding about challenges to their use of IP, 44 percent of participants (131)—nearly half of the 298 respondents answering Question 10—shared that they chose not to include desired materials in a publication because of IP concerns. Seventeen percent (50) were denied publication until certain materials were removed. In his interview, Kyle D. Stedman noted, "It almost feels a part of life to not use the first thing that comes to mind, especially when I'm doing sound work," reinforcing that IP issues are felt acutely by scholars creating multimodal scholarship (in his case, with sound). Explanatory comments suggest some changes were anticipatory, as respondents themselves forestalled potential problems, and other changes were compelled, as respondents were required by others to make changes. This finding is further borne out by 286 respondents' answers to Question 18 regarding teaching: 34 percent (96) indicated that they have changed course materials because of concerns about IP issues. These results are worth restating: Nearly one-half of participants changed publications and over one-third of participants changed teaching materials because of fears about IP violations.

The survey also reveals reasons why study participants changed publications. In open-ended explanations to their Question 10 responses, the three most popular reasons respondents provided for not including desired materials in a publication were the cost of permissions and fees (27 responses), explicit denial of the request (from the university, a publisher, the copyright holder, and so forth) (17 responses), and the hassle of obtaining permissions (15 responses). Other reasons participants offered were time (e.g., to secure permissions, to meet deadlines) (5 responses) and the inability to find the copyright holder (i.e., the works were orphaned) (5 responses). A representative response illustrating anticipated concerns about cost and hassle is:

> I avoid using anything that might require fees [for] additional permissions. It's too much hassle—identifying who to approach, then writing to them etc. and that's before the cost comes into it. In the past I found publishers to be very unhelpful in this regard, expecting authors to do all the legwork despite not having knowledge or skills in the area. [. . .] I simply avoid [use] if there is any question.
>
> (Question 10, Response 15)

This avoidance of using desired materials because of cost and hassle is part of the reason why more respondents did not indicate paying to use desired materials: They simply removed them or did not include them in the first place.

Another response exemplifies not just anticipated concerns but the full hassle of negotiating IP issues with multiple (and sometimes unknown) stakeholders:

> For my monograph I wanted to include images from websites and one from the cover of TIME Magazine. The publisher (Routledge) would not pay any royalty fees for use of these images, and would not include the images unless I secured permissions. I chose to use some, which I paid for myself, and to not use others, because of the

> prohibitive cost. I tried to argue that my use was a fair use, to both the publisher of my book and the owners of the images I wanted to include, but made no progress with that.
>
> (Question 10, Response 51)

This response illustrates the bind faced by some writing studies scholars: To publish desired materials, they must have permissions, and to get permissions, they must pay. Occasionally, they must secure permissions themselves rather than rely on publishers to do the legwork. As responses to other questions reveal, whether publishers pay such fees (and/or take them out of royalties) is sometimes invisible; therefore, in some instances, it may be that authors are unaware that publishers are providing these monies. Or publishers may simply refuse to provide such assistance. The hassle rationale is further illustrated by the following response, in which the participant reflects on a history of (perceived) hassling from an IP owner:

> Early in my career, I decided not to publish an image in an academic journal article even though it was being used for illustrative and educational purposes. The company that owned derivative rights to the image had previously sent a cease and desist letter to my student (who wanted to use a variation of the image on her personal website) and threatened to sue me if I published the image in an academic journal. If I encountered a similar situation today—knowing what I now know about intellectual property—I probably would not capitulate to the content provider's demands.
>
> (Question 10, Response 56)

Noteworthy here is both that the respondent was deterred from preparing a publication as desired "[e]arly" in that respondent's career and that the respondent reported that more knowledge of IP would have changed their[3] behavior, and potentially the outcome. This response suggests that early career scholars may be particularly susceptible to changing course due to IP fears and would especially benefit from education in IP rights and responsibilities.

Other responses illustrate explicit denial as preventing respondents from including desired materials. To answer Question 10, two respondents noted, "I was not allowed to publish an image controlled by Disney in my dissertation" (Response 41) and "I elected to remove all of the screenshots from my dissertation section on digital games because the university wouldn't clear them (even if they were fair use) without direct written permission from the companies who owned the websites [. . .] [I]n order to get it submitted, it was easier to remove them than to make an argument for fair use or get the permissions" (Response 42). Especially notable from these examples, as is reinforced in other responses to Question 10 and elsewhere, is that graduate students had their dissertations shaped by IP concerns. These novice academics, an arguably vulnerable population in academia, reported having to change their research-writing early in their careers to become full members of the field.

In his interview, Carl Whithaus made explicit that one's status in the field can affect IP decisions. He shared,

> [I]f, for instance, I was an assistant professor, I would probably have made decisions about the speed that I need to get this article out with. That would have made me drop some of the images from the get go. Because I'm where I am in my career, I'm sort of able to say it'll take the time that it takes for this thing to get out, and I'm willing to wrestle around it. So, it's interesting. I mean just the sense of what intellectual property is, particularly around images and what I could or could not possibly use, does have some bearing on what I write about and how I'm able to pursue one line of inquiry or not. And certainly as a grad student or an assistant professor I would have because of timeliness just made a decision that would have excluded some of the material that I'm thinking about now, but that's going to be a little stickier I imagine around IP.

For Whithaus, one of the luxuries of tenure is the opportunity to handle IP issues differently: He can take whatever time is necessary to "wrestle" with the IP considerations to include desired images. But he acknowledges that "as an assistant professor," he would have decided to exclude some images from his article because of "the time it takes" to handle the requisite IP issues. Novice writing studies scholars are often counseled to defer wholly digital projects and pursue mostly (or exclusively) single-authored publications to secure tenure and promotion; however, our study's responses suggest they rarely are counseled regarding ways in which IP decisions can affect their ability to meet tenure and promotion requirements. We think they should be.

Survey respondents also shared strategies for avoiding changing their publications because of IP concerns. A notable number of respondents indicated having turned to Fair Use to avoid making unwanted changes to their publications. Over half of respondents (171 of 289) indicated that they know the four guiding factors to determine Fair Use. And nearly one-fourth of respondents, 23 percent (68 of 298), indicated that they invoked Fair Use in defending use of materials in a publication. Others indicated that they assigned CC licenses to their work: 36 percent (102 of 286) reported having used CC licenses—though more than double that, 79 percent (225 of 286), reported that they are familiar with CC licenses. That 59 percent (171 of 289) reported knowing the four factors of Fair Use and 79 percent (225 of 286) indicated familiarity with CC licenses is initially heartening in that many participants indicated awareness of options for using copyrighted work and making their copyrighted work accessible on their own terms. These high percentages may reflect the population of those who self-selected to take the survey.

Survey results suggest, though, that this knowledge may not translate to practice. Only 23 percent of respondents took recourse to Fair Use and only 36 percent (102 of 286) indicated using CC licensing for their own teaching materials. While over half of participants reported knowing about Fair Use, fewer than one-fourth invoked Fair Use. Similarly, while over three-fourths of participants reported knowing about CC licenses, only one-third used them. Of course, not all uses of copyrighted material are Fair Use and not all teaching materials are appropriately shared under CC licenses, but these differing percentages suggest a disjunction between knowledge and practice among our respondents. This disparity signals that perhaps an important area of intervention for writing studies professionals regarding IP is moving them from knowledge to implementation.

Disseminating and Storing Texts

Another aspect of the knowledge-making cycle identified by study participants involves decisions regarding how and whether to disseminate and store texts. Responses to the final open-ended question of the survey (Question 20) were again especially helpful in demonstrating IP's influence on this aspect of academic knowledge-making. Several participants, for example, noted their belief that academic work should be freely shared. For instance, one offered, "I am an IP libertarian. I believe our work gains value through circulation. I am thus happy to post PDF copies of my published writing to the [W]eb. I also feel that so long as writers quote the work of others ethically and transparently, they should not have to pay to do so" (Response 75). Another similarly shared, "I tend to use permissive CC licensing for my professional blogging on teaching issues because that reflects the informal sharing teaching culture in which remixing and riffing off others['] pedagogical materials is standard practice" (Response 121). These scholars' belief that IP should be disseminated widely shaped their decisions to make their research and teaching work visible by publishing online and by using CC licenses.

Others, however, noted IP concerns caused them to circulate their work less. For example, one explained,

> I have tried to be very open in sharing course materials to other faculty members, at my university as well as at others, and to students. My current university's proposed IPP [intellectual property policy], coupled with the increasing use of faculty teaching materials by for-profit online organizations and the abuse of such materials to

> further reduce the number of full-time faculty, especially tenure/tenure-track lines, has caused me to re-think my practice. I am looking to open source/CC opportunities to share materials rather than support abusive corporate practices by those both within and outside the university.
>
> (Response 72)

For this respondent, the open sharing of work potentially jeopardizes faculty jobs, a position that echoes Krista Kennedy's concern, which we discuss in Chapter 4. This hesitance to share on account of IP concerns was particularly visible when respondents considered online work, especially (perceived) changes in university policies regarding ownership of teaching materials. One survey respondent, for instance, explained,

> I house my teaching materials and my blog on server space that I pay for, and I never applied for any of the in-house money available for designing the first online version of a course. I had fears that taking the money would make my materials work-for-hire. What I suspected would happen does happen—those faculty who took the money had their materials distributed for common use, usually after retirement. I also do not use the university's Blackboard site. [B]esides not being all that great for teaching writing, I feel queasy about the combination of university access and the university's policy on IP and faculty work. I want no ambiguity about who owns my work.
>
> (Response 140)

For this respondent, accepting university monies and resources raises "ambiguity" over the ownership of IP produced (an idea reinforced by scholars we interviewed who applied the IP as part of business practice ethical lens, which we discuss in Chapter 3). Thus, wanting to avoid such ambiguity means using personally financed blog space and refusing university course development funds.

Together, these responses illustrate that respondents were hesitant to rely on university resources both because they did not want to support particular views of IP and because they did not want to lose their own IP. An implicit tension is evidenced here between notions of the university as knowledge protector and as knowledge sharer. This respondent presents the university as claiming copyright over IP which it should not—describing the university as overreaching in protecting IP, even though the university is circulating materials potentially beneficial to other teachers.

Despite participants' concerns about using copyrighted IP, reports of cease-and-desist letters or takedown notices from entities with a claim to IP included in a publication were relatively rare. Only 18 of 301 (6 percent) respondents to Question 12 reported receiving such a complaint.[4]

However, the range of responses included under this category points to a trend of respondents conflating legal issues, attribution issues, and other writing issues. For example, in the 21 explanatory comments to Question 12, respondents mentioned receiving notices or complaints about videos, a sound clip, images, short texts, and materials on course websites, but they also reported complaints about minor typos, links included on a website, and the lack of acknowledgement to a mentor. These latter three situations, of course, are not IP issues. Among those respondents who reported receiving takedown notices, half reported them to be spurious. On the other hand, four respondents indicated that the claimed materials were removed, and five indicated that the publication was retracted (these responses may overlap). In other words, among those survey respondents who were asked to remove or take down materials, half felt the claims were baseless and about half did as asked.

When we asked survey participants whether or not they had, as authors or editors, ever initiated a takedown notice or similar complaint against another entity over IP issues, we again received a relatively low number of affirmative responses but emphatic explanatory comments. Of the 292 respondents to Question 14, 19 said "yes" to initiating IP complaints themselves; however, we received 25 explanatory comments. The comments suggesting "yes" responses pointed to multiple issues, including lack of citation, failure to recognize the correct authorship, wholesale copying or uploading of a text, direct incorporation of a reviewer's feedback without acknowledgement, and the copying of a journal's title for a new journal. Taken together, these responses suggest that while relatively few writing studies faculty have either received or initiated cease-and-desist letters or takedown notices, those that have had memorable experiences. Moreover, as with responses to the survey questions regarding cost, these low numbers may again suggest that scholars are simply choosing to avoid situations where cease-and-desist letters and takedown notices would be relevant.

The low number of takedown notices together with unsolicited mention of plagiarism/citation issues indexes a privileging of attribution and circulation over legal issues in regard to IP that was borne out by responses to other survey (and interview) questions. Some survey respondents seemed to view teaching citation conventions and plagiarism avoidance as teaching about IP (see also Lunsford and Purdy). Responses to open-ended comments illustrate. Answers to Question 18 about influences of IP on teaching show that 73 percent of participants (206 of 286) indicated that they devote instructional time to IP issues. That nearly three-fourths of respondents reported offering such instruction was surprising (and, frankly, initially heartening). However, answers to the open-ended components of Questions 14, 17, and 20 suggest that many respondents associated such instruction with teaching students about citation practices and avoiding plagiarism as opposed to teaching about copyright, other legal issues, or other aspects of IP. For instance, one answer to Question 14 was "I have been plagiarised [*sic*]—big time" (Response 24), and one answer to Question 20 was "Intellectual property concerns mostly effects [*sic*] the work our Writing Center does with students because many students are immersed in a culture of fear relative to plagiarism, and tend [to] lose interest in good argumentation as a prime concern because they are most particularly interested in citation correctness" (Response 20). Such responses suggest a tendency for scholars to default to understanding IP as primarily about attribution or to conflating IP and citation issues. While one respondent to Question 18 explicitly revealed knowledge of (and clarified) the difference—"I cover copyright to help students understand that plagiarism is NOT dependent on copyright status—because something is ou[t] of copyright, that does NOT mean that copying it verbatim and/or using it without attribution is permissible" (Response 60)—overt recognition of this distinction was not the norm among survey respondents. Such responses addressing citation and plagiarism issues are notable because we deliberately never mentioned plagiarism in our recruitment materials or survey or interview questions. This focus, of course, makes some sense given writing studies' attention to writing practices as a discipline. The field has long been concerned with source (mis)use and integration. However, it evidences a larger tendency to subordinate other IP issues to appropriate source use or to misunderstand plagiarism as a violation of IP law.

This privileging of attribution and circulation is further shown in responses expressing explicit support for OA and/or the sharing of information. One survey response illustrates: "For Pete's Sake, I live in a world of not-for-profit academic scholarship. So long as someone is properly attributing sources and not plagiarizing, information should flow freely" (Question 14, Response 9). In other words, for this respondent as long as work is not being plagiarized, academic texts should circulate widely. Plagiarism, not IP violation, is seemingly the greater concern. While the choice in practice is usually not simply one or the other, the implicit hierarchy here is telling.

There were, however, also survey responses indicating a desire to protect IP. Four participants who marked "no" to initiating IP complaints or sending cease-and-desist letters indicated that they had desired to take action or had taken informal action. For example, one remarked, "But I have thought about it. I was on the editorial board for a hymnal, and the editor-in-chief had to contend with another hymnal which copied our scores" (Question 14, Response 7). One lengthy response describes a lawsuit over a playwright's adaptation of a respondent's short story into a play despite explicit denial of permission to do so. This response notes the lack of resources available to academics to provide legal protection for their work; the lawsuit was conducted pro bono. It also notes the multiple positions that academics take in regard to IP as producers, consumers, and teachers:

> Although as an academic I am well aware of the importan[ce] of fair use, I believe that we faculty are so concerned with the necessary right to use published material in our courses that we seem to have grown quite tone-deaf to the rights of individual authors. [. . .] My point is: When copyright issues are involved, do not throw out the baby (the rights of individual authors) with the bathwater (corporate abuse of copyright law).
>
> (Question 14, Response 1)

Here this respondent shares that while they recognize the value of Fair Use as "an academic" (i.e., a teacher), they wish to protect their rights as an author. Such a response suggests that writing studies practitioners must negotiate among multiple roles when disseminating and storing texts and might make different decisions depending on whether they are foregrounding their role as author, teacher, editor, or reader, a point we discuss more fully in Chapter 3.

The relatively low number of participants who reported actively protecting their IP may be more the result of their lack of awareness of how to do so than a lack of desire to do so. Despite 62 percent of respondents (178 of 289) indicating that they know how to secure their own copyright, most participants reported not knowing how to respond to or initiate a complaint: 25 percent (72 of 289) indicated that they know what to do about takedown notices, and 17 percent (50 of 288) responded that they know how to initiate an IP complaint. These relatively low percentages may explain why so few participants indicated that they initiated a copyright complaint; according to most respondents, they do not know how. Members of the field, then, may benefit from guidance and training in options and procedures for protecting their IP, including how to formally register their copyright with the US Copyright Office and how to assign CC licenses to their work. They likewise might benefit from mentoring in options and procedures for responding to accusations of IP violations, including how to make a Fair Use claim and how to select protected venues for publishing and storing work.

Employing Materials and Technologies in Face-to-Face and Digital Classes

Responses regarding using texts and technologies in face-to-face and online classes, the final aspect of the knowledge-making cycle identified by study participants, further suggest that writing studies scholars' decisions not to teach online are tightly bound to universities' IP policies.

For instance, one respondent declined to teach online courses because the university would award release time and stipends only to faculty who signed a contract "protecting the university against any potential claims regarding copyright infringement" (Response 50). Another participant likewise responded, "Most directly, intellectual property/copyright issues have resulted in my not teaching online courses. Although members of my department are getting pressure to teach online, I refuse to do so, for if I do, I have to share exclusive rights. No. I must have exclusive rights, or I won't teach online" (Response 168). Despite public proclamations of support for online teaching from writing studies scholars (e.g., Krause), these responses suggest that policies regarding online instruction may require clearer—or different—approaches to IP, if more writing studies scholars are to participate.

Other responses reveal that IP determines the materials teachers use and ask their students to use. One participant, for instance, indicated, "I urge students to use materials licensed with appropriate Creative Commons licenses, but this of course precludes many online sources that would be useful and appropriate for class projects. It's difficult to teach about the importance of fair use to students when we see so many instances where copyright owners and large technology companies are not respectful of the concept" (Response 113). Such responses illustrate that scholars who wish to respect copyright law, including Fair Use—and to teach their students to do the same—feel they cannot use certain texts for their classes. Perhaps ironically, seeking to abide by copyright law impacts their ability to employ what they see as the best materials to teach students about respecting copyright law.

Moreover, several respondents expressed confusion about what teaching uses are appropriate under IP regulations. That is, they reported they simply are not sure what to do to obey the law, even when they want to. One, for instance, asked whether "course exercises adapted from an original exercise over 5–6, or more, years" still need to credit the original (Response 144). Another similarly questioned, "if I create a handout for a class using examples borrowed from a student's class-submitted work in order to make it relevant to that class, I feel limited by that—can I use the same handout in the future without having to update/change the examples? What if I want to post it online for others to use?" (Response 157). For these respondents, such uncertainty led them to limit their use of particular teaching materials.

Systemic, Insidious, and Pervasive Influences

When we consider as a whole the reflective responses of 393 survey respondents and the retrospective comments of 28 interview participants, a fuller picture of IP's systemic, sometimes insidious, and pervasive influence on knowledge-making in writing studies emerges.

Perhaps most significant, our study reveals that the impact of IP is systemic; that is, it affects the entire system of knowledge production, not just the end product. Scholars recounted their experiences in terms of process, touching on all aspects of the knowledge-making cycle. Our survey participants noted that IP has compelled them to select or avoid particular topics and texts to study and teach; to collect or be unable to collect particular data and materials; to include or remove images, quotes, sound clips, or other materials in publications; to select or avoid certain venues for publication; to decide whether to circulate teaching or research materials online; and to choose whether to teach online courses. These responses, taken together, illustrate a wide range of knowledge-making activities that are affected by IP.

The conclusion that IP concerns systematically affect knowledge-making in writing studies may seem unsurprising; however, while writing studies practitioners may "know" this systemic influence to be true, our study shows that writing studies practitioners do not always act with this knowledge in mind. Furthermore, published research has focused primarily on end products, and the field's legislative interventions have been mainly reactive rather than proactive, responding to particular rulings rather than telling firsthand stories and making data-driven arguments to guide the creation of legislation. To argue dismissively that academics have long faced IP issues is to ignore the increased pressure that participants reported feeling in light of changing IP legislation and university policies.

Such naturalization of the impact of IP has often led the discipline to overlook the insidious effects of IP, including more (unnecessary) self-censorship than the field has documented. Our study supports that IP's effects are often invisible. Scholars are unaware of them, largely because (and when) IP effects happen early in teaching and research processes (e.g., when scholars make the initial decision of what course to teach or what research project to pursue). Such self-censorship is especially problematic for contingent faculty and graduate students who may not have full access to university and legal resources to protect their academic freedom against IP challenges, even if those challenges are spurious.

Our study further reveals that the influence of IP is pervasive, that is, affecting all aspects of our work as writing studies professionals: teaching, research, editing, and technical and creative writing. Three survey results stand out for us in supporting that the effects of IP are pervasive. First, nearly half of respondents to Question 10—131 scholars—did not include desired materials in publications because of IP concerns. Second, nearly two-thirds of respondents to Question 20—128 scholars—indicated that IP concerns caused them to be cautious in their research and/or teaching choices. Third, over 90 percent of respondents to Question 20—183 scholars—indicated that IP had influenced their work. These are not isolated incidents. That over half of the survey's respondents took the time to provide extended explanatory comments, not only for Question 20 but throughout the survey, suggests that the IP experiences of writing studies practitioners should be taken seriously by our discipline—not dismissed as isolated occurrences or simply the way things are, but treated as shaping forces that determine the work of not only individual practitioners but the discipline as a whole. That is, what writing studies is and can do as a field is intimately connected to the decisions scholars make, are forced to make, and think they can make about IP.

Our study reveals that one extreme reaction to this pervasive influence of IP is learned helplessness. When deciding what to do, for instance, participants often reported giving up, as illustrated by the epigraph for this chapter. Not knowing other options or not seeing viable alternatives in the other options they knew, respondents reported forgoing particular research topics, data sets, teaching materials, or image use. This learned helplessness was particularly visible in our findings about cost. Our attempt through our survey to determine a quantitative measure of the literal financial costs of IP failed because we found that scholars are opting out. In other words, participants in our survey did not report having incurred significant financial costs on account of IP because they are usually deciding not to include materials in publications or not to publish at all. This learned helplessness, then, has significant outcomes for practitioners' success as teachers and scholars.

The other extreme reaction respondents reported was fearlessly ignoring IP guidelines. Though a smaller number of participants than those who reported giving up, this group reported doing whatever they wanted regardless of concerns over IP. This reaction was often motivated by the belief that Fair Use governed practitioners' work so they should not or need not worry. Other scholars who reported boldly doing as they pleased shared that they believe academic work should by its very nature circulate and be accessible freely.

We found that the impact of IP is pervasive (and potentially insidious) in another way. In addition to self-censorship, learned helplessness, and intrepid fearlessness, participants reported external compulsion coming from multiple sponsors (e.g., publishers, editors, administrators), which we explain at greater length in Chapter 4. That is, adherence to IP regulations is sometimes (en)forced. Our study reveals that writing studies scholars at all levels have been required by others to change their practices and products for IP reasons, sometimes impinging on their academic freedom and sense of empowerment and authority, and sometimes helping them be compliant with existing laws and protect their own and others' IP.

Despite the negative outcomes this learned helplessness, fearless disregard, and compelled adherence might bring (and that study participants reported have brought them), there is also potential. With an awareness of these three trends, as well as the places in the knowledge-making cycle where writing studies scholars face IP decision points, there are opportunities for sponsors, including gatekeepers, to do better—that is, to move beyond advising writing studies practitioners in ways that lead them simply to give up, give in, or pay no attention. There are also opportunities for members of the field to educate themselves about the options and possibilities opened up by ethical lenses—to have more agency in their work when selecting topics and texts to teach, collecting data and materials, negotiating procedures and products for publication, disseminating and storing texts, and employing materials and technologies in face-to-face and online classes.

Uncertainty about IP was associated with negative feelings about IP. Twenty percent of Question 20 respondents (40 of 199) indicated that IP issues created negative emotions for them, particularly anxiety, fear, and anger. Representative responses in this area include "I worry more today about IP issues" (Response 54); "I fear that in about ten years' time, we'll be acknowledging ownership even less. As that happens, I won't write and publish as much. I'll be less likely to share online what I've created" (Response 62); and "I've become increasingly angry about predatory publishers, increasingly interested in various OA alternatives, and increasingly speculative about various info-freedom futures" (Response 158). Such responses make clear that the topic of IP elicits (sometimes strong) emotional responses, and respondents view negatively what they perceive as consequences of IP: more worry, less ownership attribution, decreased scholarly productivity, and less online sharing. (The pursuit of OA publication is a marked exception that respondents reported viewing more positively.)

More knowledge about IP led participants to have more positive feelings. Six percent of respondents (12 of 199) indicated that IP concerns created positive emotions for them, for instance, boldness, confidence, empowerment, and gratitude. Representative responses include "I'm not sure I would have been skittish or on the paranoid side about using copyrighted materials in my teaching, but I'm really not at all worried about it after studying copyright and fair use so much. I'm bold about sharing my publications online, and I'm better prepared to talk about all kinds of authorship issues with students: copyright, collaboration, collage, plagiarism, etc." (Response 88) and "I teach copyright and intellectual property concerns in my journalism and writing classes, so I'm confident in this area" (Response 15). For such scholars, teaching about and studying IP led them to feel more comfortable making decisions about their own and others' IP.

Extended Examples: IP Decisions throughout the Knowledge-Making Cycle

To illustrate ways in which these pervasive, systemic, and sometimes insidious influences of IP combine to mediate a scholar's academic knowledge-making processes—and, importantly, to model more protracted, possible responses to these influences—we turn now to a longer analysis of reflections from two scholars we interviewed, Damián Baca and Cheryl E. Ball. Although they self-identify as pursuing distinct subfields in writing studies, Baca and Ball demonstrate a shared interest in the ways in which copyright law is applied to different semiotic modes (primarily, verbal versus visual, and verbal versus audio/video modes, respectively) in print and digital formats. Both Baca and Ball resist certain inherited IP "rules" and policies, as they both spent time in their interviews reflecting on how they critically analyze IP guidelines and determine when to actively oppose them. At the same time that they seek to create new solutions to IP challenges, however, both choose to follow what they consider to be IP law. Neither Baca nor Ball self-identifies as an IP scholar within the discipline, though both are knowledgeable about IP issues and have devoted considerable thought to them. Based on their experiences, each has developed a complex and strongly held ethical lens for addressing IP issues in academia. We elected to highlight their interviews in this chapter because of the clarity with which they articulated these lenses and the consistency with which they applied them in making IP decisions across aspects of the knowledge-making cycle.

As we show, despite their similar interests in multimodality and their shared dedication to developing a thoughtful stance towards IP, Baca and Ball approach IP decisions differently, in part because they differ in how they understand IP and its mediation of their work processes. Using the categories that we identified in Chapter 3, we argue that Baca makes decisions from the perspective that IP is the collective development of a culture, whereas Ball makes decisions from the perspective that IP is about disciplinary relationships. These different ethical lenses lead to equally complex and compelling reasoning, as Baca and Ball explain the decisions they have made in pursuing their academic agendas and knowledge-making. In short, the two cases illustrate that, even though IP issues are ubiquitous for academics and even though scholars may share interests, the ways in which IP challenges are manifested, interpreted, and responded to can vary widely. In pairing these two interviews, then, we do not intend to imply that these scholars would disagree with each other's positions; indeed, we speculate that Baca and Ball would align in many of their opinions about IP. Nor do we intend these cases to be oppositional. Rather, because these participants would agree on a major principle—namely, that scholarly materials should be more readily available—it is important to analyze their comments closely to understand ways in which they nonetheless differently frame IP issues and respond to them.

In our analysis, we first summarize each interview to provide the arc of each scholar's application of his or her ethical lens and to contextualize the subsequent examples. Then we present examples of ways in which each participant makes IP decisions at each stage of the knowledge-making process we identify in this chapter. These examples emerged when we coded the interview transcripts; as can be seen in Appendix B, we did not scaffold the interviews according to the knowledge-making cycle.

For Baca, taking an ethical stance means articulating and valuing non-Western perspectives towards IP, through what he called the "dual lens of [his] own research": first, the "interrogat[ion of] how dominant Western practices of knowledge-making can contribute to the dis-authorization of non-Western people" and, second, "the reactivation or restitution or reclamation of indigenous and Latino, pre-Hispanic forms of knowing in rhetorical production." In turn, he seeks to "make intellectual property as unfamiliar as possible" for his students, in part to emphasize that the very concept of IP is "imported." Although Baca referred to the historical colonization of indigenous populations, he made the point that imposed control over indigenous artifacts continues today. For instance, the "pre-Hispanic codices" that interest him are still held today in the special collections of European archives that, as he related of a colleague's experience, may refuse access to them.

Throughout the interview, Baca addressed the problem of a lack of access and permissions to materials and the need to redress this problem. Reflecting on his experiences with his own book, *Mestiz@ Scripts, Digital Migrations, and the Territories of Writing*, Baca explained how the book's central paradox came about. Although his book "has to do with how [. . .] particular symbols and graphic marks continue to make meaning in particular communities both North and South of the US-Mexican border," he was unable to acquire copyright permissions in time to include any of the "pictographic" and "ideographic" images he analyzed. "So," he laughed, "a book, *Mestiz@ Scripts*, that is concerned significantly with non-alphabetic writing systems, went into publication without even a single illustration."

Baca went on to discuss a new project for which he was then developing a funding proposal: An online archive/database that would contain both alphabetic and pictorial elements, plus an editing studio, to enable composers to create their own codices or other texts employing non-alphabetic semiotic systems. In particular, he reflected on the IP permissions issues such an online database raises, and he noted the need to respect the IP expectations of other artists and writers. He amplified his ethical lens when he spoke of introducing IP to students, saying, "I think that I see it, though, as a matter—and this is as a context of the codices and multiple scripts and multiple cultures informing these spaces—I do happen to see observances and practices of intellectual property as a kind of code-switching," as Gloria Anzaldúa defined the term. For Baca, this code-switching involves a rhetorical analysis of audiences through which he both acknowledges Western IP practices and pushes against them. Finally, Baca concluded the interview by stating that he does not consider himself to be an IP expert and wished to improve how he teaches citation practices to his students. Overall, despite this hedging about his relative IP expertise, Baca presented himself as self-aware of his role as a scholar who straddles different semiotic systems, expectations for knowledge-making, and concomitant senses of (non)ownership of intellectual activities.

For Ball, taking an ethical stance means articulating a rhetorical approach to IP that is grounded in a concern for OA. Editor of *Kairos: A Journal of Rhetoric, Technology, and Pedagogy*, which has been online and fully OA since 1996, Ball noted that her "most notable intellectual property issues" stem from her work with the journal's contributors. Because the journal specializes in multimedia webtexts (employing visual, audio, and verbal modes), and because many contributors also engage in remix scholarship, questions arise regarding Fair Use. Ball shared that typically contributors themselves raise the questions; occasionally, an external Web bot flags the use of a video clip or a song in a webtext, although the number of those flags has declined over time. Instead of stating rigid measures for determining Fair Use (such as a certain number of minutes of a film), Ball explained that "the individual use as well as the accumulative use of media assets in a webtext has to, in all cases, forward the argument in the piece in some way, right? And that way might be if we're going to refer back to Louise Rosenblatt's terms of 'efferent' and 'aesthetic': You know, are these pieces making informational—informatic-based—meaning, or are they making aesthetic-based meaning?" This emphasis on context reflects Ball's understanding that the Fair Use guidelines are flexible and that Fair Use determinations vary across different situations.

This philosophy grounds Ball's teaching as well as the collaborative workshops she provides at conferences, such as the Computers and Writing conference, to introduce new digital writers to *Kairos* and its editing processes. She shared, "We want them [workshop participants] to take away that they shouldn't be scared to use media to make their arguments." Likewise, in her "undergraduate multimodal composition classes," Ball explained that she introduces IP "at the point where they're collecting assets for their webtext projects," and she often directs her students to resources available to use under CC licenses. At this point in the interview, Ball paused to note that she had learned at a recent talk by "an open access advocate activist, Rebecca Kennison," that "the non-commercial clause in Creative Commons is actually not what people think it is" and should be reconsidered. Ball further noted her difficulty in pursuing her scholarship while abroad in Norway because certain databases were not available to her and because books published by NCTE (the National Council of Teachers of English) are not available in any electronic format.

In expanding on ways in which IP has intersected with her own scholarship beyond access to research materials, Ball explained her stance on OA publishing. She stated, "I don't publish in those kinds of [subscription-only] journals anymore because I took the stance in 2009 right before I was going up for tenure—and I realized that most of my publications were in OA locations—that I was only going to publish in locations where everyone could have access to it if they wanted. Or I was going to make it publicly available on my website." She has fulfilled this stance by insisting on SPARC (Scholarly Publication and Academic Resources Coalition) amendments to author agreements when negotiating with traditional journals seeking to publish her work. In addition, Ball recounted avoiding IP conflicts by choosing not to publish wherever an individual editor might object to her choice to make all of her work OA on her own website. She explained, "sometimes I make intellectual property decisions based on people instead of on venues. [. . .] So I'm going to respect that [editor] and I'm just going to walk away and publish somewhere else." Responding to a question about whether she was required to consider IP by her Institutional Review Board (for research involving human subjects), Ball reflected on the relationship between IRB and IP issues, and suggested that NCTE should advise its members regarding

> [h]ow people should consider usage of the data that they collect and make the potentialities of making that data public. [. . .] And then regarding media usage in scholarship, [. . .] if you're thinking about publishing, then here are the ways that you should consider rights to your work in relation to publishing, whether it's with NCTE, or whether it's with a university press, or whether it's with an independent press. What does it mean for you to retain rights or not retain rights?

Overall, Ball presented herself as comfortable in her role as an adjudicator for IP issues, one who is rhetorically aware of potential differences in approaches to IP produced by differences in locales, disciplinary societies, emergent case law, publishing practices, evolving digital media, and scholarly mandates.

As these overall summaries suggest, Baca articulated a principle that privileges collective participation in and ownership of intellectual activities and knowledge-making, even as he also acknowledged the IP rights of his Western academic colleagues, whereas Ball articulated a principle that IP practices ought to be in the service of the overall benefit of the discipline, with intellectual products openly available. Like fractals, these principles repeated throughout each aspect of the knowledge-making cycle, as we will show in our more extended analysis of Baca's and Ball's IP decisions.

Choosing Topics and Texts to Study and Teach

As scholars, both Baca and Ball are interested in the semiotic and rhetorical affordances offered by different modes of communication:

verbal, visual, and audio. These affordances are amplified by the remix culture that both of these participants also value. Texts that remix elements from other texts unexpectedly juxtapose different elements as a means to elicit reader responses, whether to forward a logical argument or to elicit affect, or both. The texts also often rely on readers' abilities to recognize the original contexts for the remixed elements, as the allusions are a component of meaning-making. Both scholars, then, value the different knowledges that different composers and readers bring to texts, and they assert that no single semiotic medium, say, alphabetic text, ought to be privileged over others, such as still photos, film excerpts, or instrumental music clips. In their interviews, each reflected carefully on the types of communication they wished to enable, the voices they wanted to foster, the types of knowledge-making that should be valued, and how IP, as traditionally practiced in Western academia, might impact their goals.

In his reflections on his proposed codex-editing archive, Baca imagined that the project would enable him to honor the complex literacies that people like his students would bring to texts. For example, he reflected on why it would be important to him to allow students to study the Marvel and DC comics characters "that are unavoidable in pop culture today":

> And it's fascinating, bringing students in whose own literacy [is] in the realm of, let's say, Marvel comics—Marvel and DC. Their own literacies are far beyond mine. So, they're able to tell—without doing any archival research—they're able to point and say, "Oh, well this depiction of this image"—in this case Superman—"this image we know comes directly from this comic and this era—1994. It comes from this volume, this series." They know the number, and they know the plot, they know what happens, how that figured in with the mythology of that figure. Things that I don't know, I don't have access to. I didn't grow up with comics. So students are able to talk about different ways of looking, different ways of seeing, and different ways of knowing that I'm simply not going to have access to. So for me, I might gravitate towards some of the alphabetic prose. I might read some of the script—the alphabetic script—first. Others, who have a wider range of literacy skills in their toolbox [. . .] may be gravitating elsewhere and pointing out details that I didn't know or did not see. So for me it's really coming down to a full range of ways of creating that is not limited to a logosyllabic notion of expression.

In other words, for Baca the codex-editing archive was intended to allow scholars to choose to employ literate practices and engage in knowledge-making activities that might otherwise be suppressed in traditional academic logosyllabic venues.

Baca anchored this discussion in the specific context of wanting to include a particular text in the archive. He did not claim that he was negotiating to make Marvel and DC character images available in the archive. Rather, he had another specific goal for this project. He mentioned that he was talking with an "artist, Delilah Montoya, about the possibility of digitally scanning her codex and then having some elements that appear in her codex that are hers made available in a database that users might be able to access to create and recreate themselves." A significant work in the Chican@ movement, the *Codex Delilah* (1992) represented an important voice to be remembered and reanimated by being made available through Baca's editing studio—as well as a text that in itself would continue to be studied and taught as it provided allusions for future codices. Even though Baca was interested in making the *Codex Delilah* a part of the collective database to support future work, he was sensitive to the artist's own needs for traditional IP protections and recognition:

> So in that conversation, before I had it, I was trying to think through and thinking about her as an artist and as a creator and she is a professor in the art department at the University of Houston. [. . .] So I was thinking that if we were to move forward, then the only way to do this—the way I would feel comfortable—is that the ownership of this *Codex Delilah* would remain hers. So it would still remain her intellectual property. And with her permission, there would be some portions that we might be able to . . . that we would make available in the digital editing studio.

In other words, in this decision of texts to study and teach, academic IP practices intervene in a collective approach to culture building, as that cultural knowledge might be generated through the proposed archive and editing studio. Baca's comments illustrate that he was simultaneously aware of the codex's position as a remixed, culturally significant text and of the artist's position as a creator in a Western academic setting—a simultaneous awareness that he referred to as IP code-switching.

Ball's reflections regarding selecting texts to study and teach came from her perspective as an editor of a flagship journal in the discipline. Ball described her aims to encourage authors to study and produce multimodal publications fearlessly—and to enable the long-term success of such publications for the discipline. She explained that at her conference workshops, she and her co-presenters witnessed a shift in how potential contributors raise IP issues in the Q&A after the journal editor presentations. The editors still received queries "about our copyright and Fair Use policies" that focused not on general practices, but on specific, anticipated plans, phrased, in Ball's words, as " 'I want to use X media in my webtext. Is that okay?'" However, Ball continued, "The frequency with which we have those discussions has decreased over the years." From this decrease, Ball concluded, "So that's kind of cool that people are beginning to know that they can do stuff in *Kairos.*" Instead of questions about allowability—such as, "Is that okay?"—Ball commented that she wants contributors to focus on questions about what materials are needed to communicate effectively. She explained, "[It's] an educational process for us to teach folks that they can use the media that they need to use to make their argument." According to Ball, then, contributors should privilege their discipline's expectations for making effective multimodal arguments above any general, abstract copyright concerns.

Ball went on to explain that the discipline falters if journals and contributors unquestioningly prioritize IP over academic choices about what to study and how to develop that scholarship. She empathized with potential contributors' questions, saying, "And I know that's not always the case with all the other Web textual publications in our field, so that's also a learning curve for authors to know which journals can I publish certain things in and which can't I." However, Ball's experiences warned her that self-censorship out of excessive caution about IP matters can backfire. She contrasted her editorial approach to that of another journal: "[T]he one journal that I know of that had a much more strict policy on copyright—in that, for a while they were saying you can't use anything that's not original or you can't use anything that doesn't appear in a media commons or something like that. It is now defunct. They only lasted a year, so . . . part of what played into their demise because that's just not how we compose these days." Blanket, restrictive policies about IP are ineffective and counterproductive for Ball, especially when applied to new modes and genres of communication that scholars should be researching and teaching. Thus, she makes decisions about what texts to study and teach (and advises others to make decisions about what texts to study and teach) based on this belief.

Collecting Data and Materials

For both interviewees, considering research experiences in Europe amplified their concerns that IP issues may interfere with collecting information for legitimate scholarship. Baca noted that "there's a geopolitics to intellectual property," with definitions of IP imported to the Americas from Europe (a point reinforced by other interviewees as well, including Palmquist and Whithaus). He commented that the original codices that he studies in his scholarship are inaccessible: "[Of] the pre-Hispanic codices, we have really only a couple, a dozen or so. And those are not available. They are not in Mexico. They are not in the United States. They are not in North America. They are not in the Western Hemisphere. They are in Europe, in special collections. And I have not attempted to access the original manuscripts." Baca noted that a US colleague who did follow the regulations for gaining access to an archive—spending "nine months in preparation, a great deal of grant money, a lot of paperwork ahead of time"—was denied access upon arrival. He received "conflicting reports" about why, but indicated that "part of the reason" given was that the materials were "too old" for the public to handle.

Another reason, though, Baca commented, is that archival materials are subject to a ritualistic handling that emphasizes an entity's ownership. Echoing Anne Ruggles Gere's experience of being presented with guarded materials at an archive owned by a women's group, which we discuss in Chapters 3 and 4, Baca described his own encounter with an "Old Spanish translation of the original Latin translation of the *Popol Vuh*" at Chicago's Newberry Library:

> [Y]ou go in to look at a document that is rare and you are not allowed to touch it, but you have an employee standing next to you at all times wearing gloves, and the manuscript is on a felt, protected stand that is almost like a miniature podium that's placed on top of a large table. And you are permitted to look at the document—you can lean over it and look—but you cannot turn the pages. The employee would do that for you. So it is a very curious culture surrounding these "protected" documents.

Even this ritualistic access, however, did not apply to the indigenous materials Baca wished to see, as he reiterated, "And so for the codices, they're just not available. They're not on this continent, and they're not available to those who attempted to see them. So what we have in place are facsimiles of the codices." Ultimately, Baca was able to pursue his scholarship using these facsimiles, but his reflections indicate how archival ownership of materials mediated all of his research efforts; that is, the ways in which collecting data and materials were possible (and impossible) directly shaped his scholarship.

Like Baca, Ball was concerned throughout her interview about issues of access; however, instead of focusing on manuscripts in special collections, Ball expressed concern about how researchers and students could gain and maintain access to discipline-specific, contemporary materials. For one example, she mentioned talking with her graduate students about the importance and tenuousness of gaining access to research articles via university library databases:

> One of the easiest examples I can give to [. . .] my US students, 'Look when I'm in Norway, and I'm working for the architecture and design school in Norway, I don't have access to JSTOR, to EbscoHost, and to all these major databases that y'all, as students, assume you will always have access to. But the second you graduate you won't have access to those anymore.' And the reason why I don't have access to them when I'm over there is because the Norwegian school that I'm

> working for is too specific. [. . .] It's a professional school that only focuses on architecture and design and urban planning and so they only have databases that are relevant to that kind of work.

As Ball commented, researchers can be naive in assuming that they will have prolonged and consistent access to materials, particularly digital materials. Because students may not have cause to consider how their university library manages the IP licenses for important research assets, those processes remain invisible until they can no longer access the scholarship they need. Moreover, researchers accustomed to the liberal arts core curriculum required at the majority of US universities may not consider the disciplinary restrictions on IP licenses at more vocational institutions or institutions located in other countries. As a counter-example to these restrictive licensing practices, Ball praised the Norwegian national mandate "that all scholarship that you publish as a researcher in the country must be deposited into an open access repository," namely, the CRIStin repository run by the Norwegian Ministry of Education and Research.

Drawing upon her own difficulty with acquiring research materials while she was living in Norway, Ball concluded that it would be more equitable and beneficial if research in writing studies were more readily available: "[M]aking our work open access means making it available to the world—like to people who can't afford it, who don't otherwise have access for either material or economic reasons, etc." This stance is borne directly from her experience with IP access across geographic and institutional boundaries: Possibilities for knowledge-making work depend upon geographic and institutional restrictions on collecting data and materials. Whereas Baca explicitly interpreted these restrictions as the continued ramifications of colonialism and imperialism, Ball interpreted them as inimical to a discipline that, in her opinion, should value collaboration and effective communication practices.

Negotiating Procedures and Products for Publication

Both Baca and Ball spoke at length about their experiences negotiating IP issues with publishers and potential contributors to projects, especially issues that involved incorporating others' IP into new texts. For each, the decision whether to incorporate another scholar's materials into a text begins with a rhetorical judgment about how that IP figures into the text's purpose and argument. Here we highlight two examples.

Speaking from the perspective of an author, Baca focused on a central paradox for his book: "I'm publishing on the question of, the potential potency of non-alphabetic scripts and forms of writing while doing so entirely alphabetically" because of IP issues. Baca had identified images from contemporary codices that he wanted to reproduce in his book, and he had worked hard to acquire the necessary IP permissions. The materials that interested him were peppered with visual references to Western cultural symbols as well as references to the pre-Hispanic codices (i.e., the *Codex Mendoza*):

> I think you might have seen the [contemporary] codex. There is a film with pop culture symbolism, so there [are] DC properties, properties from DC, properties from Marvel, properties from Disney. So Mickey Mouse is there, Minnie Mouse is there, you have Goofy, Wonder Woman, Superman, Spider-Man intermixed, juxtaposed with indigenous images directly from the *Codex Mendoza*—these pictographic and ideographic forms. So it's a very clever. And, of course, there is a great deal of satire running through.

For his argument, then, Baca analyzed the significance of this juxtaposition of imagery within the contemporary codex. Despite his efforts, however, he could not secure the permissions in time to include reproductions of the images themselves.

When asked about how the lack of reproduced visuals affected his scholarship, Baca answered with an extended meditation on this decision's impact. He explained that, on one hand,

> It really wasn't a drastic shift. I would say that there were minor shifts that are virtually unnoticeable. And so there isn't a time when, in my close reading, in my textual analysis, that I rely on heavily, which is actually quite—, pretty conventional method of analysis. When I'm doing that, there is no point where I had to go back and edit out, 'See references this,' or 'See image here.' So it wasn't written out that way; it wasn't drafted that way from the beginning.

Baca went on to say that, when considering the question of the book's audience, it was appropriate that few edits were required when he realized that the images would be unavailable. Because he had described the images thoroughly, the book was appropriately detailed and argued for the other scholars he was addressing. From the stance of a conventional form of Western academic knowledge-making, then, the book successfully accomplished its goal of presenting a close reading.

On the other hand, however, Baca questioned whether the traditional, logosyllabic approach he had taken was truly adequate for analyzing the subject matter he explored. He mused, "And maybe [the book] really should have been" drafted so that removing images would have had more impact on the argument. He continued, "There's some possible critique there that I probably should have crafted it in such a way where maybe it would have had written analysis that could not have moved forward [without the images], and then also that [the book] could not have been put forward in the absence of [the images]." Given the cultural resonances of images in the codices, he reflected, was it true to the subject matter to allow them to be eliminated?

Baca imagined, though, that the images would have been included as distinct excerpts to illustrate written points, and that plan likewise would have been inadequate:

> I was still uncomfortable with it [using the images to illustrate points], I have to be honest with you. I was so uncomfortable with it because we are still left with a dichotomy that we're still very comfortable in: annotation and illustration itself. [. . .] I was wanting to bring a heavy degree of doubt to call that binary opposition into question.

In other words, while writing the book and working with its IP implications, Baca discovered that no traditional, print form of argumentation—whether he included the images or not—would be adequate for analyzing the visual modes of communication that are integral to codices. No logosyllabic approach can fully replace the acts of experiencing and interpreting the culturally significant visuals. Moreover, from his perspective, logosyllabic elements should not be allowed to dominate visual elements, as when images are regulated to be labeled figures or illustrations or appendices. Although Baca was proud of his book's scholarship and satisfied with how it communicated with a specific, scholarly audience, his experiences with struggling over the IP permissions for the images exacerbated his dissatisfaction with print modes of argumentation. From these experiences, Baca developed his plan to build a new digital archive and editing studio that would more effectively support both alphabetic and non-alphabetic forms of communication and argumentation.

As an editor, Ball worked to forestall some of the IP issues that Baca experienced as an author. *Kairos* is a digitally native, OA journal that publishes webtexts, a genre of scholarly communication that treats all modalities as relevant for academic meaning-making. The journal relies on the Fair Use practices embedded within US copyright law that are intended to protect scholarly work. In fact, the IP issues that Ball encountered primarily arose not from academic practices but from corporate policies, as digital companies developed new IP policies alongside their emergent technologies. For example, Ball mentioned the consequences for *Kairos* when the video platform YouTube began experimenting with copyright bots as a tool to identify potential IP violations:

> At the time, I think YouTube was still in court over that Prince video with the little baby dancing, and so that hadn't been resolved yet, so they were being pretty feisty about their takedown notices. But they had implemented an area of the website where you could write in and argue against the takedown. And so we did, and we cited Fair Use and said [. . .] the reasons why the person who was the

> author was using this song in this video had rights to use it fairly in their webtext: They were critiquing something, they were using a very small amount that wasn't going to impact the market value of the original piece, etc. And so that did the trick, and YouTube stopped bothering us for that thing.

Kairos's policies and Ball's role as an editor evolved as YouTube's approaches to IP did. When copyright bots were first introduced, they flagged a range of materials that YouTube would then automatically remove from the platform.[5] At the time of the interview, a Fair Use case was still making its way through the court systems, a case in which a mother had posted a brief video of her baby dancing to the background music of a song by Prince. The case centered on whether YouTube needed to consider Fair Use claims before removing materials, or, in Ball's words, whether YouTube was being too "feisty about their takedown notices."[6] As Ball explained, at the time of the interview, YouTube had already changed the platform to include a "website where you could write in and argue against the takedown." Ball was able to protect the contributor's rhetorical choices by citing factors of Fair Use, such as the use of the materials for scholarly critique, the amount used, and the lack of impact on the materials' original market.

Beyond relying on these legal criteria for Fair Use, Ball developed editorial policies that rested not on rigid "rules," such as those proposed by the CONFU (Conference on Fair Use) Guidelines (Lehman), but on interpretive judgments about the role of specific materials in an academic argument. At first, she jokingly explained, "[T]his is one of the silly reasons why I call *Kairos* webtexts scholarly porn. It's like, 'You know it, when you see it.' It works or not." More seriously, she went on to explain that she and her editorial team encourage contributors to avoid facile reproduction of others' IP: "But when we go back to an author and say, 'This is too much,' it's because there's too much. [. . .] One of the typical judgments against over usage of media is that it becomes bells and whistles." Ball's editorial decisions, then, are concerned about others' IP not so much because of legal consequences, as the reproduction typically can be justified by Fair Use, but because of the argument's suitability for *Kairos*'s readers. As a leading journal of digitally native scholarship, *Kairos* shapes and is shaped by a discipline that is developing criteria for multimodal argumentation.

One instance Ball shared in her interview illustrates. Ball offered an extended example of how she worked with one contributor to strengthen their webtext, an example that she reported sharing at her workshops at the Computers and Writing Conference:

> An author sent us a webtext for consideration once that was using ten, fifteen ten-minute clips of a Hollywood movie to make their argument. Well that was, in essence, the entire movie. And we were, like, there's

> not enough scholarly engagement to warrant you showing this roughly entire movie in ten-minute clips. [. . . You] don't need that to make your argument. Your argument is actually much smaller in scope, and so how can we trim these clips in such a way that will make your argument actually more robust and will make people want to read it?

When asked whether *Kairos* had an editorial policy about restricting the use of media to pre-specified lengths (such as ten-minute clips from movies), Ball reiterated that the editorial advice was based on judgments about a webtext's rhetorical effectiveness and about readers' experiences, not on rigid, CONFU-oriented guidelines about reproducing multimedia:

> It doesn't. I mean, one: [the ten-minute rule] is a myth and two: it's meaningless. [. . .] I talk about the ten minutes of the video of the Hollywood movie that was chunked over—and maybe that's why that person chose to only give a ten-minute segment because that was ten percent of the movie. I don't know what their reasoning was in splitting them up, but almost all the clips were ten minutes long. But no, *Kairos* doesn't use any sort of timeframe or fraction value for evaluating when a media element is rhetorically useful or not. It's a matter of evaluating in the context that it's being presented in and evaluating it in terms of the argument being made.

In her approach to YouTube and IP guidelines, then, Ball emphasized that she protected both the right and the need for scholars—not entities beyond academia—to define what materials are appropriate for scholarly critique. Fair Use, in her opinion, is a matter for negotiation, based on evaluations about "when a media element is rhetorically useful or not" for "the context that it's being presented in." Because many of these rhetorical contexts were experimental, as *Kairos* contributors explored how to compose effective multimodal webtexts, Ball acted as an arbiter. At the same time she resisted overly zealous appropriations of IP by corporate entities, she also resisted egregious use of others' IP by contributors to the academic journal. These beliefs in the importance of scholars having freedom to use IP to make scholarly arguments, the necessity of grounding this use in argumentation rather than adornment, and the contextual application of Fair Use judgments determined the ways in which she negotiated with *Kairos* contributors regarding their products for publication.

Disseminating and Storing Texts

As shown in the previous sections, both interviewees were interested in the infrastructures that support academic knowledge-making. For different reasons, Baca and Ball commented that they were dissatisfied with traditional venues for communicating scholarly work, especially because these venues were bounded by IP practices that were no longer serving their academic goals. As a result, both articulated and worked to build new venues that would allow them to realize more fully their academic intentions. These intentions had implications not only for final products of scholarly work—that is, publications—but also for academic IP created before and after a manuscript is published.

In his interview Baca again referenced his monograph as an example. Drawing on his experiences with writing his book, Baca decided that he needed a venue that would support multimodal argumentation. More than that, though, he explained that he was interested in fostering texts that relied on shared, culturally significant materials. He commented on the impetus for his proposed codex-editing studio:

> [W]hat I couldn't do with my book—what I wasn't able to do with the majority— [. . .] all of my publications that I have been unable to do—why not just put into practice what I'm analyzing by actually doing it? And to do it, we would need to build a digital editing studio to invent and draw from rich resources alphabetic and non-alphabetic, all of the above.

In other words, Baca did not just want to enable multimodal publication, as with a new journal, or just to enable remix argumentation techniques, although those were important for his project. Rather, he emphasized that the digital editing studio would allow users "to invent" materials and to "draw from rich resources alphabetic and non-alphabetic" stored in the archive. Baca wanted "all of the above," a place to borrow, construct, publish, and share culturally significant elements that would allow endless recombinations of Western and non-Western semiotic systems. He wanted a place that offered a new model of disseminating and storing texts.

Developing that new place to disseminate and store texts—the codex-editing studio—was proving difficult, Baca explained, because he was working through a series of difficult IP decisions about materials he wanted to disseminate and store in the shared archive. In addition to considering the impact of the studio on the IP of contemporary artists, such as Delilah Montoya, Baca was also concerned about including snippets from the pre-Hispanic and later codices whose physical copies were not available to him for replication. In consulting IP sponsors, including "the head librarian at the special collections," Baca reported "getting some conflicting reports" about what materials would be allowed under Fair Use. "Some are arguing," he explained, "that some of the earlier codices are public domain, and so they are much easier to use." However, the versions of the codices he could access were digital copies:

> There are a couple databases online [. . .] that offer some partial scans and it's not very interactive at all. It's just a few scans, if you

> just wanted to see them. I would say that some of these databases are not much different than the equivalent of going to Google images and then just typing in *Codex Mendoza* and just seeing what images pop up.

Including these inferior images in his studio, in Baca's opinion, would be a compromise, as their "pixels are not that hot, the size isn't that great, but at least you're able to see it." In addition to being concerned about their quality, Baca reported he was uncertain whether even these images would be available to him, as he was unsure of their own IP status: "In terms of rights and permissions, I'm wondering if [the database owners] might have to remove them, if they were asked. I'm not sure. I'm not entirely sure." In other words, he mused that if the database owners did not own the IP in these incomplete copies of the codices, then they could not legitimately grant him replication rights either. Ultimately, Baca concluded that, in terms of IP, "I have to admit to you there's a great deal of unanswered questions and over the next two years I hope that I would be able to provide some more detailed answers." At the time of the interview, these unanswered IP questions were stalling the development of an innovative, scholarly platform for sharing and collectively developing texts.

Ball's concerns regarding disseminating and storing texts likewise touched on issues of access to the IP in databases but centered more on a need for international commitments to OA. In reflecting on her experiences conducting research both in the US and Norway, where she was thwarted from accessing desired materials because particular institutions of higher education did not subscribe to the databases that housed these materials, Ball shared her commitment to an OA stance. She summed up: "And I'm just like, 'Put it all online.' Everybody!" For her, this experience as a researcher shaped her stance as an author. A desire to disseminate her scholarly IP OA was a primary factor in deciding where and how to publish her work.

Beyond that stance about final publications, however, Ball was interested in IP implications for research datasets. In response to a question about what IP resources the NCTE should develop, Ball argued that the NCTE should issue policies about the raw data that writing researchers collect:

> I would really like to see us starting to share our datasets more. [. . . T]his is a discussion that's been going on for a couple years now within writing studies, but it's not gone very deep because most people just get completely freaked out and don't know what you're talking about when you start talking about data. Well, I'm talking about student texts and [. . .] the survey questions that you create and the answers to those, and, like, we have all this information. This is the

> idea on which the Research Exchange was founded, right? We have all this [. . .] boutique data that we collect from writing programs and from teaching and from doing our own scholarly research. But we don't share that data as raw data.

As Ball mentioned, writing scholars were becoming involved in conversations about sharing their research data, but the discipline did not have a common understanding of what data might (or should) be shared. Her gloss on what ought to be included—"student texts and the survey questions that you create and the answers to those"—contained both raw data (texts and answers) and the instruments that produced data (survey questions), as, from her perspective, all would be valuable to the discipline as shared information. One attempt to build the needed infrastructure for making these scholarly materials more visible and readily available for reuse, the Research Exchange, was not fully incorporated into the field's research practices.

In Ball's opinion, the cost of not sharing this type of scholarly IP was wasted effort and lost research opportunities. She continued,

> And there's a lot of value that could be found in that raw data. And people are like, "but that's my data . . ." Like, yeah, but you could only answer five research questions out of that dataset in your lifetime. There may be 27 research questions that could be answered. [G]ive it to somebody else and let people aggregate their data and see what it looks like across [datasets].

Writing researchers, Ball suggested, should resist a humanistic inclination towards single authorship and single ownership of material, in other words, the stance "but that's my data." Instead, by urging researchers to "aggregate their data and see what it looks like," Ball echoed Richard Haswell's call for writing studies to move towards conducting more replicated, aggregated, data-driven (RAD) research. That said, "we need the mechanisms in order to be able to do that," Ball acknowledged. She had supported yet another infrastructure project, "rhetoric.io," which, she noted, "just simply, for time reasons, it hasn't gone much of anywhere. But it's still lingering in the back." Thinking about what would make such an IP-sharing repository successful, Ball indicated that another institutional infrastructure might provide motivation: "But in order for people to invest their time and their data in something like rhetoric.io or any sort of data repository, they have to have written into their IRB plans what they are going to do with that data." According to Ball, the mandates for data-sharing from an Institutional Review Board, which approves research plans involving human subjects and implements governmental policies, might be the push needed to move the discipline to new data-sharing practices. Both Ball and Baca, then, imagined new possibilities for making texts and research materials associated with texts more readily accessible to all future users, with Ball intent on restructuring (inter)disciplinary repositories, and Baca intent on creating a new authoring platform that would honor community commitments.

Employing Materials and Technologies in Face-to-Face and Digital Classes

When asked about how they would teach undergraduate and graduate students about IP issues, both interviewees indicated that they understood IP as a set of enculturated practices. Not only did they need to teach students techniques for handling others' and their own IP, but they also wished to teach students appropriate attitudes towards IP. As a result, both Baca and Ball made choices about which materials and technologies to introduce in classes based on which enculturated practices they associated with IP. As the following examples demonstrate, they both respected academic IP, but they framed their approaches with different ethical lenses.

Baca's initial response highlighted a theme that we identified throughout the survey and interview responses, which we analyze earlier in this chapter and at length elsewhere (see Lunsford and Purdy): the association of plagiarism avoidance instruction with IP instruction. In our survey and interview prompts, we identified IP as copyright, patents, trademarks, and proprietary knowledge (trade secrets). We did not mention the terms plagiarism, citation, or attribution. Nonetheless, when asked about their teaching, a majority of respondents equated IP with these themes, as Baca did, when he imagined himself addressing his undergraduates: "'Hey, listen, when you're reading something, and you want to paraphrase, and if you paraphrase enough and you're not citing the page number of that passage that you just paraphrased, that can be seen as a form of plagiarism.'" However, the rules of paraphrasing, as Baca emphasized about understanding of IP in general, are not universal. He continued, "And so it's not as though this is something that's going to be inherent, that students are just going to know—they have to be told, right?" Instead, he explained, "[Students] have to be taught about [. . .] how this particular cultural activity functions in this particular space and this is why." Baca elaborated on his claim that IP is a "particular" rather than a universal cultural activity, saying, "I see it though as a matter—and this is as a context of the codices and multiple scripts and multiple cultures informing these spaces—I do happen to see observances and practices of intellectual property as a kind of code-switching." By "code-switching," he went on to explain, he meant Gloria Anzaldúa's definition, indicating that he had in mind more than switching certain words or phrases, but alternating among and straddling cultural stances.

To participate in a specific practice associated with IP, according to Baca, is to align with just one possibility among the "multiple scripts and multiple cultures" that Baca sees himself and his students inhabiting.

Ball likewise interpreted IP practices as particular to certain spaces and privileged disciplinary venues in thinking about these contexts. She characterized her instruction as "a lot about venue and audience and *disciplinary values and community values* in media-rich pieces" (emphasis added). Speaking of how she teaches undergraduates, Ball commented that "about two thirds of the way through the semester we have a week in my undergraduate multimodal composition classes devoted to intellectual property. And it's at the point where they're collecting assets for their webtext projects." Because students are searching the Web for "assets"—texts, images, music, video—it is an opportunity for Ball to ask them to think carefully about different IP policies. For example, she explained, "we stop and say, 'Okay, here's what Creative Commons looks like and here's how you might find pieces that are tagged 'Creative Commons.'" Beyond pointing students to items governed by Creative Commons licenses, though, Ball asks students to carefully evaluate IP practices across locations: "'[N]ow go look at the policies that these different journals have, which are your potential venues,' and so venue matters a lot, right?" She expanded on this principle with several examples to indicate the variability of how IP laws may be applied:

> So if you're just throwing something on YouTube as a person—not as a scholar for a particular journal, but as just as somebody in the world, you have to attend to YouTube's intellectual property's laws or guidelines. If you are doing it for *Kairos*, you have to attend to *Kairos's* guidelines, which are fairly wide open. If you're submitting to a print-based journal as a scholar, your copyright and intellectual property guidelines are much more restrictive for all sorts of reasons, and so you have to attend to those. So we talk about the rhetorical context in which the media artifacts will eventually live.

For Ball, because the products of IP "live" in particular rhetorical contexts, teaching universal rules about the use and integration of others' IP does not make sense. Instead, she reported emphasizing with students that attention to the venue of publication, particularly whether digital or print, shapes ways in which IP can be used—precisely because these media allow for circulation and storage of IP in different ways.

Before we leave our analysis of Baca's and Ball's interviews, we, in a gesture back to the focus of Chapter 4, want to note the range of IP sponsors who mediated their IP decisions. We note human (colleagues, editors, copyright holders), institutional (publishers/presses, IRB offices, libraries/archives, OA policies, Creative Commons, time, governmental agencies), and technological (YouTube, repositories) sponsors playing mediating roles throughout their academic knowledge-making experiences. In some instances, the interviewees described the IP sponsor as helpful, as when Baca reported looking to colleagues for models for his own IP decisions, and when Ball articulated how important the four factors of Fair Use are for her journal. However, in some cases, the IP sponsor prevented an initial plan, as when Baca discovered he could not include desired images in his book, and Ball discovered that entire books and journal databases were unavailable to her in Norway. These setbacks caused both scholars to build alternatives more amenable to their academic goals. Throughout the IP decisions they reported, each maintained their ethical lens, which informed how they went about finding the alternatives they needed. Each interviewee also served as an IP sponsor—as teachers, but also as scholars who introduce other scholars to the alternatives that they desire.

We focused on these two scholars' reflections because, together, they capture several of the main arcs of this book. First, IP decisions are enculturated into the work of academics, and decisions that seem natural are based on histories of negotiating interests among creators, distributors, and audiences. Second, IP decisions are complex and contextual, resisting universal rules and requiring reasoned deliberation from particular ethical lenses. Third, IP decisions do not happen in isolation; they are mediated by human, institutional, and technological sponsors, some of which explicitly identify in this role while others do not. Fourth, IP decisions are recurrent. Practitioners encounter them again and again in academic knowledge-making. Last, but not least, IP decisions are malleable: Scholars may accept setbacks under specific circumstances, but they may also be inspired to change the circumstances of their knowledge-making.

Conclusion

This chapter draws on survey and interview data to illustrate ways in which IP decisions shape academic knowledge-making from conception and invention through publication and dissemination. In particular, this chapter shows the pervasive, systemic, and sometimes insidious ways in which IP issues and concerns influence writing studies practitioners' work while choosing topics and texts to study and teach, collecting data and materials, negotiating procedures and products for publication, disseminating and storing texts, and employing materials and technologies in face-to-face and digital classes. This list of knowledge-making activities is not exhaustive; rather, it indicates the activities around which survey and interview responses cohered. However, it usefully demonstrates the wide range of sites throughout academic knowledge-making where IP concerns play a role. We ultimately argue that IP considerations have significant influence far earlier in academic knowledge-making than is often realized (or at least has been documented). Writing studies practitioners, in other words, do not just encounter IP choices when seeking to secure copyright permissions to publish an image or deciding whether to publish in an OA journal, though these are important IP decisions. Writing studies practitioners also make choices about what texts and topics to include on their syllabi or even what research projects to pursue based on IP considerations. The entire academic knowledge-making enterprise is shaped by IP issues.

Thus, when IP choices are invisible or are made for writing studies practitioners by others, the consequences are considerable. For instance, we found in our study that reactions to the pervasive, systemic, and insidious influence of IP include self-censorship, learned helplessness, intrepid fearlessness, and compelled compliance. Writing studies practitioners reported deciding not to engage in particular knowledge-making activities because they were concerned about violating IP laws (real or perceived). For instance, before they even asked for permission to use a particular textbook or to include a particular epigraph, they just removed it themselves, even if such actions were ultimately unnecessary per IP law. Writing studies practitioners also reported simply giving up particular pursuits rather than undertake the time, effort, and cost involved to do their desired work. For instance, once they learned that reproducing an image would require paying expensive permission fees or tracking down a copyright holder whose identity is not readily known, they felt helpless and their work stalled. Conversely, other writing studies practitioners, particularly those study participants who reported greater knowledge of IP law and policies, pursued their academic knowledge-making activities without worry. In some cases, this intrepid fearlessness was borne of negative experiences with their own IP, when they felt inadequately compensated or acknowledged and thereby decided to just do what they wanted, even if their decisions potentially ran afoul of IP law. In other cases, this intrepid fearlessness came from confidence that they could defend their decisions as compliant with IP law (e.g., Fair Use guidelines), even if these decisions were not supported by particular IP sponsors, such as colleagues or editors. Other such respondents felt invigorated to teach certain courses, pursue certain research agendas, or create certain resources to meet IP needs, for example, to teach students about Fair Use, to research university intellectual property policies, or to establish new archives. Finally, writing studies practitioners sometimes felt bullied into making particular IP decisions. They reported feeling a lack of agency to do as they wanted, perhaps because IP sponsors had more power than they did or because they lacked the knowledge to justify their choices.

We contend that offering and documenting examples of colleagues thinking through IP issues—at moments throughout their academic knowledge-making—can help move practitioners past unnecessary self-censorship, learned helplessness, and bullied compliance. In turn, these practitioners can then become better IP sponsors for others, including their students and colleagues. IP conundrums do not often have easy answers; thus, providing models of others engaging this complexity is crucial.

Notes

1. For each question, we report the number of respondents who completed that question, as not all respondents completed all twenty questions. Question 20 was completed by 201 respondents, but two of the responses were uncodable.
2. See Appendix B for the interview questions and transcription conventions; see Appendix C for the position titles and affiliations of interview participants from at the time of their interviews.
3. As we note in earlier chapters, we use *they* as a singular inclusive pronoun.
4. This percentage is identical to the percentage in Rife's study, where 6 percent of her participants likewise reported receiving takedown notices (*Invention* 42).
5. See Chapter 4 for analysis of Cruz Medina's reflections on the evolving IP policies of YouTube and YouTube's role as an IP sponsor.
6. See Chapter 3 for discussion of the *Lenz v. Universal Music Corporation* case Ball referenced.

6 Conclusion

[IP issues] have made me more aware of what it means to be an author, and what are the relationships of business, ownership, and knowledge-building in the world.
—*(Question 20, Response 87)*

A Call for Increased and Broadened Focus on IP in Writing Studies

In this book, we argue that IP considerations play a critical, and often invisible, role in the scholarly, pedagogical, and editorial work of writing studies professionals. Our nationwide survey and semi-structured interviews empirically support that conceptions of IP have become enculturated in the academic work of knowledge production of professionals in the field. In particular, writing studies practitioners make decisions to avoid infringing on IP—from abandoning research and teaching pursuits to choosing (where) not to publish—which can limit the research and teaching pursued by members of the discipline. But the story is not all bad. In contrast, writing studies practitioners make decisions to study, engage with, or challenge prevailing Western approaches to IP—from directing research and teaching agendas to creating new publication venues—which can enrich their scholarly and pedagogical pursuits. This book seeks to make explicit the tacit thinking behind such decisions. Its chapters focus on four overarching questions about decisions regarding IP: 1) What histories and legislation set the parameters for an IP decision? (Chapter 2); 2) What values guide this decision? (Chapter 3); 3) Who and what offers guidance about this decision, and what advice do they offer? (Chapter 4); and 4) When are such decisions made in academic knowledge-making? (Chapter 5).

While the notion that IP issues are part of academic work is not new, this book provides data to substantiate the real, tangible ways in which writing studies practitioners are affected by—and affect—IP. It demonstrates these effects through documentation and analysis of, in Chapters 3, 4, and 5, respectively, the ethical lenses writing studies practitioners apply, the sponsors they encounter and become, and the activities of the knowledge-making process in which they engage. These data allow us to show colleagues and administrators in higher education, as well as legislators and the public, that academic work in writing studies (and beyond) is inextricably bound up in what practitioners can do—or think they can do—with their and others' IP. Given that IP decisions are often based on myths about IP law, IP laws that are driven by the interests of entertainment industries rather than educational institutions, and IP laws themselves that are ever-changing and open to interpretation, as we discuss in Chapter 2, we profess that writing studies practitioners need to be aware of, and pay attention to, the ways in which IP decisions influence their academic practices. That way, they can make proactive choices rather than merely react. The work writing studies practitioners want (and need) to do is made more difficult when their IP choices are dictated by others, are based on unexamined assumptions, or when practitioners lack knowledge of their IP rights and responsibilities. By identifying the multiple cultural histories of IP; the ethical lenses writing studies practitioners can apply; sponsors they can use, avoid, or challenge; and processes of academic knowledge-making they can engage in with renewed consideration of IP's influence, this book provides a means for cultivating the awareness and providing the information that members of the field can use to make proactive decisions.

In this spirit of proactivity, we open this concluding chapter by calling for three changes in the way writing studies approaches IP. First, as we found in our study that early career professionals feel especially vulnerable when making IP decisions, we argue for increased consideration of IP earlier in practitioners' careers—that is, as part of graduate school and pre-tenure/early-career training. That way, practitioners enter their professional lives knowing ways in which to make informed IP decisions. This training might take the form of orientation workshops, professional development, and/or courses. Equally as important, we call for expanding the field's sense of the times and sites of IP influence in academic work. We argue not just for considering IP issues when producing and circulating the end products of scholarly and pedagogical work, but also for viewing IP issues as fundamental at the beginning and throughout research, teaching, and editorial endeavors, as we found in our study that IP considerations play crucial roles in this early work. Third, as we also discuss elsewhere (see Lunsford and Purdy), we call for moving the teaching of IP beyond plagiarism and citation to address the legal, historical, economic, and personal dimensions of IP—that is, to teach IP to students and colleagues as shaped by legislation, historical developments, capitalist interests, and sociocultural forces.

Challenges of Increased and Broadened Focus on IP in Writing Studies

We understand these changes will not happen overnight. To explain, we turn, as we have throughout our project, to one of our study participants.

In her interview, Joyce Locke Carter explained three related reasons why members of the field may resist attending to IP. The first reason Carter addressed is that members of the discipline may not see and treat their work as "intellectual property" because they classify it otherwise:

> I think that people still generally, in the humanities, appear to me to bristle at thinking about their work as intellectual property. I think there's a lot of work to be done. . . . You know, they say, "I don't make intellectual property. I write stories; I connect with people; I teach students; I engage my audience." And all of that is true.

Thus, the very term *intellectual property* can feel uncomfortable to members of the field. A second reason Carter mentioned is that members of the field may be unsure of or intimidated by the "legal processes" associated with IP. She continued, "I would imagine if you took a poll of a vast number of members of the CCCC, NCTE, or RSA,[1] they would say they probably know what the term [intellectual property] means; they might even recognize what it does. I don't think they would particularly like it." Practitioners may feel overwhelmed and confused by IP. Indeed, our survey and interviews support that a prevailing response to IP concerns is for teacher-scholars simply to give up. They embrace a learned helplessness as tackling IP issues can be difficult, time consuming, and expensive. Carter shared a third reason: the association of IP with commercialism. She explained, "I think people see intellectual property as part of . . . It's not a homogenous thing, but my impression is that people see intellectual property—talking about intellectual property—as part of a commercialization of education." While IP allows academics to make money for their work, some academics dislike a business model for higher education because it is seen to privilege profit over pedagogy and savings over scholarship.

This book goes some way toward redressing these three challenges. We do not offer legal advice (we are not attorneys), but we draw together data and reflections that provide evidence, advice, and guidance. For instance, we address the first challenge in Chapter 2, where we untangle IP's complex histories to clarify that there are two prevailing Western approaches to IP, the Anglo-American and the Continental systems, that differ in important ways, especially regarding which element of the rhetorical situation (author, distributor, or audience) they privilege. In Chapter 2, we also identify some of the myths that circulate surrounding IP, particularly regarding Fair Use, to help equip writing studies practitioners to respond to sponsors who may misinform them (intentionally or not) about IP policies, regulations, and rules. These sponsors are the focus of Chapter 4.

To respond to the second challenge, we address some of the potential reasons writing studies professionals might spurn the concept of

IP. These reasons include the perplexing history (or, more accurately, the multiple histories) and myths of IP, which we review in Chapter 2; the sometimes competing ethical lenses that can be applied in making IP decisions, which we discuss in Chapter 3; the range and layering of sometimes invisible IP sponsors, which we outline in Chapter 4; and the widespread (and sometimes insidious) effects of IP on the academic knowledge-making cycle, which we address in Chapter 5. With more clarity about these potential sources of discomfort, we hope IP might seem less intimidating and, in turn, colleagues will be less likely to give up particular pursuits because of IP concerns, bullying, or misinformation.

To address the third challenge Carter identifies, we share extended examples of writing studies scholars thinking through their IP decisions, many of which entail consideration of or intersect with the commercialization of education. In Chapter 3, we analyze the reflections of several interviewees who used ethical lenses for approaching IP that attend to IP's role in economic systems and in business pursuits. Their reflections can serve as examples of ways to think through commercial IP issues in writing studies—and in higher education more broadly. They articulate approaches to making IP decisions that highlight and (in some cases) mitigate the tension between economic/corporate and scholastic motivations behind IP decisions. Additionally, in Chapter 4, we analyze Cruz Medina's reflections on his teaching, which touch on issues regarding the monetization of blogs, the commercial interests of YouTube, and the ownership of memes. His consideration of these issues, alongside reporting on the IP sponsors that shape his and his students' IP decisions, offers an example of seeing economically driven choices as having both positive and negative effects. His reflections remind us that such economic choices exist on a spectrum, rather than a binary, with pedagogically and scholastically driven decisions. Finally, in Chapter 5, we report ways in which two of our interviewees, Damián Baca and Cheryl E. Ball, made IP decisions, consciously and unconsciously, throughout all stages of their academic knowledge-making work. Their work entails decisions about how and whether to profit from scholarship and/or teaching by securing financial and cultural capital.

Notwithstanding these challenges, our study also found successes. From our survey and interviews, we are struck that many members in the field work to forward pedagogical and scholastic endeavors in the discipline despite IP challenges. There is a generosity of spirit in light—or in spite—of IP restrictions: Writing studies practitioners were generous in their time and in their practices. For instance, they were generous in sharing their reflections with us, both in taking the survey and in participating in interviews. Moreover, they were generous in taking on copyright permission costs themselves (e.g., Blair); creating and overseeing archival spaces for research and teaching, such as the DALN and FSU Card Archive, that seek to simplify and make transparent IP concerns (e.g., McCorkle, Selfe, Yancey); and teaching students and colleagues about IP issues, including Fair Use and open access (OA) (e.g., Amidon, Ball, Berry, Medina, Silver). This formal and informal teaching extended to combating myths about IP (e.g., Logie), sharing strategies for protecting one's IP (e.g., Galin, Kennedy, Palmquist, Pemberton), and introducing students and colleagues to alternative perspectives to prevailing treatment of IP, including non-Western and copyleft approaches (e.g., Baca, Cushman, Lowe). We also found that there is genuine excitement about the possibilities of IP as a subject of research and teaching in writing studies. It is precisely these kinds of actions and approaches that we seek to document in this book to provide examples, ideas, and hope for writing studies practitioners to take up moving forward with their future research, teaching, and editing.

Heuristics

In considering ways to help writing studies colleagues with this future work, we offer heuristics. As we contend throughout this book, IP decisions are complex and contextual and, therefore, cannot be resolved with a simple checklist or flowchart; thus, examples of practitioners thinking through their IP decisions are crucial. We see heuristic questions as a next step in practically applying insights gained from these reflections. In providing these heuristics, we again turn to the work of IP scholar Martine Courant Rife. Just as her research on the power of myths about IP law ("Copyright") serves as a useful frame for our project's focus on scholars' reflections (rather than just the law), her work to create a "fair use heuristic for the use of the visual" to guide writing studies scholars' use of images ("Ideas" 148–50) serves as a productive framework for ways in which scholars might move forward based on these reflections. In "Ideas Toward a Fair Use Heuristic: Visual Rhetoric and Composition," Rife works to establish "some basic guidelines" based on her analysis of four "key" court cases regarding the copyright of visual material (148, 138). We follow her lead here in offering heuristics to readers. Though we offer prompting questions rather than declarative statements, we likewise endeavor to provide guidance based on analysis of findings from our survey responses and interviews. We organize these questions by the foci of our chapters: ethical lenses, sponsors, and steps of academic knowledge-making.

First, in Table 6.1 we offer questions for writing studies practitioners to answer in considering the ethical lenses they apply—or might apply—in making IP decisions.

As an example of how these questions can serve as a heuristic to help guide writing studies practitioners' future IP choices with attention to

Table 6.1 Heuristic Questions for Ethical Lenses

Lens	*Questions*
IP as part of business practice	• Is this IP decision situated in a business or an educational context (or both)? What are the unique considerations of each context? • To what extent is it appropriate or useful to treat higher education as a business in making this decision? • To what extent is it appropriate or useful to treat higher education as distinct from business in making this decision?
IP as part of economic systems	• What are the economic consequences of making this IP decision? What are the gains and costs? To whom? • What, if any, financial benefits will I or others receive from making this decision? To what extent are these benefits reasonable and useful? • What, if any, financial benefits will I or others lose from making this decision? To what extent are these losses reasonable and useful? • In what ways will the labor associated with this decision be funded? By whom?
IP as fundamental to democracy	• To what extent does this IP decision lead to "the Progress of Science and the useful Arts" (USC, Article I, § 8, Clause 8)? • In what ways does this decision influence the agency of others to have a democratic voice (at local, national, and global levels)? To what extent is preserving this democratic voice useful or appropriate?
IP as protecting individual expertise	• To what extent does this IP decision value and/or protect my individual expertise and the creations that communicate that expertise? • To what extent does this IP decision value and/or protect the individual expertise of others and their creations that communicate that expertise? • To what extent do my or others' creations need to be protected?

Lens	*Questions*
IP as part of ethical systems	• In what ethical systems do I participate (e.g., religious, disciplinary, military)? • In what ways is this IP decision consistent with or divergent from the conventions or guidelines of those ethical systems? • To what extent am I comfortable with these consistencies or divergences? • In what ways does this IP decision affect my ethos (i.e., my credibility and honor)?
IP as collective development of a culture	• In what cultures is this IP decision situated? • In what ways can and should those cultures and their beliefs (particularly about property, authorship, and ownership) be valued? • To what extent is making decisions that abide by or challenge US law useful and appropriate? • What assumptions does this decision reflect for who can own property and for what purposes?
IP as about disciplinary relationships	• What disciplinary relationships does this IP decision affect and in what ways? • To what extent are these consequences useful and appropriate? In what ways will they affect future scholarly, teaching, and editing work in writing studies (and its subfields)? • What disciplinary beliefs/stances about (co)authorship and ownership does this decision reflect?

the ethical lenses they use or might use, we apply them to one of the vignettes from our introduction:

> A faculty member is considering whether to publish a textbook. On one hand, they[2] need the financial boost (and CV line for promotion) that a successful textbook would provide. On the other hand, their materials were inspired by documents openly shared by colleagues in their program. They debate about their responsibilities to those who have developed materials before them.

Using the heuristic questions provided, this author would consider the disciplinary relationships affected by publishing a textbook that draws on materials shared by colleagues in their program. To answer the question *What disciplinary relationships does this IP decision affect and in what ways?*, the author would note that these relationships would include not only program colleagues, but also their department/program chair as well as potential readers/users of the textbook. To answer *To what extent are these consequences useful and appropriate?* and *In what ways will they affect future scholarly, teaching, and editing work in writing studies (and its subfields)?* the author would consider that these stakeholders might appreciate having their materials adapted and shared with attribution but decry not being compensated financially for their work.

This heuristic would also ask the author to think about approaches to collaborative authorship and Fair Use valued by writing studies as a discipline. In answering the question *What disciplinary beliefs/stances about (co)authorship and ownership does this decision reflect?*, the author would note that collaborative authorship is generally valued in the discipline and is itself considered an area of scholarship inquiry, but that tenure and promotion decisions, at least at most research-oriented institutions but even increasingly at teaching institutions as well, are frequently based on the publication of IP attributed to a single individual. The author then might consider a range of ways to acknowledge their colleagues' contributions, from making them co-authors to citing their materials to working only with materials published to more public audiences. While other questions from the heuristic provided might be asked as well, this hypothetical example helps to show in what ways this heuristic can be useful.

Next, in Table 6.2 we offer questions for writing studies practitioners to answer in considering the human, technological, and institutional sponsors that mediate their IP decisions. (See also Amidon et al.; though they do not explicitly discuss "sponsors," they offer another heuristic for considering the influences of mediating forces in IP decisions.)

As an example of how these questions can serve as a heuristic to help guide writing studies practitioners' future IP choices with attention to the sponsors that mediate their choices, we again apply them to one of the vignettes from our introduction:

> An instructor receives a forwarded email from a student. The email is from an online source that claims a copyright violation because the student has posted a music clip to a website designed for the class. The student's final project—a remixed visual essay analyzing a current political movement—has been removed by an outside entity.

In considering how to advise this student, this instructor would use the heuristic provided to ask *What people are my sources of information or*

Table 6.2 Heuristic Questions for IP Sponsors

Type of Sponsor	*Questions*
Human	• What people are my sources of information or guidance about IP for this decision? • What are these people's motivations in offering information or guidance? What are their sources of information about IP? • In what ways do their guidance or information facilitate or thwart my work? • What are consequences of following their guidance or basing my decision on their information?
Technological	• What technologies are involved in this IP decision? • What beliefs about IP do these technologies instantiate? What treatment of my IP do I agree to by using these technologies? • What do these technologies encourage or allow me to do with my IP? What do they discourage or prevent? • What are their possible motivations for treating my IP this way? • To what extent does this treatment of my IP facilitate or thwart my work? To what extent am I comfortable with this treatment of my IP?
Institutional	• What institutions are involved in this IP decision? • What treatment of my IP do I agree to by aligning or affiliating with these institutions? • What do these institutions encourage or allow me to do with my IP? What do they discourage or prevent? • What are their possible motivations in treating my IP this way? • To what extent does this treatment of my IP facilitate or thwart my work? To what extent am I comfortable with this treatment of my IP?

guidance about IP for this decision?, What technologies are involved in this IP decision?, and *What institutions are involved in this IP decision?* Upon identifying these sponsors, the instructor would then ask additional questions in order to decide who or what to trust and follow: *What are these people's motivations in offering information or guidance?, What are their sources of information about IP?, What beliefs about IP do these technologies instantiate?, What treatment of my IP do I agree to by using these technologies?*, and *What treatment of my IP do I agree to by aligning or affiliating with these institutions?* These questions would allow the instructor to ascertain motivations of these knowledge sources to understand better why they might share the information or offer the guidance that they do.

Likewise, the instructor would consider the online source's motivations as an IP sponsor. Why did they remove the project before issuing a takedown notice? Must this action be accepted? Answering the heuristic questions *What are consequences of following these people's guidance or basing my decision on their information?*, *What do these institutions encourage or allow me to do with my IP?*, and *What do these technologies encourage or allow me to do with my IP?* would also help the instructor consider possible consequences of response options. For the instructor, these response actions might entail encouraging the student to repost the project and make an argument that using the music constitutes Fair Use, challenging the online entity that removed the project (instead of encouraging the student to do so), or advising the student simply to accept the takedown. Answering these questions could help the instructor reflect on what view of IP these response options signal and, in turn, communicate to the student—as well as which approach to IP they wish to privilege. For instance, reposting the project and making a Fair Use argument signals a belief in Fair Use as a right—and as a powerful sponsor for making IP decisions. Accepting the takedown and not reposting the project emphasizes the power of the online entity as a gatekeeping sponsor as well as recognizes the time and effort involved in challenging claims of copyright violation. With the heuristic question *To what extent does this treatment of my IP facilitate or thwart my work?*, the instructor would also consider their own motivations as a human sponsor advising the student: Why do they want the student to respond in a particular way? What course of action is best for the student? To what extent is this different than what is best for the instructor?

Finally, in Table 6.3 we offer heuristic questions for writing studies practitioners to answer in considering the sites and times of IP decisions in their academic knowledge-making processes.

As an example of how these questions can serve as a heuristic to help guide writing studies practitioners' future IP choices with attention to the processes of academic knowledge-making in which they engage, we again apply them to one of the vignettes from our introduction:

> A newly hired adjunct is given an employment contract to sign, a contract that includes work-for-hire claims over teaching materials, including materials for online courses.

Using the heuristic questions provided, this contingent faculty member would ask *Who owns the copyright to the materials I have created?*, *What are the stipulations of my contract?*, and *What is my university's intellectual property policy?* These questions would allow the contingent faculty member to determine who owns the copyright to their teaching materials. They would likely find that, in such a work-for-hire arrangement, the institution of higher education would, in most instances, be the copyright holder. The contingent faculty member would then use this heuristic to ask *To what extent am I comfortable with these conditions?* For instance, does the faculty member plan to publish them (in a textbook, in a journal

Table 6.3 Heuristic Questions for Steps of the Academic Knowledge-Making Cycle

Steps	*Questions*
Choosing topics and texts to study and teach	• In what ways are my choices of what to do for this research project or this course based on IP concerns? • To what extent are these concerns based in the law? To what extent are these concerns well founded? Or are they based in myths? • If I cannot teach or research as I intend, what macro- and micro-level alternatives are available? • What would I teach or research differently were the IP I need and/or the IP I produce to be freely available?
Collecting data and materials	• Will I be able to access the materials I need to in order to complete this academic knowledge-making work? • What will be the financial and labor costs of accessing these materials or securing permissions to use them? • Who can I contact to find out the answers to these questions?
Negotiating procedures and products for publication	• Who will own the copyright to what I am publishing (e.g., me, the journal, the publisher, the editor)? • To what extent am I happy with the terms of my publishing contract? What are consequences of accepting them? • To what extent can I propose alternative terms? If I can, what would those terms be? • What concessions or restrictions are reasonable to accept in order to publish as I want or need to (e.g., for tenure and promotion, for work to appear in a high-impact journal or press)? • What are possible consequences if I refuse to publish as stipulated?
Disseminating and storing texts	• How do I want my IP to be available to others (e.g., by OA, under Creative Commons licenses, in high-profile closed journals)? • What are consequences of this decision? • In what ways will my IP be protected based on where it is stored? To whom will it be available for use?

(*Continued*)

Table 6.3 (Continued)

Steps	*Questions*
Employing materials and technologies in face-to-face and digital classes	• To whom are my course materials accessible? • Who owns the copyright to the materials I have created? What are the stipulations of my contract? What is my university's or employer's intellectual property policy? • To what extent am I comfortable with these conditions? • For what changes, if any, do I want to argue to have the copyright ownership of teaching materials that I desire?

article)? Are they teaching at other universities where they plan to use these same materials? If so, would that be permissible? Do they want to share their materials more freely or have them more protected than the ways the institution allows? In what ways would their teaching materials continue to be used by the university in their absence? Would these materials be attributed to them?

The faculty member might then consider what changes they would ask for in the contract by answering the heuristic question *For what changes do I want to argue to have the copyright ownership of teaching materials that I desire?* These changes might include a stipulation that they are permitted to use the same teaching materials elsewhere or to publish them. If the faculty member chose to accept and sign the contract, they would use the question *In what ways are my choices of what to do for this class based on IP concerns?* to decide what texts and topics they would want to teach and to what extent they would change these based on the terms of the employment contract. More specifically, the contingent faculty member might then consider if there are curricular units or particular handouts or lessons over which they would not want their employer to have copyright ownership. Applying this heuristic to this example helps to illustrate that writing studies practitioners need not answer these questions in the order in which they are provided (i.e., in the order of steps of the academic knowledge-making cycle that we present in Chapter 5). As these steps are recursive, practitioners can ask and answer these questions in whatever order makes most sense for their IP decisions.

Future Trajectories of IP

In this next section of the conclusion, we continue to look at the future, particularly to consider the future developments of IP. IP will continue to evolve. Thus, in this section we address three future trajectories of

IP that make crucial an awareness of the ethical lenses available to guide IP decisions, the sponsors that mediate IP decisions, and the aspects of the knowledge-making cycle affected by IP decisions. There are certainly more issues than the three identified here that we might discuss, but these three trends strike us as especially important for writing studies practitioners.

Nonhuman Agents

One future trajectory is nonhuman agents becoming authors/copyright holders. The 2017 monkey selfie case (*Naruto et al. v. Slater*) provides an example. This case raises questions about whether animals and, by extension, other nonhuman agents can (or should) be able to copyright texts they "create," as well as what roles the digital tools used in textual creation play in how copyright is assigned. That the Ninth Circuit Court of Appeals refused to throw out this case precisely because this is a "developing area of the law" (*Naruto et al. v. Slater* 2) suggests that future copyright decisions will need to contend with these issues.

Naruto et al. v. Slater is a case of monkeys and money, cameras and creativity. In this case, PETA (People for the Ethical Treatment of Animals) sued photographer David J. Slater on behalf of Naruto, a crested macaque from Indonesia who, in 2011, took a selfie photo with Slater's camera. Slater had copyrighted the photo in the United Kingdom, his place of residence, and, upon seeing it published on the Web, asked that it be taken down (Propen 10, Jiang). The publishing websites refused. Among other places, the photo was published to Wikipedia, which contended the photo was not copyrightable because it was taken by an animal, and animals cannot own copyrights. Wikipedia reasoned that the photo was, therefore, part of the public domain (Stewart).

PETA, however, took a different stance. PETA argued Naruto's copyright (rather than Slater's copyright) was infringed by this republishing of the photo (Berlinger). Slater did not agree. He argued his company, Wildlife Personalities Ltd., for whom he was on assignment when the photo was taken, owned the "worldwide commercial rights" to the photo because it was taken with Slater's camera. US District Judge William Orrick III ultimately ruled in favor of Slater, concluding that "while Congress and the President can extend the protection of law to animals as well as humans, there is no indication that they did so in the Copyright Act" (Osborne). PETA appealed, but the case was ultimately settled out of court, so the appeal did not proceed. Amy D. Propen reports that, as a result, who ultimately owns the copyright in such a situation (where a nonhuman actor is a major agent) is unclear, as different media outlets have reported different outcomes (12).[3] Slater's website signals his belief that he (still) owns the copyright. At the time of this writing, Slater continues to "assert" "his right to be identified as the author of all images published" on the website, including Naruto's selfie. (Slater, however, refers to the macaque as "Ella" rather than "Naruto," the name PETA used.) Slater's website includes the copyright symbol along with the photo. He also includes hyperlinked text where readers are directed to "Click to read the original story about how I created my famous monkey 'selfie.'" His use of "I created" and "my" to reference the photo emphatically affirms his claim to copyright ownership.

The *Naruto v. Slater* case highlights the range of entities that are and can become sponsors in making IP decisions. In this ruling, PETA, Wildlife Personalities Ltd., Judge Orrick III, the US Constitution, and even Wikipedia/Wikimedia all served as sponsors. PETA, upon learning that Slater published photos of Naruto in his book *Wildlife Personalities*, argued that Naruto be assigned copyright because nonhuman animals are protected by US copyright law. In particular, PETA, invoking the next friend principle (which allows people to file a lawsuit for someone else who is not able to do so), argued that it should be permitted to use proceeds from the sale of the photos to fundraise for Naruto and other macaques (Kravets). Additionally, Wikipedia acted as a sponsor in arguing that the images are not copyrightable because they were taken by a nonhuman and, therefore, fall in the public domain. Judge Orrick also became a sponsor in offering his ruling that nonhuman agents are not covered by US copyright law, which he based, at least in part, on another mediating sponsor, the US Constitution. We anticipate that future cases will likewise call attention to the complex interrelationships of human, technological, and institutional sponsors. Thus, we profess that the field's understanding of IP sponsors must be broadened to account for nonhuman agents.

Artificial Intelligence and Bots

Animals are not the only nonhuman agents for whom IP, particularly copyright, issues will arise in the future. The work of writing studies practitioners is ever more dependent on digital technologies that increasingly rely on artificial intelligence (AI) and robots (bots). By complicating notions of authorship and ownership, these new technologies complicate what IP is and means. Carl Whithaus, for instance, noted in his interview, "I don't know that four years ago that we would have had a discussion about Tumblr in relationship to IP, but now you have to have a discussion about Tumblr, so I doubt that it's something I could have known beforehand." Indeed, knowing ethical lenses for approaching IP, sponsors that mediate IP decisions, and points in the knowledge-making cycle affected by IP is crucial precisely because the pace of technological development makes it impossible to know everything about IP "beforehand." Writing studies practitioners frequently encounter new rhetorical situations that call upon new IP decisions.

Take the case of AI and bots. The *Naruto v. Slater* case suggests that the question of whether nonhuman agents are authors—and, therefore, can be owners of copyright—is contestable, which applies to questions of whether the AI and bot algorithms that are part of the digital writing and publishing landscape can (or should) be seen as authors or own property. In short, does AI get to have IP? The answer has significant consequences as the digital spaces where writing studies professionals compose, circulate, and read texts often involve AI. Heidi A. McKee and James E. Porter assert, "More frequently than people realize, our communications are occurring not just with fellow humans but with AI agents" (*Professional* 2). Jialei Jiang addresses this issue by using the *Naruto v. Slater* case to devise a framework for thinking about distributed authorship. Timothy R. Amidon and Jessica Reyman likewise provide an example in their analysis of social media, particularly regarding ways in which the terms of service of social media position users as owners of their content but not of their data. Though they do not use language of AI explicitly, they argue for seeing social media activities, including automatically generated "content-related" and "site-specific" data, as co-authored between users and social media sites, including their bots (110–12, 118). While the thrust of their argument is that users should have ownership of, and thereby access to, the data they generate through social media activities, one implication of their argument is that the AI that serves to co-author social media content and data would, even should, also have a claim to copyright ownership of that content and data.

Other scholars have likewise explored the increasing presence and role of bots as producers and consumers of texts. Bill Hart-Davidson, Mike McLeod, and Jeff Grabill, in their section of the article "Computers and Composition 20/20: A Conversation Piece, or What Some Very Smart People Have to Say about the Future," quip, "You see, the robots are coming. And they want us to tell them what to do" (Walker et al. 336). James Grimmelmann, in "Copyright for Literate Robots," argues that the robots are already here, and copyright law is working to account for them—or, as he argues, not account for them. He contends that "copyright law has concluded that it is for humans only: reading performed by computers doesn't count as infringement" (656). Law scholar Amir H. Khoury agrees in arguing that IP laws should not apply to what Khoury call "Hubots," or "Human-Like Robots," as Hubots are "equivalent to things found in nature" (636). For him, their creations should "forever rest in the public domain" (668). The parallel of this logic with the monkey selfie case decision is striking: Naruto, as a monkey and, therefore, a thing "found in nature," was likewise found not to have IP rights and, according to Wikipedia at least, her creations should be part of the public domain. While the consistency of these positions might suggest that the possibility for AI and bots to be treated as copyright owners is closed, we think this question is far from decided, especially as humans play a direct role in designing AI and bots, a point Khoury addresses only indirectly in labeling humans as "masters" of Hubots (636).

Grimmelmann eloquently summarizes what is at stake in considering bot IP. He declares, "paying attention to robotic readership refocuses our attention on the really fundamental questions: what is copyright, and what is it for? To say that human readers count and robots don't is to say something deep about the nature of reading as a social practice, and about what we want robots—and humans—to be" (681). These stakes could not be higher. As a discipline, writing studies is invested in treating reading and writing as social practices as well as in respecting and preserving the agency of people. Therefore, following Grimmelmann's logic, members of the field would seem to support that bots should not be seen as agents and, therefore, not as capable of owning texts or copyright. Yet the popularity and impact of writing studies scholarship drawing on actor network theory and materialist rhetorics, which affirm the role, power, and agency of nonhuman tools and technologies, complicates this position.

Thus, we contend that questions of copyright's applicability to bots are only beginning and will increasingly become an issue when considering robots as writers as well as readers. Bots already write content for both Facebook and Twitter. For instance, Russian bots wrote material for Facebook in the 2016 presidential election (Shane) and continue to produce anti-vaccination messages on Twitter (Johnson). Meme generators create and circulate memes (Vie). And, as Krista Kennedy has discussed, bots write articles in Wikipedia. As scholars in writing studies, we need to be prepared to address the role of bots and AI in writing and reading activities, including what it means to see them as authors and copyright holders (or not). The heuristic questions we offer in this book provide a means of responding to and preparing for this thorny issue—and those that we cannot yet envision.

If computer programming, such as that behind AI and bot technologies, becomes a literacy, or part of our broader definition of literacy, as Annette Vee argues it might (or even should), then the decision of whether code-driven creations like AI and bots can own IP will have massive consequences. Indeed, her assertion that "ignorance about code" has real legal consequences, including for IP (210, 221–23), will only be amplified in the future, as coding decisions are increasingly and inextricably bound up in IP decisions—and vice versa. Vee explains, for instance, that existing IP law in the US allows software processes to be patented, which can "bar others from writing code." She elaborates, "The aggressive behavior of so-called patent trolls and companies who vigorously defend their patents with cease-and-desist letters threatening costly legal battles can make it potentially dangerous for people to write and publish code" (222). Vee's concern here is that possibilities for coding literacy will, therefore, be stifled because such "[o]verbearing intellectual property laws are well-known barriers to accessing raw materials for any creative endeavor, including programming" (222). We would add that such laws can likewise serve as barriers to meaning making for writing studies practitioners and, by extension, the students they teach.

Licensing

Another future trajectory of IP important to writing studies professionals is the increasing role of licensing. Much of the infrastructure with which writing studies practitioners now work is licensed rather than owned. Specialized course management and multimedia authoring software require licenses. Ebooks and database subscriptions require licenses. To do their daily work, writing studies practitioners (or the institutions or organizations where they work) must pay licensing fees and agree to stipulated terms of use. For instance, Adobe's website, image, and video authoring software programs (e.g., Dreamweaver, Photoshop, Illustrator), which are frequently used by writing studies practitioners to create multimodal and multimedia webtexts, are now available only through the Adobe Creative Cloud via a subscription-based license, which is tied to a particular device or to a particular institutional site ("Creative"). People can no longer purchase CDs or digital downloads of this software (at least to use the most current versions). Thus, in order to continue projects that depend on these software programs, writing studies practitioners must continue to re-up their subscriptions to renew their licenses for use. Otherwise, they risk being unable to access or continue their work.

The University of California State System of Higher Education's termination of its contract with Elsevier, which we discuss in Chapter 2, serves as a cautionary example. The UC System, like many colleges and universities, paid an annual licensing fee for its faculty and students to access scholarly databases published and hosted by Elsevier. The system did not purchase physical copies of these texts but rather paid for the right to access them, paying millions of US dollars for those materials over time. Fortunately, the licensing agreements between the UC System and Elsevier contained clauses guaranteeing perpetual access to most issues of journals purchased by the end of 2018. When the UC System terminated its contract with Elsevier in Spring 2019, its faculty and students lost access to only some of the licensed materials (McKenzie, "UC"). However, as of this writing, one of the conditions under contention is whether the UC System will need "to forgo perpetual access to a significant number of Elsevier journals" (Office of Scholarly Communication, "Open").

Such licensing makes time a commodity. With licensing, what users pay for is the distribution of certain software, databases, or content to them and the opportunity to access these materials for a particular period of time. Therefore, users become subscribers rather than owners. In this way, such licensing privileges access and distribution over ownership. Those who purchase Adobe Creative Cloud do not own a physical or digital product. They simply have the privilege to access it—as long as they continue to pay. Those who access eBooks through their college or university library can read those books only for a specified period of time—until they are automatically "returned" (i.e., the access period is up) and as long as the college or university continues to pay the vendor who distributes the books. The institution may pay higher fees upfront for perpetual access to the materials, but those agreements depend on some distributor being able to provide a system to be accessed. What happens if the distributor is, as in the case of Elsevier, no longer interested in providing perpetual access, or becomes no longer solvent or is sold? Those answers, too, must be negotiated, and we predict that scholars should anticipate new layers of IP complications as licensed materials are shuffled to new servers and copyright holders, and access to these materials is similarly shuffled. Thus, as IP comes less and less to be physically or digitally owned, the role ownership plays in our understanding of IP will potentially shift. This diminishing role of ownership flies in the face of US IP law, which is based on the notion that IP is property whose copyright can be individually owned. New legislation may consider more directly the role of licensing in IP.

Especially pertinent to our audience, this shift also flies in the face of many US college and university reward structures. Tenure and promotion decisions, as well as intellectual property policies, for most research-oriented institutions are based on the production of IP for which the ownership is clearly ascertainable. For example, though scholars from multiple disciplines, including writing studies, have argued otherwise, the gold standard for tenure and promotion at many research institutions continues to be the single authored print monograph—a product for which the copyright owner can be easily determined (whether it is the author or, more likely, the publisher). We proffer that this shift from ownership to access/distribution brought about by increased reliance on licensing could—and should—compel changes in the kinds of IP colleges and universities privilege and the ways they conceive of and measure the value of IP—less by its form (e.g., as a print book) and more by its distribution (e.g., how frequently it is accessed, reused, or cited). Gabriela Raquel Ríos and Donnie Johnson Sackey's discussion of biocultural diversity as offering an alternative lens for understanding IP in a way that is more respectful of indigenous populations seems especially relevant here. By applying their call for an approach to understanding IP that does not measure IP in terms of textual production (220–21) to a different context (academic reward structures rather than indigenous populations) we want to be careful not to appropriate or misapply their work. However, we contend that considering the value of IP to be more than just a thing produced that can be sold both allows for respecting indigenous populations' perspectives on IP that look beyond monetary valuation and allows for broadening academic institutions' understanding of what and how IP should be counted for tenure and promotion decisions, merit raises, and course reappointed time. That is, embracing a more inclusive approach to IP potentially benefits both indigenous populations and academics at Western academic institutions, including writing studies practitioners.

What We Learned from Writing This Book: Our Own Ethical Lenses, Sponsors, and Knowledge-Making Cycle Decisions

We close this book with two reflections: one on our own IP decisions and experiences in writing this book and another on what we might call the politics of IP. In a book about the influences of IP on academic work in writing studies, we would be remiss in not discussing some of own IP choices. As we have emphasized throughout this book the value of reflections in helping writing studies practitioners learn to make decisions regarding IP, we offer our own reflections on the process of writing the book. In particular, we identify the IP issues that we encountered.

Perhaps the most visible IP decision we made was to publish with a closed, for-profit publisher, Routledge. This choice may seem ironic given the findings of our study, which include that writing studies practitioners are sometimes thwarted in their academic work because of such publishers and that many of the participants we surveyed and interviewed support OA publishing. We published with Routledge, however, for several reasons. First, there is precedent for doing so for IP scholarship in writing studies. Jessica Reyman's *The Rhetoric of Intellectual Property: Copyright Law and the Regulation of Digital Culture*, a foundational work of scholarship on IP in the field, is also published with Routledge, and we see our book as a companion text to Reyman's. Thus, it seemed advantageous to pursue the same publishing opportunity. Second, we wanted the book to be recognized for promotion decisions. For better or for worse, we both felt we had the best chance of this book "counting" for promotion at our respective institutions if we published with a respected academic publisher, even if that publisher did not publish the work OA. We did have the opportunity to pay to make one of the book chapters OA. Yet, because this cost was not covered by our institutions and, therefore, was a significant out-of-pocket expense, we, applying the ethical lenses IP as part of economic systems and IP as about disciplinary relationships, decided not to do so. However, we also resolved to balance this choice with a commitment to make openly accessible other scholarship based on this research. To that end, we have published about our study in the fully OA journal *Kairos: A Journal of Rhetoric, Technology, and*

Pedagogy (Lunsford and Purdy). Moreover, we have each also published other scholarship in OA venues (e.g., *Across the Disciplines*, *First Monday*).

In addition to our IP decision regarding where to publish our book, we also encountered several gatekeeping sponsors during our research. For instance, Jim, though he teaches at Duquesne University, was unable to access the *Duquesne Law Review* through the University's library holdings for articles written by Jacob H. Rooksby (previously also a faculty member at Duquesne)—while Karen was able to access it through the University of California library system. Karen, however, encountered her own problems with gatekeeping sponsors. As a faculty member at the University of California Santa Barbara, she was threatened with losing access to materials published by Elsevier when the UC System decided not to renew its contract with Elsevier in March 2019 (McKenzie "UC"). As a member of the editorial board for *Computers and Composition*, which is published by Elsevier, she was then faced with the difficult decision of whether she should remain on the editorial board. Both of us also had tremendous difficulty accessing *The SAGE Handbook of Intellectual Property* (David and Halbert)—even at research universities—without purchasing it for $185.

In addition to our IP decisions regarding where to publish the book and how to work with gatekeeping sponsors of particular research sources, we also decided what content to include in the book based on IP concerns. In particular, we redacted information from quotations and left out examples to protect the identity of respondents and interviewees who we felt could potentially be identified. In these instances, we privileged the ethical lens of IP as about disciplinary relationships to protect colleagues (whether known personally to us or not) who we believed could suffer negative consequences based on information they disclosed, even though study participants knew we would be using the material provided for our study and signed permissions forms. In some cases, we felt removing this material lessened the impact of examples or arguments, but we felt compelled to prevent any possible negative repercussions for our study participants, even if the possibility of those repercussions was slight. These choices speak to the power (we might say the chilling effect) of punishments for potential copyright violations—even for us, scholars who know more about IP than others and who feel confident in making Fair Use defenses.

During our publication process, we also encountered a nascent IP issue that we anticipate other writing scholars (and humanities scholars more generally) will need to develop strategies for resolving: a trend among academic and university presses to issue blanket bans on using epigraphs in front of articles and chapters. Indeed, the checklist of author guidelines for this book stated that any epigraphs should be removed because they often elicit copyright issues and litigation. Anecdotally, we know that such blanket bans are being adopted elsewhere, as Jim had encountered a similar ban when publishing a journal article, and academic colleagues have alerted us to their own experiences with negotiating these restrictions. In the case of our book, we were able to argue successfully that the chapter epigraphs are quotations from our dataset and thus unlikely to cause copyright concerns. Given these experiences, we are now beginning to research what led major IP sponsors like scholarly presses to overturn an academic argumentation practice that is centuries old.

Of course, the overall IP decision driving this book is our sense that writing studies scholars benefit from being more aware of the ways in which IP choices are enculturated into academic knowledge-making practices, that this is a topic worth researching and teaching. In turn, they benefit from having a toolkit of ethical lenses to apply in making IP decisions, knowledge of the multiple kinds of IP sponsors that can facilitate or thwart academic work, and understanding of the multiple sites and times throughout the academic knowledge-making processes when IP choices wield influence. That is why we wrote this book.

The Politics of IP

In our introductory chapter, we reference Lawrence Lessig's run for president of the United States to demonstrate the centrality of IP in our current cultural moment. To conclude, we turn again to a story that connects IP, particularly copyright, and the presidential office of the United States. The Register of Copyrights Selection and Accountability Act (Senate Bill 1010, House Bill 1695) was proposed in 2017 to "amend[] federal copyright law to require the President, with the advice and consent of the Senate, to appoint a Register of Copyrights." In other words, the bill gives the president, rather than the librarian of Congress, the authority to appoint the register of copyrights.

While the shift may seem incidental, we believe it is not. As Lisa Peet reports in *Library Journal*, critics of the bill, which include the American Library Association, the Library Copyright Alliance, and the Society of American Archivists, contend it "will give the executive branch too much power over the Copyright Office" and, therefore, "the interests of commercial stakeholders, such as the entertainment industry, would be disproportionately represented." This shift, in other words, further serves to make IP legislation and policy attuned to industry rather than to education. However, supporters of the bill, including the Association of American Publishers, the Authors Guild, and numerous entertainment industry groups, praise the bill for making the register of copyrights accountable to Congress (Peet).

We agree with the Electronic Frontier Foundation's (EFF's) position that this change converts a "non-political job" to a "political appointee" (Harmon). One might suggest that the EFF's objection would be less vehement were a Democratic rather than Republican president in office at the time this legislation is being considered. However, this move to align the register of copyrights—and arguably by extension the Copyright Office—with a political agenda of any persuasion (Democrat or Republican) has potentially troubling implications. While the EFF's characterization of the register of copyrights as currently "apolitical" is perhaps overstated or naive, their point that converting the position into a presidential appointee makes it "highly partisan" and the Copyright Office "another political bargaining chip" likely is not. The register of copyrights has two primary responsibilities: "[R]egistering copyrightable works and providing information on copyright law to the government" ("Don't"). When this work is aligned with a particular political agenda, it potentially threatens the rights of creators and users of IP, and privileges the rights of distributors and publishers. Most pressing from our perspective is that the needs of educational institutions, including faculty and students who engage in knowledge production, are likely minimized. Though writing studies practitioners may be unable to combat the lobbying strength of the entertainment industries to change this or other bills, they can educate themselves about the ways in which IP affects their knowledge-making practices, be cognizant of the ethical lenses they can apply in making informed and proactive IP decisions, and recognize the many sponsors that mediate the IP decisions that they can make. Moreover, the success of the outcry against other IP legislation, including SOPA (the Stop Online Piracy Act, HR 3261) and PIPA (the Preventing Real Online Threats to Economic Creativity and Theft of Intellectual Property Act, or Protect IP Act, S 968), suggests that being an outspoken voice can matter.

Applying the heuristics we offer in this conclusion to make arguments to elected representatives and university administration about such bills—as well as about the IP of software, data, AI, and nonhuman agents and tools—is an important step in protecting academic work in writing studies for the future. Part of our argument in this book is that the multifaceted and complex nature of IP precludes a one-size-fits-all answer to all IP decisions. Thus, we cannot offer here what those arguments should be. They are contingent, based on a variety of historical, social, infrastructural, and other contextual forces, including those we outline in Chapters 2, 3, 4, and 5. However, we do contend that writing studies practitioners can take several steps to make better arguments to support an approach to IP education and scholarship that values, promotes, and protects writing and writers:

- Understand the histories of IP, including its competing Anglo-American and Continental models—as well as the existence of other non-Western approaches.

- Recognize and apply the various ethical lenses available for approaching IP decisions, including democratic, economic, business, non-Western, religious, disciplinary, and relational perspectives.
- Identify and engage (or avoid) the human, institutional, and technological sponsors that mediate IP decisions.
- Recognize and attend to the multiple aspects of academic knowledge-making affected by IP decisions, from selecting topics to research and teach to selecting or creating venues to publish the products of scholarly work.

More broadly, we need to continue to gather and record examples of writing studies practitioners thinking through IP decisions so that members of the field have examples, like those we provide in this book. One particular area where such models are lacking is how to go about protecting copyright if someone feels that their copyright has been violated. There is more work to do.

While the evolving and complex nature of IP and IP law can frustrate and overwhelm, we profess that this dynamism of IP opens up opportunities for response and intervention. If IP were static, writing studies practitioners would have little agency. As members of a discipline already especially attuned to process, writing studies practitioners are well positioned to study, engage, and shape the ever-evolving entity that is IP.

Notes

1. CCCC, NCTE, and RSA are the Conference on College Composition and Communication, the National Council of Teachers of English, and the Rhetoric Society of America, respectively, the major professional organizations with which writing studies professionals are affiliated.
2. As we note in earlier chapters, we use *they* as an inclusive singular pronoun.
3. There are other inconsistencies in the coverage of this case. For example, the Associated Press reports that "Slater and PETA announced in September that they had reached a settlement under which Slater agreed to donate 25 percent of any future revenue from the images to charities dedicated to protecting crested macaques in Indonesia," whereas Slater's own website declares, "As of July 2017, I will be donating 10% of your purchase [of photographs of the macaques] towards a monkey conservation project in Sulawesi."

Appendix A
Survey Questions

SurveyMonkey was used to host the following survey. The first two screens presented the informed consent information. The definitions of intellectual property and permissions appeared at the top of the first question:

We are interested in learning how emergent practices involving intellectual property may be affecting teachers-scholars and editors in writing studies. "Intellectual property" refers to copyrights, patents, trademarks, and trade secrets/proprietary knowledge. We are interested in hearing about both print and digital practices.

"Permissions" are fees paid to the owners of copyrights, patents, trademarks, and trade secrets/proprietary knowledge to allow the reuse of materials in your own works. For example, you may need to pay permission fees to an archive to allow the reprint of a certain image or a letter held by that archive. Or you may pay permission fees to a publisher to reprint a text or a dataset or a proprietary survey in your own work. Sometimes, these fees are paid to the IP holder directly; sometimes, they are negotiated through your own publisher.

Questions 1–9: Costs Associated with Permissions and Open-Access Fees

This question refers to publications OTHER THAN textbooks.

1. Have you ever had to pay (personally, and/or through funding from your institution or external source) to secure permissions to include material in a publication(s)? Please consider all potential types of print or digital material: images, audio/video clips, epigraphs or other quoted text, proprietary data or survey protocols, etc.
   Yes/No
2. If permissions had to be paid for, which types of materials were involved? (Check all that apply. Include all publications except for textbooks.)

   ___ Audio clip
   ___ Epigraph (i.e., a quotation used before or after your main text)

___ Font (any proprietary font type, whether print or digital)
___ Image (e.g., any still image—photograph, artwork, figure, table, etc.)
___ Proprietary data
___ Readings or reprints (i.e., Full or lengthy passages from previously published materials)
___ Quotation (within your main text, endnotes/footnotes, appendices)
___ Survey protocol (e.g., any copyrighted survey questions or protocols)
___ Video clip
___ Other (please specify) ______________________

3. If permissions had to be paid for, please estimate the TOTAL amounts for all of your publications (except textbooks) from the following sources. We would like to know your career totals in US dollars. [Participants could select increments of costs, from $1–$250 through $50,001–above.]

   Estimated total amount you have spent out of pocket
   Estimated total amount your university has provided
   Estimated total amount an external grant agency (agencies) has provided
   Estimated total amount a publisher provided and/or deducted from royalties

4. This question refers to TEXTBOOKS.

   Have you ever had to pay (personally, and/or through funding from your institution or external source) to secure permissions to include material in a textbook(s)? Please consider all potential types of print or digital material: images, audio/video clips, epigraphs or other quoted text, proprietary data or survey protocols, etc.
   Yes/No

5. If permissions had to be paid for, which types of materials were involved? (Check all that apply for all textbooks.)

   ___ Audio clip
   ___ Epigraph (i.e., a quotation used before or after your main text)
   ___ Font (any proprietary font type, whether print or digital)
   ___ Image (e.g., any still image—photograph, artwork, figure, table, etc.)
   ___ Proprietary data
   ___ Readings or reprints (i.e., Full or lengthy passages from previously published materials)
   ___ Quotation (within your main text, endnotes/footnotes, appendices)
   ___ Survey protocol (e.g., any copyrighted survey questions or protocols)

___ Video clip
___ Other (please specify) ________________________________

6. If permissions had to be paid for, please estimate the TOTAL amounts (for all of your textbooks, all editions) from the following sources. We would like to know your career totals in US dollars. [Participants could select increments of costs, from $1–$250 through $50,001–above.]

   Estimated total amount you have spent out of pocket
   Estimated total amount your university has provided
   Estimated total amount an external grant agency (agencies) has provided
   Estimated total amount a publisher provided and/or deducted from royalties

7. Open-access fees are potential charges separate from fees for permissions to replicate published materials. They are required by some publishers if you wish to allow your publication to be free to readers. In some cases, the open-access material is posted by the publisher (on a sponsored website). In other cases, the open-access fees allow you to make your publication available to readers through an institutional repository, a centralized database (such as PubMed), or your own website.

   Have you ever had to pay open-access fees (personally, and/or through funding from your institution or external source) for your publication(s), including textbooks?

   ___ Yes
   ___ No
   ___ I was offered the option, but declined
   ___ I am not certain

8. This question refers to publications OTHER THAN TEXTBOOKS.

   If you have had to pay open-access fees for publications other than textbooks, please estimate the TOTAL amounts for all publications from the following sources. We would like to know your career totals in US dollars. [Participants could select increments of costs, from $1–$250 through $50,001–above.]

   Estimated total amount you have spent out of pocket
   Estimated total amount your university has provided
   Estimated total amount an external grant agency (agencies) has provided

9. This question refers to TEXTBOOKS.

   If you have had to pay open-access fees for a textbook(s), please estimate the TOTAL amounts (for all textbooks, all editions) from the following sources. We would like to know your career totals in US dollars. [Participants could select increments of costs, from $1–$250 through $50,001–above.]

Estimated total amount you have spent out of pocket
Estimated total amount your university has provided
Estimated total amount an external grant agency (agencies) has provided
Estimated total amount a publisher provided and/or deducted from royalties

Questions 10–16: IP Issues and Decisions about Publishing Materials

10. As an author, have you ever done the following (Please check all that apply.)

   ___ Decided NOT to include desired material in a publication because of intellectual property concerns?
   ___ Invoked Fair Use principles in defending use of material in a publication?
   ___ Been unable to include desired material in a publication because of intellectual property concerns (e.g., you were denied publication unless you removed certain material)?
   ___ N/A—None of these apply

   If you checked any of the above besides N/A, please explain ______________________

11. As an editor of a book, journal or other venue, have you ever done the following (Please check all that apply.)

   ___ Asked a contributing author(s) to remove material from a text because of intellectual property concerns
   ___ Decided NOT to include desired material in a publication because of intellectual property concerns without consulting a contributing author(s)
   ___ Involved Fair Use principles in defending use of material in a publication
   ___ Been unable to include desired material in a publication because of intellectual property concerns (e.g., the press refused to go forward with publication unless you removed certain material)
   ___ N/A—I have not been an editor OR none of these apply

   If you checked any of the above besides N/A, please explain ______________________

12. After a piece has been published, have you ever received a take-down notice or complaint from an entity with a claim to intellectual property included in the publication?

    Yes/No
    Please explain____

13. If you have received a take-down notice or complaint, how was the claim resolved? (Please check all that apply)

    ___ The take-down notice or complaint has not been resolved
    ___ I responded to a take-down notice or complaint, and simply never heard from the claimant again
    ___ The take-down notice or complaint was demonstrated to be spurious
    ___ The issue was settled through formal or informal arbitration
    ___ Permissions from the claimed material were subsequently acquired
    ___ The claimed material was altered (e.g., a font was changed, a quotation was shortened or paraphrased, etc.)
    ___ The claimed material was removed
    ___ The publication was retracted
    ___ N/A—have not received a take-down notice or complaint
    ___ Other (please specify) ______________________________

14. As an author or editor, have you ever initiated a take-down notice or other complaint against another entity over IP issues?

    Yes/No
    Please explain____

15. If you initiated an action against another entity over IP issues, what was the outcome? (Please check all that apply)

    ___ The issue has not been resolved
    ___ I have not heard back about my claim
    ___ The issue was settled through formal or informal arbitration
    ___ Permissions for the claimed material were subsequently acquired
    ___ The claimed material was altered (e.g., a font was changed, a quotation was shortened or paraphrased, etc.)
    ___ The claimed material was removed
    ___ The publication was retracted
    ___ N/A—I have not initiated an action against another entity over IP issues
    ___ Other (please specify) ______________________________

16. Has your IRB/Human Subjects review office ever (please check all that apply):

    ___ Asked you to address IP concerns in your research protocol before approval

___ Rejected a research protocol outright based on IP concerns
___ Asked you specifically to address in your research protocol students' copyrights for their own texts
___ Questioned your ability to quote materials provided by participants
___ N/A—I have not submitted a research protocol for review by an IRB/Human Subjects board OR none of these apply

If you checked any of the options besides N/A, please explain the circumstances. Likewise, if your IRB/Human Subjects board has raised any other IP concerns in regard to your protocol, please explain. ______________________________

Questions 17–19: Knowledge and Teaching of IP

17. For these questions, your answers should indicate the knowledge you currently have (i.e., you would not need to ask someone or use Google to find the information): [Participants could check Yes or No for each question.]

    Do you know the four guiding factors in determining Fair Use?
    Do you know how to secure copyright on your own text?
    Do you know who owns the copyright for the teaching materials you create at your university?
    Do you know what to do if you receive a take-down notice or other IP complaint?
    Do you know what to do if you wish to initiate a take-down notice or other IP complaint?
    If you have any comments, please explain ______________

18. These questions address how IP issues affect your teaching (or not): [Participants could check Yes or No for each question.]

    Do you devote instructional time to intellectual property issues (e.g., copyright protections, Fair Use, OA, Creative Commons, patents, trademarks, trade secrets)?
    Have you ever changed course materials because you or someone else raised IP concerns?
    Are you familiar with Creative Commons licenses?
    Have you used Creative Commons licenses for any of your own teaching materials?
    Please explain/provide examples ______________

19. Have you or students in any of your classes encountered problems publishing course projects in online venues because of intellectual property issues? (If yes, please check all that apply for yourself and/or your students.)

___ Blog
___ Course Management System (e.g., Blackboard)
___ Facebook
___ YouTube
___ Website
___ Wikipedia
___ N/A—have not used any online venues or have not encountered problems

Please explain/provide examples/list other venues where problems were encountered ________________________

Question 20: Final Response

20. As you reflect on your career, in what ways have intellectual property concerns shaped your teaching, research-writing practices, and/or your editorial decisions? ________________________

The survey ended with a thank-you screen.

Appendix B

Interview Questions and Transcription Conventions

Questions

Participants were provided with copies of the interview questions prior to the interview, either over email or in person.

1. What is your name?
2. What is your institutional affiliation and position?
3. Tell us the salient part of your IP story. As you reflect on your career, in what notable ways have intellectual property concerns shaped your teaching, research-writing practices, and/or your editorial decisions?
4. What do you think is most important for writing studies teacher-scholars to know about IP?
5. What do you wish you had known before about IP that you know now? Why? What do you still wish you knew?
6. What role should an IRB /Publisher /Teacher take in addressing IP issues?
7. What do you think students should leave writing classes—either first-year writing or writing major classes—knowing about IP, Fair Use, and/or OA? Why?
8. What do you teach students in your classes or programs about IP, Fair Use, and/or OA? Why?
9. Did you receive a take-down notice or challenge to a Fair Use argument for something you published? If so, how did you respond to the notice? What actions did you take? What happened as a result of them? Did you change future actions based on this experience?
10. What materials should CCCC or NCTE develop as a resource for teachers and researchers in explaining IP issues to IRBs/Publisher/CCCC or NCTE members?
11. What should we be teaching the novice members of our field about ways in which to design and implement studies that effectively consider and account for IP concerns?

Transcription Conventions

Transcripts were lightly edited for clarification; for example, we removed some self-corrections, “uhs” and “ums,” and vocal feedback (“umhmm,” “yes”) from the interviews.

‘words’	Words in single quotation marks indicate places where a speaker constructs or ventriloquizes dialogue.
(words)	Words in parentheses indicate uncertainties in the transcription.
[words]	Words in brackets indicate explanatory comments; frequently, they replace pronouns or acronyms.
wor-	A word with a hyphen indicates a self-interruption, except when it is used to indicate a line break.
[. . .]	Bracketed ellipses indicate that words have been deleted.
. . .	Unbracketed ellipses indicate verbal pauses

Appendix C
Interview Participants

Names and affiliations given for participants are as of the time of their interview in 2015. Several participants now have different positions at different institutions.

Table C.1 Interview Participants and Their Institutional Affiliations

Name	*Position(s)*	*Institutional Affiliation*
Timothy R. Amidon	Assistant Professor of English in Rhetoric and Composition	Colorado State University
Damián Baca	Associate Professor of English in the Rhetoric and Composition Program	University of Arizona
Cheryl E. Ball	Associate Professor of Digital Publishing, Editor of *Kairos*	West Virginia University
Patrick W. Berry	Assistant Professor of Writing and Rhetoric, Senior Editor of Computers and Composition Digital Press	Syracuse University
Kristine L. Blair	Professor of English, Editor of *Computers and Composition* and *Computers and Composition Online*	Bowling Green State University
Hugh Burns	Professor Emeritus; Holland H. Coors Endowed Chair in Technology	Texas Woman's University; Air Force Academy
Joyce Locke Carter	Associate Professor of Rhetoric and Technical Communications	Texas Tech University

(*Continued*)

Table C.1 (Continued)

Name	*Position(s)*	*Institutional Affiliation*
Ellen Cushman	Dean's Professor of Civic Sustainability and the Director of Civic Sustainability, Diversity, and Inclusion Initiatives; Editor of *Research in the Teaching of English*	Northeastern University
Michele Eodice	Director of the Writing Center and the Associate Provost for Academic Engagement	University of Oklahoma
Jeffrey R. Galin	Associate Professor of English	Florida Atlantic University
Anne Ruggles Gere	Gertrude Buck Collegiate Professor in the School of Education, Professor of English Language and Literature, Arthur F. Thurnau Professor; Director of the Joint PhD Program in English and Education; and Director of the Sweetland Center for Writing	University of Michigan
Donna J. Kain	Associate Professor of English, Editor of *Technical Communication Quarterly*	East Carolina University
Diane Kelly-Riley	Assistant Professor of English and the Director of Composition, Editor of *The Journal of Writing Assessment*	University of Idaho
Krista Kennedy	Assistant Professor of Composition and Cultural Rhetorics	Syracuse University
John Logie	Associate Professor of Rhetoric	University of Minnesota Twin Cities
Charles Lowe	Associate Professor of Writing	Grand Valley State University
Ben McCorkle	Associate Professor of English and Writing Program Administrator	The Ohio State University, Marion
Cruz Medina	Assistant Professor of Rhetoric and Composition	Santa Clara University

Name	*Position(s)*	*Institutional Affiliation*
Christa J. Olson	Associate Professor of Composition and Rhetoric	University of Wisconsin—Madison
Mike Palmquist	University Distinguished Teaching Scholar, Associate Provost for Instructional Innovation, Professor of English, Editor of the *WAC Clearinghouse*	Colorado State University
Michael A. Pemberton	Professor of Writing and Linguistics, Editor of *Across the Disciplines*	Georgia Southern University
Cynthia L. Selfe	Humanities Distinguished Professor of English	The Ohio State University
Naomi Silver	Associate Director of the Sweetland Center for Writing	University of Michigan
Kyle D. Stedman	Assistant Professor of English	Rockford University
Joonna Smitherman Trapp	Senior Program Coordinator for the Writing Program, Co-editor of *The Journal for the Assembly on Expanded Perspectives on Learning*	Emory University
Bob Whipple	Professor of English	Creighton University
Carl Whithaus	Professor of Writing and Rhetoric	University of California Davis
Kathleen Blake Yancey	Professor of English and Distinguished Research Professor	Florida State University

Appendix D
Open Letter to Journal Publishers

September 2001

We support the establishment of an online public library that would provide the full contents of the published record of research and scholarly disclosure in medicine and the life sciences in a freely accessible, fully searchable, interlinked form. Establishment of this public library would vastly increase the accessibility and utility of the scientific literature, enhance scientific productivity, and catalyze integration of the disparate communities of knowledge and ideas in biomedical sciences.

We recognize that the publishers of our scientific journals have a legitimate right to a fair financial return for their role in scientific communication. We believe, however, that the permanent, archival record of scientific research and ideas should neither be owned nor controlled by publishers, but should belong to the public, and should be freely available through an international online public library.

To encourage the publishers of our journals to support this endeavor, we pledge that, beginning in September 2001, we will publish in, edit or review for, and personally subscribe to only those scholarly and scientific journals that have agreed to grant unrestricted free distribution rights to any and all original research reports that they have published, through PubMed Central and similar online public resources, within 6 months of their initial publication date.

Harold Varmus, Nobel Laureate, Director, National Cancer Institute
Patrick O. Brown, Professor, Stanford University School of Medicine
Michael Eisen, Assistant Professor, University of California, Berkeley

Available from www.plos.org/open-letter. Harold Varmus won the Nobel Laureate in Physiology or Medicine in 1989. Patrick Brown is a biochemist, whereas Michael Eisen is an evolutionary biologist.

As stated on its website, PLOS content is licensed for use under a Creative Commons Attribution (CC BY) license: "Unless otherwise indicated, articles and accompanying materials published by PLOS on the PLOS Sites, including peer reviews, are licensed by the respective authors for use and distribution by you subject to citation of the original source in accordance with the Creative Commons Attribution (CC BY) license" ("PLOS"). We provide it as Appendix D in accordance with that license.

Appendix E

Reported Costs for Publication Fees

Table E.1 Career Total Amounts for All Publications (Except Textbooks), by Source of Funding

	Estimated total, out of pocket	*Estimated total, provided by university*	*Estimated total, provided by grant*	*Estimated total, publisher has provided and/or deducted from royalties*	*Total respondents (Note: respondents could choose more than one column.)*
$1–$250	32	9	2	4	40
$251–500	11	3	1	2	15
$501–$750	1	3	1	1	5
$751–$1,000	2	2			4
$1,001–$2,000	1				1
$2,001–$3,000	1	2			3
$3,001–$4,000				2	2
. . .					
$20,001–$25,000				2	2

Table E.2 Career Total Amounts for Textbooks, by Source of Funding

	Estimated total, out of pocket	*Estimated total, provided by university*	*Estimated total, provided by grant*	*Estimated total, publisher has provided and/or deducted from royalties*	*Total respondents (Note: respondents could choose more than one column.)*
$1–$250	6	3	1	3	11
$251–500	2			4	6

	Estimated total, out of pocket	*Estimated total, provided by university*	*Estimated total, provided by grant*	*Estimated total, publisher has provided and/or deducted from royalties*	*Total respondents (Note: respondents could choose more than one column.)*
$501–$750		1			1
$751–$1,000	1			4	5
$1,001–$2,000				2	2
$2,001–$3,000				1	1
$3,001–$4,000		1		2	3
$4,001–$5,000	1			1	2
$5,001–$10,000				1	1
$10,001–$15,000	1			3	4
$15,001–$20,000			1	4	5
$20,001–$25,000	1			2	2
$25,001–$30,000				1	1
$30,001–$35,000				1	1
$35,001–$40,000					
$40,001–$45,000					
$45,001–$50,000					
$50,001–above			2	2	4

Table E.3 Comparing Materials for Which Permissions Were Paid (Respondents could select more than one type.)

Type of material	*Scholarship*	*Textbooks*
Audio clip	1	3
Epigraph (i.e., a quotation used before or after the main text)	4	0
Font (any proprietary font type, whether print or digital)	2	1
Image (e.g., any still image—photograph, artwork, figure, table, etc.)	46	29
Proprietary data	1	3
Readings or reprints (i.e., full or lengthy passages from previously published materials)	24	39
Quotation (within your main text, endnotes/footnotes, appendices)	10	7
Survey protocol (e.g., any copyrighted survey questions or protocols)	1	1
Video clip	2	2
Other	5	0
	Total respondents: 73	Total respondents: 52

Appendix F

Reported Costs for Open-Access Fees

Table F.1 Career Total Amounts for Access Fees for Non-Textbook Publications, by Source of Funding

	Estimated total, out of pocket	*Estimated total, provided by university*	*Estimated total, provided by grant*	*Total respondents (Note: respondents could choose more than one column.)*
\$1–\$250	9	2	1	10
\$251–500	1	1		2
\$501–\$750	1			1
\$751–\$1,000			1	1
\$1,001–\$2,000		1		1
\$2,001–\$3,000			1	1
. . .				
\$10,001–\$15,000		1		1

Table F.2 Career Total Amounts for Access Fees for Textbook Publications, by Source of Funding

	Estimated total, out of pocket	*Estimated total, provided by university*	*Estimated total, provided by grant*	*Estimated total, publisher has provided and/or deducted from royalties*	*Total respondents (Note: respondents could choose more than one column.)*
\$1–\$250	6	2	1	2	7
\$251–500	1				1
. . .					
\$1,001–\$2,000		1			1
. . .					
\$10,001–\$15,000		1	1		1

Works Cited

Aaron, Lynn S., and Catherine M. Roche. "Intellectual Property Rights of Faculty in the Digital Age—Evolution or Dissolution in 21st Century Academia." *Journal of Educational Technology Systems*, vol. 43, no. 3, 2015, pp. 320–41.

"About." *FSU Card Archive.* fsucardarchive.org/about.

"About Us." *Copyright Clearance Center.* 2019, www.copyright.com/about/.

Ahmadi, Shafiqa. "Faculty Rights to Courses and Digital Courseware." *New Directions for Higher Education*, vol. 177, 2017, pp. 25–37.

Amidon, Timothy R., and Jessica Reyman. "Authorship and Ownership of User Contributions on the Social Web." *Cultures of Copyright*, edited by Dànielle Nicole DeVoss and Martine Courant Rife, Peter Lang, 2015.

Amidon, Timothy R., Les Hutchinson, TyAnna Herrington, and Jessica Reyman. "Copyright, Content, and Control: Student Authorship Across Educational Technology Platforms." *Kairos: A Journal of Rhetoric, Technology, and Pedagogy*, vol. 24, no. 1, Fall 2019, Special issue on *Ownership, Authorship, and Copyright*, edited by Karen J. Lunsford, John Logie, and TyAnna Herrington, technorhetoric.net/24.1/topoi/amidon-et-al/index.html.

Amore, Paul, et al. *Copywrite, Plagiarism, and Intellectual Property.* Special issue of *Kairos: A Journal for Teachers of Writing in Webbed Environments*, vol. 3, no. 1, 1998, kairos.technorhetoric.net/3.1/index.html.

Anderson, Paul V. "Simple Gifts: Ethical Issues in the Conduct of Person-Based Composition Research." *College Composition and Communication*, vol. 49, no. 1, 1998, pp. 663–89.

Armstrong, Tracey. "Copyright Clearance Center: Providing Compliance Solutions for Content Users" *Journal of Library Administration*, vol. 42, nos. 3–4, 2005, pp. 55–64, doi:10.1300/J111v42n03_04.

Arola, Kristin L., and Adam C. Arola. "An Ethics of Assemblage: Creative Repetition and the 'Electric Pow Wow.'" *Assembling Composition*, edited by Kathleen Blake Yancey and Stephen J. McElroy, National Council of Teachers of English, 2017, pp. 204–21.

Associated Press. "Federal Appeals Court Rejects Monkey Selfie Suit." *NBC News*, 23 April 2018, www.nbcnews.com/news/us-news/federal-appeals-court-rejects-monkey-selfie-suit-n868501.

Association of Research Libraries. *Code of Best Practices in Fair Use for Academic and Research Libraries.* January 2012, www.arl.org/focus-areas/copyright-ip/fair-use/code-of-best-practices.

Authors Guild, Inc. v. Google Inc., No. 13-4829-cv (2d Cir. Oct. 16, 2015).

Baca, Damián. *Mestiz@ Scripts, Digital Migrations, and the Territories of Writing.* Palgrave Macmillan, 2008.

Baldwin, Peter. *The Copyright Wars: Three Centuries of Trans-Atlantic Battle.* Princeton University Press, 2014.

Ballentine, Brian D. "In Defense of Obfuscation: Questioning Open Source and a New Perspective on Teaching Digital Literacy in the Writing Classroom." *Composition and Copyright: Perspectives on Teaching, Text-Making, and Fair Use,* edited by Steve Westbrook, State University of New York Press, 2009, pp. 68–89.

———. "Writing in the Disciplines Versus Corporate Workplaces: On the Importance of Conflicting Disciplinary Discourses in the Open Source Movement and the Value of Intellectual Property." *Across the Disciplines,* vol. 6, 2009, wac.colostate.edu/atd/technologies/ballentine.cfm.

Basgier, Christopher. "The Author-Function, the Genre Function, and the Rhetoric of Scholarly Webtexts." *Computers and Composition,* vol. 28, no. 2, 2011, pp. 145–59.

Bazerman, Charles. "The Case for Writing Studies as a Major Discipline." *Rhetoric and Composition as Intellectual Work,* edited by Gary A. Olson, Southern Illinois University Press, 2002, pp. 32–38.

Bazerman, Charles, David Blakesley, Mike Palmquist, and David Russell. "Open Access Book Publishing in Writing Studies: A Case Study." *First Monday,* vol. 13, no. 1, January 2008, firstmonday.org/ojs/index.php/fm/article/view/2088/1920.

Bergstrom, Carl T., and Theodore C. Bergstrom. "The Economics of Ecology Journals." *Frontiers in Ecology and the Environment,* vol. 4, no. 9, 2006, pp. 488–95.

Berlinger, Joshua. "PETA, Photographer Reach Settlement in 'Monkey Selfie' Case." *CNN,* 12 September 2017, www.cnn.com/2017/09/12/asia/monkey-selfie-settlement/index.html.

Brandt, Deborah. *Literacy in American Lives.* Cambridge University Press, 2001.

———. *The Rise of Writing: Redefining Mass Literacy.* Cambridge University Press, 2015.

Bruce, Bertram C., et al. "The Inquiry Page: Bridging Digital Libraries to Learners." *Knowledge Quest,* vol. 31, no. 3, January/February 2003, pp. 15–17.

Burns, Hugh. "Four Dimensions of Significance: Tradition, Method, Theory, Originality." *Computers and Composition,* vol. 21, no. 1, 2004, pp. 5–13.

Burnside, Elkie. "Little Dear and Intellectual Property." *Digital Archive of Literacy Narratives,* www.thedaln.org/#/detail/5bd73fbf-fae4-4cca-98f6-74f4d4ed5232.

California Legislature Assembly. *An Act to Amend Section 51871.5 of the Education Code, Relating to Education Technology,* AB 307. 2005–2006 Reg. Sess. (18 September 2006). *California State Assembly,* www.leginfo.ca.gov/pub/05-06/bill/asm/ab_0301-0350/ab_307_bill_20060918_chaptered.html.

Cambridge University Press et al. v. Becker. No. 1:08-cv-01425-ODE (N.D. Ga. Mar. 31, 2016).

Cambridge University Press et al. v. Patton. 769 F.3d 1232 (11th Cir. 2014).

Cantwell, Brendan, and Ilkka Kauppinen, editors. *Academic Capitalism in the Age of Globalization.* Johns Hopkins University Press, 2014.

Chilling Effects Amici Curiae Brief in Support of Appellee. Perfect 10, Inc. v. Google. Electronic Frontier Foundation, 2010, www.eff.org/document/chilling-effects-amicus-brief.

Christou, Corilee. "Copyright Clearance Center at 40." *Information Today*, January/February 2018, www.infotoday.com/it/jan18/Christou-Copyright-Clearance-Center-at-40.shtml.

Comer, Kathryn, Michael Harker, and Ben McCorkle, editors. *The Archive as Classroom: Pedagogical Approaches to the Digital Archive of Literacy Narratives.* Computers and Composition Digital Press/Utah State University Press, 2019, ccdigitalpress.org/book/archive-as-classroom.

Conference on College Composition and Communication. *CCCC Guidelines for the Ethical Conduct of Research in Composition Studies,* March 2015, cccc.ncte.org/cccc/resources/positions/ethicalconduct.

———. "Guidelines for the Ethical Treatment of Students and Student Writing in Composition Studies." *College Composition and Communication,* vol. 42, no. 3, 2001, 485–90.

———. "Resolution 5." *2012 Resolutions & Sense of the House Motions.* CCCC Annual Business Meeting, 24 March 2012, St. Louis, MO, www.ncte.org/cccc/resolutions/2012.

Conference on College Composition and Communication Caucus on Intellectual Property. *CCCC Intellectual Property Annual,* 2005–present, escholarship.org/uc/ucsb_writing_program_ipa.

———. "Use Your Fair Use: Strategies Toward Action." *College Composition and Communication,* vol. 51, no. 3, 2000, pp. 485–88.

Consent to Participate & Release of Materials. *Digital Archive of Literacy Narratives,* www.thedaln.org/#/create/rights.

Copyright Clearance Center v. Commissioner, 79 T.C. 793 (1982), www.leagle.com/decision/198287279aytc7931822.

"Creative Cloud Plans & Pricing." *Adobe,* 2019, www.adobe.com/creativecloud/plans.html.

Crews, Kenneth D. *Copyright Law for Librarians and Educators: Creative Strategies and Practical Solutions.* 3rd ed., American Library Association, 2012.

———. "The Law of Fair Use and the Illusion of Fair-Use Guidelines." *Ohio State Law Review,* vol. 62, 2001, pp. 599–702.

Curb, Lisa A., and Charles I. Abramson. "An Examination of Author-Paid Charges in Science Journals." *Comprehensive Psychology,* vol. 1, no. 4, 2012, pp. 1–6.

David, Matthew, and Debora Halbert, editors. *The SAGE Handbook of Intellectual Property.* Sage, 2015.

DeVoss, Dànielle Nicole. "Academia, Academe, and Intellectual Property." *Academe,* November–December 2015, www.aaup.org/article/academia-academe-and-intellectual-property.

———. "English Studies and Intellectual Property: Copyright, Creativity, and the Commons." *Pedagogy,* vol. 10, no. 1, 2010, pp. 201–15.

DeVoss, Dànielle Nicole, and James E. Porter. "Why Napster Matters to Writing: Filesharing as a New Ethic of Digital Delivery." *Computers and Composition,* vol. 23, no. 2, 2006, pp. 178–210.

DeVoss, Dànielle Nicole, and Suzanne Webb. "Media Convergence: *Grand Theft Audio*: Negotiating Copyright as Composers." *Computers and Composition,* vol. 25, no. 1, 2008, pp. 79–103.

Dewey, John. *Experience and Education.* Macmillan, 1938.

Donoghue, Frank. *The Last Professors: The Corporate University and the Fate of the Humanities.* Fordham University Press, 2008.

Dubisar, Abby M., and Jason Palmeri. "Palin/Pathos/Peter Griffin: Political Video Remix and Composition Pedagogy." *Computers and Composition*, vol. 27, no. 2, 2010, pp. 77–93.

Edwards, Dustin. "Framing Remix Rhetorically: Toward a Typology of Transformative Work." *Computers and Composition*, vol. 39, no. 1, 2016, pp. 41–54.

Edwards, Mike, and Jessica Reyman. "Open Access and the Economics of Scholarship in Rhetoric and Composition Studies." *Rhetoric Review*, vol. 37, no. 2, 2018, pp. 212–25.

Enoch, Jessica, and Jean Bessette. "Meaningful Engagements: Feminist Historiography and the Digital Humanities." *College Composition and Communication*, vol. 64, no. 4, 2013, pp. 634–60.

Farivar, Cyrus. "'Dancing Baby' Lawsuit Finally Settles, Baby Is Now a Middle-School Student." *Ars Technica*, 28 June 2018, arstechnica.com/tech-policy/2018/06/dancing-baby-lawsuit-finally-settles-baby-is-now-a-middle-school-student/.

Galin, Jeffrey R. "Keep on Keeping on: Georgia State Fair Use Case Faces a New Metric for Assessing Fair Use." *The CCCC-IP Annual: Top Intellectual Property Developments of 2014*, June 2015, pp. 21–29, escholarship.org/uc/item/2z35m4hc.

———. "Own Your Rights: Know When Your University Can Claim Ownership of Your Work." *Composition and Copyright: Perspectives on Teaching, Text-making, and Fair Use*, edited by Steve Westbrook, State University of New York Press, 2009, pp. 190–216.

Galin, Jeffrey R., and Joan Latchaw. "From Incentive to Stewardship: The Shifting Discourse of Academic Publishing." *Computers and Composition*, vol. 27, no. 3, 2010, pp. 211–24.

Geismar, Haidy. *Treasured Possessions: Indigenous Interventions Into Cultural and Intellectual Property*. Duke University Press, 2013.

Ginsberg, Benjamin. *The Fall of the Faculty: The Rise of the All-Administrative University and Why It Matters*. Oxford University Press, 2011.

Greenemeier, Larry. "Remembering the Day the World Wide Web Was Born." *Scientific American*, 12 March 2009, www.scientificamerican.com/article/day-the-web-was-born/

Grimmelmann, James. "Copyright for Literate Robots." *Illinois Law Review*, vol. 101, 2016, pp. 657–81.

Gurak, Laura J., and Johndan Johnson-Eilola, editors. *Intellectual Property*. Special issue of *Computers and Composition*, vol. 15, no. 2, 1998, pp. 121–274.

H.R.1695—Register of Copyrights Selection and Accountability Act of 2017. 115th Congress (2017–2018), www.congress.gov/bill/115th-congress/house-bill/1695.

H.R.3261—Stop Online Piracy Act. 112th Congress (2011–2012), www.congress.gov/bill/112th-congress/house-bill/3261.

Harmon, Elliot. "Don't Make the Register of Copyrights Into a Presidential Pawn." *Electronic Frontier Foundation*, 25 September 2018, www.eff.org/deeplinks/2018/09/dont-turn-register-copyrights-presidential-pawn.

Haswell, Richard H. "NCTE/CCCC's Recent War on Scholarship." *Written Communication*, vol. 22, no. 2, 2005, pp. 198–223.

Herrington, TyAnna K. "The Interdependency of Fair Use and the First Amendment." *Computers and Composition*, vol. 15, no. 2, 1998, pp. 125–43.

Hobbs, Renee. "Best Practices Help End Copyright Confusion." *The Council Chronicle*, March 2009, pp. 12–13, 27.

"Home." *Digital Archive of Literacy Narratives.* www.thedaln.org/#/home.

Housewright, Ross, Roger C. Schonfeld, and Kate Wulfson. *Ithaka S+R | Jisc | RLUK: UK Survey of Academics 2012.* 16 May 2013, doi.org/10.18665/sr.22526.

———. *Ithaka S+R U.S. Faculty Survey 2012.* 8 April 2013, doi.org/10.18665/sr.22502.

Internet Archive. archive.org.

"Internet Scout Research Group." *The Scout Report*, vol. 22, no. 11, 18 March 2016, scout.wisc.edu/report/2016/0318.

Jaszi, Peter. "Fair Use and Education: The Way Forward." *Law and Literature*, vol. 25, no. 1, 2013, pp. 33–49.

Jiang, Jialei. "What Monkeys Teach Us About Authorship: Toward a Distributed Agency in Digital Composing Practices." *Kairos: A Journal of Rhetoric, Technology, and Pedagogy*, vol. 24, no. 1, Fall 2019, Special issue on *Ownership, Authorship, and Copyright*, edited by Karen J. Lunsford, John Logie, and TyAnna Herrington, kairos.technorhetoric.net/24.1/topoi/jiang/index.html.

Johnson, Carolyn Y. "Russian Trolls and Twitter Bots Exploit Vaccine Controversy." *The Washington Post*, 23 August 2018, www.washingtonpost.com/science/2018/08/23/russian-trolls-twitter-bots-exploit-vaccine-controversy.

Joseph, Heather. "Future of the Research Library: Heather Joseph on Open Access." *SPARC*, 10 April 2014, sparcopen.org/news/2014/future-of-the-research-library-heather-joseph-on-open-access/.

———. "The Open Access Movement Grows up: Taking Stock of a Revolution." *PLoS Biology*, vol. 11, no. 10, 2013, doi.org/10.1371/journal.pbio.1001686.

Kamdar, Adi, Daniel Nazer, and Vera Ranieri. *Defend Innovation: How To Fix Our Broken Patent System.* Electronic Frontier Foundation Whitepaper. February 2015, www.eff.org/wp/defend-innovation-how-fix-our-broken-patent-system.

Keller, Deidré A., and Anjali S. Vats. "Centering Education in the Next Great Copyright Act: A Response to Professor Jaszi." *Duquesne Law Review*, vol. 54, no. 1, 2016, pp. 173–95.

Kennedy, Krista. "Textual Machinery and Bot-Written Texts in Wikipedia." *The Responsibilities of Rhetoric: Proceedings of the 2008 Rhetoric Society of America Conference*, edited by Michelle Smith and Barbara Warnick, Waveland Press, 2010, pp. 303–9.

Kennedy, Krista, and Rebecca Moore Howard, editors. *Western Cultures of Intellectual Property.* Special issue of *College English*, vol. 75, no. 5, 2013, pp. 461–69.

Khoury, Amir H. "Intellectual Property Rights for Hubots: On the Legal Implications of Human-like Robots as Innovators and Creators." *Cardozo Arts & Entertainment Law Journal*, vol. 35, 2017, pp. 635–68.

Kimbrough, Julie L., and Laura N. Gasaway. "Publication of Government-Funded Research, Open Access, and the Public Interest." *Vanderbilt Journal of Entertainment & Technology Law*, vol. 18, no. 2, 2015, pp. 267–302.

Kirsch, Gesa, and Patricia A. Sullivan, editors. *Methods and Methodologies in Composition Research.* Southern Illinois University Press, 1992.

Kirsch, Gesa E., and Liz Rohan, editors. *Beyond the Archives: Research as a Lived Process.* Southern Illinois University Press, 2008.

Krause, Steven D. "Why I Teach Online (Even though I Don't Have to)." *Inside Higher Ed*, 14 March 2018, www.insidehighered.com/digital-learning/views/2018/03/14/professor-describes-why-he-teaches-online-opinion.

Kravets, David. "Will the Real Monkey Who Snapped Those Famous Selfies Please Stand up?" *Ars Technica*, 10 November 2015, arstechnica.com/tech-policy/2015/11/will-the-real-monkey-who-snapped-those-famous-selfies-please-stand-up/.

Lehman, Bruce A. "The Conference on Fair Use: Final Report to the Commissioner on the Conclusion of the Conference on Fair Use." November 1998, https://www.uspto.gov/sites/default/files/documents/confurep_0.pdf.

Lenz v. Universal Music Corp., 801 F.3d 1126 (9th Cir. 2015).

"Lenz v. Universal Music Corp." *Harvard Law Review*, vol. 129, no. 2289, 10 June 2016, harvardlawreview.org/2016/06/lenz-v-universal-music-corp/.

Lessig, Lawrence. *Free Culture: How Big Media Uses Technology and the Law to Lock Down Culture and Control Creativity*. Penguin Press, 2004.

———. *The Future of Ideas: The Fate of the Commons in a Connected World*. Vintage, 2002.

———. "Innovation Policy." *Lessig on the Issues*, 15 October 2015, medium.com/lessig-on-the-issues/innovation-policy-a070db1d2d8d#.mkfan719s.

———. *Remix: Making Art and Commerce Thrive in the Hybrid Economy*. Penguin Press, 2008.

———. "Why I Dropped out." *The New Yorker*, 28 January 2016, www.newyorker.com/news/news-desk/why-i-dropped-out.

———. "Why I Want to Run." *Lessig*, 11 August 2015, lessig2016.us/why-i-want-to-run/.

Leverenz, Carrie S. "Design Thinking and the Wicked Problem of Teaching Writing." *Computers and Composition*, vol. 33, no. 1, 2014, pp. 1–12.

Logie, John. *Peers, Pirates, and Persuasion: Rhetoric in the Peer-to-Peer Debates*. Parlor Press, 2006.

Lowe, Charles. "A Brief History of Open Source: Working to Make Knowledge Free." *Kairos: A Journal for Teachers of Writing in Webbed Environments*, vol. 6, no. 2, Fall 2001, kairos.technorhetoric.net/6.2news/opensource.html.

———. "Considerations for Creative Commons Licensing of Open Educational Resources: The Value of Copyleft." *Computers and Composition Online*, Fall 2010, cconlinejournal.org/open.

———. "Copyright, Access, and Digital Texts." *Across the Disciplines*, vol. 1, 2004, wac.colostate.edu/atd/articles/lowe2003/index.htm.

Lowe, Charles, and Pavel Zemliansky, editors. *Writing Spaces: Readings on Writing*. Vol. 1 and 2, WAC Clearinghouse, 2009 and 2010, wac.colostate.edu/books/writingspaces.cfm.

Lunsford, Andrea A., and Susan West. "Intellectual Property and Composition Studies." *College Composition and Communication*, vol. 47, no. 3, 1996, pp. 383–411.

Lunsford, Karen J. "Another Piece in the Open-Access Puzzle: The California Access to Publicly Funded Research Act (AB609)." *The CCCC-IP Annual: Top Intellectual Property Developments of 2014*, March 2015, pp. 34–37, https://escholarship.org/uc/item/2z35m4hc.

Lunsford, Karen J., and James P. Purdy. Webtext design by Erika Carlos. "Mapping the IP Landscape: Reflections on Ownership, Authorship, and Copyright for Writing Instruction." *Kairos: A Journal of Rhetoric, Technology, and Pedagogy*, vol. 24, no. 1, Fall 2019, Special issue on *Ownership, Authorship, and Copyright*, edited by Karen J. Lunsford, John Logie, and TyAnna Herrington, kairos.technorhetoric.net/24.1/topoi/lunsford-et-al/index.html.

Lunsford, Karen J., John Logie, and TyAnna Herrington, editors. *Ownership, Authorship, and Copyright.* Special issue of *Kairos: A Journal of Rhetoric, Technology, and Pedagogy*, vol. 24, no. 1, Fall 2019, kairos.technorhetoric.net/24.1/coverweb/lunsford-et-al/index.html.

Marback, Richard. "Embracing Wicked Problems: The Turn to Design in Composition Studies." *College Composition and Communication*, vol. 61, no. 2, 2009, pp. W397-W419.

McClure, Randall, and James P. Purdy, editors. *The Future Scholar: Researching and Teaching the Frameworks for Writing and Information Literacy.* Information Today, 2016.

McCorkle, Ben. "Hindered Hope: Shepard Fairey, the Associated Press, and the Missed Opportunity to Help Clarify U.S. Copyright Law." *Cultures of Copyright*, edited by Dànielle Nicole DeVoss and Martine Courant Rife, Peter Lang, 2015, 54–63.

McKee, Heidi A. "Ethical and Legal Issues for Writing Researchers in an Age of Media Convergence." *Computers and Composition*, vol. 25, no. 1, 2008, pp. 104–22.

McKee, Heidi A., and James E. Porter. "The Ethics of Archival Research." *College Composition and Communication*, vol. 64, no. 1, 2012, pp. 59–81.

———. "The Ethics of Digital Writing Research: A Rhetorical Approach." *College Composition and Communication*, vol. 59, no. 4, 2008, pp. 711–49.

———. *The Ethics of Internet Research: A Rhetorical, Case-Based Process.* Peter Lang, 2009.

———. *Professional Communication and Network Interaction: A Rhetorical and Ethical Approach.* Routledge, 2017.

McKenzie, Lindsay. "Another 'Big Deal' Bites the Dust." *Inside Higher Ed*, 24 May 2019, www.insidehighered.com/news/2019/05/24/lsu-ends-elsevier-bundled-journal-subscription.

———. "An Elsevier Pivot to Open Access." *Inside Higher Ed*, 24 April 2019, www.insidehighered.com/news/2019/04/24/elsevier-agrees-first-read-and-publish-deal.

———. "Florida State Cancels Bundled Journal Deal With Elsevier." *Inside Higher Ed*, 26 April 2018, www.insidehighered.com/quicktakes/2018/04/26/florida-state-cancels-bundled-journal-deal-elsevier.

———. "UC Drops Elsevier." *Inside Higher Ed*, 1 March 2019, www.insidehighered.com/news/2019/03/01/university-california-cancels-deal-elsevier-after-months-negotiations.

McSherry, Corynne. "After More Than a Decade of Litigation, the Dancing Baby Has Done His Part to Strengthen Fair Use for Everyone." *Electronic Frontier Foundation*, 27 June 2018, www.eff.org/deeplinks/2018/06/after-more-decade-litigation-dancing-baby-ready-move.

Merica, Dan. "Harvard Professor Lawrence Lessig Is Exploring a Long Shot Presidential Bid." *CNN*, 11 August 2015, www.cnn.com/2015/08/11/politics/larry-lessig-presidential-campaign-exploration/index.html.

Millward, Jody, Lois Powers, and Rebecca Crump. "TYCA Two-Year College Facts and Data Report: 2005." *National Council of Teachers of English.* TYCA Research Committee, 2005, http://www.ncte.org/library/NCTEFiles/Groups/TYCA/TYCA_DataReport.pdf.

Montoya, Delilah. *Codex Delilah, Six-Deer: Journey from Mexicatl to Chicana.* Presented at The Mexican Museum, San Francisco, 1992.

Morris, Emily Michiko. "The Many Faces of Bayh-Dole." *Duquesne Law Review*, vol. 54, no. 1, 2016, pp. 81–132.

Mortensen, Peter, and Gesa E. Kirsch. "On Authority in the Study of Writing." *College Composition and Communication*, vol. 44, no. 4, 1993, pp. 556–72.

Mowery, David C., and Arvids A. Ziedonis. "Numbers, Quality, and Entry: How Has the Bayh-Dole Act Affected U.S. University Patenting and Licensing?" *Innovation Policy and the Economy*, vol. 1, 2000, pp. 187–220.

Naruto v. Slater, No. 16–15469 (9th Cir. 2018).

Neal, Michael, Katherine Bridgman, and Stephen J. McElroy. "Making Meaning at the Intersections: Developing a Digital Archive for Multimodal Research." *Kairos: A Journal of Rhetoric, Technology, and Pedagogy*, vol. 17, no. 3, Special issue on *Multimodal Research Within/Across/Without Borders*, edited by Karen J. Lunsford, Summer 2013, kairos.technorhetoric.net/17.3/index.html.

Newfield, Christopher. *The Great Mistake: How We Wrecked Public Universities and How We Can Fix Them.* Johns Hopkins University Press, 2016.

———. *Unmaking the Public University: The Forty-Year Assault on the Middle Class.* Harvard University Press, 2008.

Office of Scholarly Communication, University of California. "Open Statement: Why UC Terminated Journal Negotiations With Elsevier." *UC OSC Blog*, 20 March 2019 (revised 25 April 2019), osc.universityofcalifornia.edu/2019/03/open-statement-why-uc-terminated-journal-negotiations-with-elsevier/.

Oral History Association. "Best Practices." 2019, www.oralhistory.org/best-practices/.

———. "Principles and Best Practices." 2009, www.oralhistory.org/about/principles-and-practices-revised-2009/.

Osborne, Samuel. "'Monkey Selfie' Case: Photographer Wins Two Year Legal Fight Against Peta Over the Image Copyright." *Independent*, 12 September 2017, www.independent.co.uk/news/world/americas/monkey-selfie-david-slater-photographer-peta-copyright-image-camera-wildlife-personalities-macaques-a7941806.html.

Peet, Lisa. "New Bills Would Let President, Not Librarian of Congress, Name Copyright Register." *Library Journal*, 18 May 2017, www.libraryjournal.com/?detailStory=new-bills-would-let-president-not-librarian-of-congress-name-copyright-register.

"Plans and Pricing." *Getty Images*, 2019, www.gettyimages.com/plans-and-pricing.

"PLOS Terms of Use." *PLOS*, 22 May 2019, www.plos.org/terms-of-use.

Porter, James E. "MOOCs, 'Courses,' and the Question of Faculty and Student Copyrights." *The CCCC-IP Annual: Top Intellectual Property Developments of 2012*, March 2013, pp. 2–18, https://escholarship.org/uc/item/7h72f4ht.

Powell, Malea. "Dreaming Charles Eastman: Cultural Memory, Autobiography, and Geography in Indigenous Rhetorical Histories." *Beyond the Archives: Research as a Lived Process*, edited by Gesa E. Kirsch and Liz Rohan, Southern Illinois University Press, 2008, pp. 115–27.

Poynder, Richard. "The OA Interviews: Jeffrey Beall, University of Colorado Denver." *Open and Shut?* 11 July 2012, poynder.blogspot.com/2012/07/oa-interviews-jeffrey-beall-university.html.

———. "The OA Interviews: Michael Eisen, Co-founder of the Public Library of Science." *Open and Shut?* 19 February 2012, poynder.blogspot.com/2012/02/oa-interviews-michael-eisen-co-founder.html.

Propen, Amy D. "Going Bananas Over Copyright: Monkey Selfies and the Intersections of Rhetoric, Intellectual Property, and Animal Studies." *The CCCC-IP Annual: Top Intellectual Property Developments of 2017*, May 2018, escholarship.org/uc/item/3fc6t3d6.

Public Library of Science. "PLOS Open Letter." www.plos.org/open-letter.

———. "The PLOS Story." www.plos.org/history.

Purdy, James P. "Anxiety and the Archive: Understanding Plagiarism Detection Services as Digital Archives." *Computers and Composition*, vol. 26, no. 2, 2009, pp. 65–77.

———. "Calling Off the Hounds: Technology and the Visibility of Plagiarism." *Pedagogy: Critical Approaches to Teaching Literature, Language, Composition, and Culture*, vol. 5, no. 2, 2005, pp. 275–95.

———. "What Can Design Thinking Offer Writing Studies?" *College Composition and Communication*, vol. 65, no. 4, 2014, pp. 612–41.

Quinn, Michele Myatt. "Open Access in Scholarly Publishing: Embracing Principles and Avoiding Pitfalls." *The Serials Librarian*, vol. 69, no. 1, 2015, pp. 58–69.

Ramsey, Alexis E., et al., editors. *Working in the Archives: Practical Research Methods for Rhetoric and Composition*. Southern Illinois University Press, 2010.

Ratliff, Clancy. "Open Source and the Access Agenda." *Computers and Composition Online*, Fall 2010/Spring 2011, cconlinejournal.org/OpenSourceAccess_Ratliff/OpenSourceAccess.html.

Reyman, Jessica. "Property, Theft, Piracy: Rhetoric and Regulation in *MGM Studios v. Grokster*." *Composition and Copyright: Perspectives on Teaching, Text-Making, and Fair Use*, edited by Steve Westbrook, State University of New York Press, 2009, pp. 9–30.

———. *The Rhetoric of Intellectual Property: Copyright Law and the Regulation of Digital Culture*. Routledge, 2010.

Reyman, Jessica, and Mary Lay Schuster, editors. *Technical Communication and the Law*. Special issue of *Technical Communication Quarterly*, vol. 20, no. 1, 2010.

Ridolfo, Jim, and Dànielle Nicole DeVoss. "Composing for Recomposition: Rhetorical Velocity and Delivery." *Kairos: A Journal of Rhetoric, Technology, and Pedagogy*, vol. 13, no. 2, 2009, kairos.technorhetoric.net/13.2/topoi/ridolfo_devoss/index.html.

Rife, Martine Courant. "Copyright Law as Mediational Means: Report on a Mixed Methods Study of U.S. Professional Writers." *Technical Communication*, vol. 57, no. 1, 2010, pp. 44–67.

———. "The Fair Use Doctrine: History, Application, and Implications for (New Media) Writing Teachers." *Computers and Composition*, vol. 24, no. 2, 2007, pp. 154–78.

———. "Ideas Toward a Fair Use Heuristic: Visual Rhetoric and Composition." *Composition and Copyright: Perspectives on Teaching, Text-Making, and Fair Use*, edited by Steve Westbrook, State University of New York Press, 2009, pp. 133–53.

———. *Invention, Copyright, and Digital Writing*. Southern Illinois University Press, 2013.

———. "Why *Kairos* Matters to Writing: A Reflection on Its Intellectual Property Conversation and Developing Law During the Last Ten Years." *Kairos: A Journal of Rhetoric, Technology, and Pedagogy*, vol. 11, no. 1, Spring 2006, kairos.technorhetoric.net/11.1/binder.html?topoi/rife/index.html.

Rife, Martine Courant, Shaun Slattery, and Dànielle Nicole DeVoss, editors. *Copy(write): Intellectual Property in the Writing Classroom.* WAC Clearinghouse and Parlor Press, 2011, wac.colostate.edu/books/copywrite/.

Rife, Martine Courant, et al., editors. *Copyright, Culture, Creativity, and the Commons.* Special issue of *Computers and Composition,* vol. 27, no. 3, September 2010, pp. 161–246.

Ríos, Gabriela Raquel, and Donnie Johnson Sackey. "Biocultural Diversity and Copyright: Linking Intellectual Property, Language, Knowledges, and Environment." *Cultures of Copyright,* edited by Dànielle Nicole DeVoss and Martine Courant Rife, Peter Lang, 2015, pp. 211–25.

Rittel, Horst W.J., and Melvin M. Webber. "Dilemmas in a General Theory of Planning." *Policy Sciences,* vol. 4, no. 2, 1973, pp. 155–69.

Rizor, Sara L., and Robert P. Holley. "Open Access Goals Revisited: How Green and Gold Open Access Are Meeting (Or Not) Their Original Goals." *Journal of Scholarly Publishing,* vol. 45, no. 4, 2014, pp. 321–35.

Rooksby, Jacob H. *The Branding of the American Mind: How Universities Capture, Manage, and Monetize Intellectual Property and Why It Matters.* Johns Hopkins University Press, 2016.

———. "Copyright in Higher Education: A Review of Modern Scholarship." *Duquesne Law Review,* vol. 54, no. 1, 2016, pp. 197–221.

———. "Intellectual Property and the University: An Introduction." *Duquesne Law Review,* vol. 54, no. 1, 2016, pp. 1–5.

Rowley, Jennifer, et al. "Academics' Behaviors and Attitudes Towards Open Access Publishing in Scholarly Journals." *Journal of the Association for Information Science and Technology,* vol. 68, no. 5, May 2017, pp. 1201–11.

Rubin, Zick. "Let's Spread the Word About Fair Use." *The Chronicle of Higher Education,* 23 September 2012, www.chronicle.com/article/Lets-Spread-the-Word-About/134544/.

S.968—PROTECT IP (Preventing Real Online Threats to Economic Creativity and Theft of Intellectual Property) Act of 2011. 112th Congress (2011–2012). www.congress.gov/bill/112th-congress/senate-bill/968.

Sag, Matthew. "Copyright Trolling, an Empirical Study." *Iowa Law Review,* vol. 100, no. 3, 2015, pp. 1105–1147, ilr.law.uiowa.edu/print/volume-100-issue-3/copyright-trolling-an-empirical-study/

Samuels, Robert. "The Future Threat to Computers and Composition: Nontenured Instructors, Intellectual Property, and Distance Education." *Computers and Composition,* vol. 21, no. 1, 2004, pp. 63–71.

———. *Why Public Higher Education Should Be Free: How to Decrease Cost and Increase Quality at American Universities.* Rutgers University Press, 2013.

Sano-Franchini, Jennifer, Robyn Tasaka, and Lehua Ledbetter. "Toward a Reflexive Approach to Remix—or—What Hawai'i Creole English and Corporate Tourism Can Teach Us About Copyright." *Cultures of Copyright,* edited by Dànielle Nicole DeVoss and Martine Courant Rife, Peter Lang, 2015, pp. 226–42.

Schaffner, Derek J. "The Digital Millennium Copyright Act: Overextension of Copyright Protection and the Unintended Chilling Effects on Fair Use, Free Speech, and Innovation." *Cornell Journal of Law and Public Policy,* vol. 14, no. 1, 2004, pp. 145–69.

Schneider, Richard A., et al. *Declaration of Rights and Principles to Transform Scholarly Communication.* University Committee on Library and Scholarly Communication, University of California, 25 April 2018.

Schonfeld, Roger C. "Read and Publish: Is It Good for the Academy?" *The Scholarly Kitchen: What's Hot and Cooking in Scholarly Publishing*, 4 September 2018, scholarlykitchen.sspnet.org/2018/09/04/read-publish-good-academy/.

Schwartz, Meredith. "Georgia State Copyright Case: What You Need to Know—and What It Means for E-Reserves." *Library Journal*, 17 May 2012, www.libraryjournal.com/?detailStory=georgia-state-copyright-case-what-you-need-to-know-and-what-it-means-for-e-reserves.

Shane, Scott. "The Fake Americans Russians Created to Influence the Election." *The New York Times*, 7 September 2017, www.nytimes.com/2017/09/07/us/politics/russia-facebook-twitter-election.html.

Shetler, Angela M. "Authorship Abroad: Considering Copyright Across Cultures." *Cultures of Copyright*, edited by Dànielle Nicole DeVoss and Martine Courant Rife, Peter Lang, 2015, pp. 243–53.

Shirk, Henrietta Nickels, and Howard Taylor Smith. "Emerging Fair Use Guidelines for Multimedia: Implications for the Writing Classroom." *Computers and Composition*, vol. 15, no. 2, 1998, pp. 229–41.

Slater, David J. "The Monkey Selfie." *DJS Photography*, 2017, www.djsphotography.co.uk/monkeyselfie.htm.

———. *Wildlife Personalities*. Blurb, 2014.

Society of American Archivists. "A Guide to Deeds of Gift." 2019, www2.archivists.org/publications/brochures/deeds-of-gift.

SPARC (Scholarly Publishing and Academic Resources Coalition). *Who We Are*. 2018, sparcopen.org/who-we-are/.

Spigelman, Candace. "Habits of Mind: Historical Configurations of Textual Ownership in Peer Writing Groups." *College Composition and Communication*, vol. 49, no. 2, May 1998, pp. 234–55.

Stedman, Kyle. "Creative Commons Plus: Increasing Options for Content Creators." *The CCCC-IP Annual: Top Intellectual Property Developments of 2009*, March 2010, pp. 17–22, https://escholarship.org/uc/item/2bn7p292.

Stewart, Louise. "Wikimedia Says When a Monkey Takes a Selfie, No One Owns It." *Newsweek*, 21 August 2014, www.newsweek.com/lawyers-dispute-wikimedias-claims-about-monkey-selfie-copyright-265961.

Stoltz, Mitch. *Collateral Damages: Why Congress Needs To Fix Copyright Law's Civil Penalties*. Electronic Frontier Foundation Whitepaper, 24 July 2014, www.eff.org/wp/collateral-damages-why-congress-needs-fix-copyright-laws-civil-penalties.

Suber, Peter. *Open Access*. Massachusetts Institute of Technology Press, 2012.

Theimer, Kate. "Archives in Context and as Context." *Journal of Digital Humanities*, vol. 1, no. 2, Spring 2012, journalofdigitalhumanities.org/1-2/archives-in-context-and-as-context-by-kate-theimer/.

Ulman, H. Lewis. "A Brief Introduction to the Digital Archive of Literacy Narratives (DALN)." *Stories That Speak to Us: Exhibits from the Digital Archive of Literacy Narratives*, edited by H. Lewis Ulman, Scott Lloyd DeWitt, and Cynthia L. Selfe, Computers and Composition Digital Press/Utah State University Press, ccdigitalpress.org/book/stories/chapters/introduction/.

US Constitution. Art. I, Sec. 8.

Vaidhyanathan, Siva. *Intellectual Property: A Very Short Introduction*. Oxford University Press, 2017.

Vee, Annette. *Coding Literacy: How Computer Programming Is Changing Writing*. Massachusetts Institute of Technology Press, 2017.

Vie, Stephanie. "One Does Not Simply Make Memes and Not Consider Intellectual Property Issues: Social Media, Memetic Circulation, and Writing Studies." *Media Commons,* 16 October 2016, mediacommons.org/fieldguide/question/what-intellectual-property-challenges-do-you-expect-your-discipline-will-be-confronting–10.

WAC Clearinghouse. "Welcome to the WAC Clearinghouse." 2019, wac.colostate.edu.

Walker, Janice R., et al. "Computers and Composition 20/20: A Conversation Piece, or What Some Very Smart People Have to Say about the Future." *Computers and Composition,* vol. 28, no. 4, 2011, pp. 327–46.

Weigel, David. "Larry Lessig Ends Presidential Campaign, Citing Presidential Debate Rules." *Washington Post,* 2 November 2015, www.washingtonpost.com/news/post-politics/wp/2015/11/02/larry-lessig-ends-presidential-campaign-citing-unfair-debate-rules/.

Welch, Nancy, and Tony Scott, editors. *Composition in the Age of Austerity.* Utah State University Press, 2016.

Westbrook, Steve, editor. *Composition and Copyright: Perspectives on Teaching, Text-Making, and Fair Use.* State University of New York Press, 2009.

———. "Introduction." *Composition and Copyright: Perspectives on Teaching, Text-Making, and Fair Use,* edited by Steve Westbrook, State University of New York Press, 2009, pp. 1–5.

———. "Visual Rhetoric in a Culture of Fear: Impediments to Multimedia Production." *College English,* vol. 68, no. 5, 2006, pp. 457–80.

Westbrook, Steve, and James Ryan. "Permissions and Precedents: A Cautionary Tale from Art Publishing." *Cultures of Copyright,* edited by Dànielle Nicole DeVoss and Martine Courant Rife, Peter Lang, 2015, pp. 91–107.

Willinsky, John. *The Access Principle: The Case for Open Access to Research and Scholarship.* Massachusetts Institute of Technology Press, 2006.

Wolff, Christine, Alisa B. Rod, and Roger C. Schonfeld. *Ithaka S+R US Faculty Survey 2015.* 4 April 2016, doi.org/10.18665/sr.277685.

Woodmansee, Martha, and Peter Jaszi, editors. *The Construction of Authorship: Textual Appropriation in Law and Literature.* Duke University Press, 1994.

———. "The Law of Texts: Copyright in the Academy." *College English,* vol. 57, no. 7, 1995, pp. 769–87.

Woodworth, E.D. "Teaching IP Literacy Narrative." *Digital Archive of Literacy Narratives,* www.thedaln.org/#/detail/9ebfc92e-8d9e-462a-80e3-473f3aaaf1c3.

@YouTube Spotlight. *YouTube Copyright School.* YouTube, LLC, 24 March 2011, www.youtube.com/copyright_school.

Yancey, Kathleen Blake, editor. *A Rhetoric of Reflection.* Utah State University Press, 2016.

Zimmerman, Traci. "The Future of Copyright? A Look at the First Decade of Creative Commons." *The CCCC-IP Annual: Top Intellectual Property Developments of 2013,* March 2014, pp. 36–39, https://escholarship.org/uc/item/6ng4h3mj.

Index

Note: **Bold** page numbers denote references to tables.

For Product Safety Concerns and Information please contact our EU
representative GPSR@taylorandfrancis.com
Taylor & Francis Verlag GmbH, Kaufingerstraße 24, 80331 München, Germany

www.ingramcontent.com/pod-product-compliance
Ingram Content Group UK Ltd.
Pitfield, Milton Keynes, MK11 3LW, UK
UKHW022000180926
475701UK00003B/119

* 9 7 8 1 0 3 2 4 0 0 9 2 1 *